Marine of Revolution
& Consulate

Marine of Revolution & Consulate

The Recollections of a French Soldier
of the Revolutionary Wars
1791–1804

Moreau de Jonnès

translated by
Cyril Hammond

LEONAUR

Marine of Revolution & Consulate: the Recollections of a French Soldier of the Revolutionary Wars 1791-1804
by Moreau de Jonnès

First published under the title
Adventures in the Revolution and Under the Consulate

Published by Leonaur Ltd

Text in this form and material original to this edition
copyright © 2008 Leonaur Ltd

ISBN: 978-1-84677-470-6 (hardcover)
ISBN: 978-1-84677-469-0 (softcover)

http://www.leonaur.com

Contents

Lafayette & the National Guards

The town of Rennes, that Armorican city already old in days of Julius Caesar, and the capital of the Duchy of Brittany, still possessed in 1788 a part of its ancient walls and the big towers which flanked them. It had also a Municipal Council which offered a furious resistance to the usurpations of the Court. Finally it could lay claim to a College whose solid merits were roundly admitted and a Legal Institute which had nourished many famous men. At this particular time, Moreau, the future conqueror of Hohenlinden, the Xenophon of the finest retreat known to modern times, was head of the Law School, in other words one of those young lawyers destined to uphold the honour of the Bar at Rennes.

Theoretically, a town which has mothered so many well-known men should possess a University peopled by many and studious undergraduates. Not at all. With the exception of a few small groups scribbling shamefully in dark corners, nobody paid any attention to lectures, and the intelligence available was employed at forced draught to avoid efforts which would have brought success under normal pressure.

The school was divided into two sets. The first affected a *rakish* existence. Its members' time was divided between the café and the fencing-master, followed, when they had money or credit, by gallantries, brawls, duels, debts and melancholia.

The other class constituted the *plebs*, and I had the expensive privilege of belonging to it. It was a turbulent and thoroughly undisciplined collection which rendered intelligence entirely superfluous. The one daily ambition was to play some trick successfully and not to suffer for it. The Beadle was the constant object of pleasantries of a dubious character. Apples were foregone, books were sold, in order to buy the hooks necessary to the harpooning of his wig and its translation, if not to Heaven, like the tresses of Berenice, at least to the classroom ceiling. The desired result was obtained as a general rule, but it took more time, ingenuity and perseverance to hook that wig than would have sufficed for a translation of Cicero. The critical moment of the entire day was the *break*, and it was extremely difficult to get away without fighting somebody or being beaten by someone else. The most peacefully inclined frequently arrived home with a black eye, bleeding nose, bruised figurehead and clothes in rags. It may be added that this state of affairs was not always appreciated by the parents, and was known to carry with it the privilege of being beaten all over again.

If one follows the biographer of Bertrand du Guesclin, Constable of France, it will be remarked that five hundred years ago in Brittany, youth behaved in precisely the same manner; presumably, therefore, French civilisation has not progressed since the Middle Ages. Nevertheless one should not take this too seriously, since even if our studies suffered, these far from effeminate habits fitted us well for the rude ordeal of war which we were destined shortly to undergo.

The town was garrisoned by the Regiment of Rohan-Soubise, under the command of Colonel Count d'Hervilly. He was bitterly hated because he had expelled the judges from the Palais de Justice and closed its doors against them. We retaliated by closing the cafés against the officers, we hissed the soldiers whenever we met them, and we called out their Colonel. He was a little, dry, yellow man, booted to the thighs, and his arrogant manner rendered him superlatively disagreeable. He accepted all challenges and disarmed his opponent almost by the movement with which he put himself on guard, using a thrust of which the provincial Schools of Fence were entirely ignorant. Three or four of us suffered the same fate. Twenty were ready to take their places, but were forbidden to do so, because the College feared that a possible success might be interpreted as an ambush.

Recognising, nevertheless, that the troubles in Brittany were becoming menacing, the Ministry altered its policy, re-established Parliament, and sent away those who had been guilty of violence towards it. The departure of the Regiment of Rohan-Soubise was accompanied by the maledictions of the populace, and its Colonel narrowly escaped death by stoning. I met him three times afterwards, and always in sanguinary circumstances; the first time he was at the head of the Knights of the Dagger, introduced into the Tuileries to carry off the King. They were thrown out by the National Guard in a most disrespectful manner. On the second occasion, the 10th August, he was in charge of the defence of the Tuileries; and the last, at Quiberon, where he perished.

At the beginning of 1791, when I was working hard and really endeavouring to put my studies to practical use, I was obliged to leave for Paris. Although I was then only a school-boy I had been brought up in the midst of public unrest in Brittany, and this had hardened my outlook. Furthermore, my studies had developed my capacity to observe the events to which I might be a party. Misrepresented as they have so often been, it is not perhaps without interest to have them related by an impartial eyewitness.

At the beginning of 1791 the Revolution was supposed to be at an end and the constitutional monarchy solidly established. If this was not an actual fact it was at least public opinion, and well-informed people in Paris shared it. In the provinces the conviction was less hearty. In Brittany in particular it was somewhat shaken by the sinister predictions of our old nobility, who swore that the whole affair was merely a large uprising and that those responsible for it would be sent to the gibbet by Act of Parliament. It is true that the students of Rennes looked very darkly on these prophets of evil, whom we regarded as fanatics, and that more than once we predicted that the civil war which they so ardently desired would bring upon their own heads the blood that would be shed thereby. This prophecy came back to me in bitterness when I saw it fulfilled under my very eyes upon the sands of Quiberon.

When I reached Paris in February the appearance of the city in no way suggested the gloomy future. The populace was calm, confident and cheerful, and, furthermore, business was daily improving. Undoubtedly the noble tenants of the Faubourg St. Germain were absent and its houses deserted; but the popular and mercantile quarters were scarcely aware of this, for business was good. Sundays were real feast days. There were crowds at all the public places, and the Boulevard du Temple, then in the height of fashion, was practically blocked. The great attraction consisted in a new play which was all the rage. It was called "Nicodemus in the Moon," a species of allegorical comedy, the subject of which was a peaceful revolution brought about in the interests of everybody. The public seized with delight upon every allusion, and during its run of a hundred nights never ceased applauding the verses in praise of the King, who was compared to a rose! This kind of poetic licence was not to the taste of everybody, but its success proved that Louis XVI had not lost the affection of his people.

It is interesting to remark that this period was characterised by a peculiar penchant towards the idyllic and all that is most naive in literary endeavour; a return to the Golden Age, in fact—Florian's pastorals and Berquin's verses for the young. The eighteenth century romances had completely disappeared. Instead of *Heloïse, Zadig* and *Manon Lescaut,* one read cheerfully *Zélie dans le Désert, L'Enfant de la Nature* and the *Epreuves du Sentiment.* This leaning towards the romantic side of life at the moment of its most terrible reality resembled those dreams which we always try to prolong and which are interrupted by the chaos of a storm.

The security of Paris seemed beyond question; it reposed upon a foundation which no other capital had ever known. There were 60,000 bayonets, ready, devoted and intelligent and which asked neither pay, barracks nor any other thing which to ordinary troops is essential. That great institution the Paris National Guard had become the Palladium of the city. At the first tap of drum each house disgorged a citizen whose military bearing compared favourably with that of a soldier belonging to a *corps d'élite*. They were not only fine troops but fine fellows, who fought as though they had done nothing else all their lives, and whom I have seen stand up for three hours to the fire of the finest infantry in Europe. This army, which is entitled to remembrance, was drilled by the French Guard and organised by General Lafayette. Their services received just recognition. Instructors of the National Guard have been promoted to the highest grades in the service, and so far as the General is concerned, the people's gratitude made him king of Paris for two years. It is impossible nowadays to realise how he was idolised. The only explanation of the fascination which he exercised is to be found in the youthful heart and spirit of a populace newborn, so to speak, to the party politic. Whenever Lafayette appeared he was greeted by an immense crowd which surrounded him and cheered him to the echo. All wished to touch him and to pat his white horse which, like his master, met this hero-worship with untiring patience and unfailing good temper.

Those who only knew Lafayette during the latter part of his life will be inclined to think that in describing him as we saw him at this epoch we have been embroidering an historic personality. No! The fact is that he had greatly changed. The dungeons of Olmutz had broken both his body and his spirit. To their work must be added forty years of hope deferred, of plans gone wrong, of fatal errors and possibly the fear of an unkindly judgement by posterity—this after contributing to the freedom of two great nations at the risk of his life and the sacrifice of his freedom, his fortune and his happiness.

In 1791 he was a charming gentleman some thirty-five or thirty-six years old, slim, distinguished and thoroughly aristocratic. He was fair in colouring, his face was pale, and his fair powdered hair, dressed *à l'oiseau royal,* was curled at the sides and hid his ears. When he was pleased and interested he made the most charming and favourable impression. It was only when irritated that one remarked on his forehead signs of a quick temper and on his mouth rather a disdainful expression; but these minor characteristics were quite overshadowed by the air of kindness and gentleness which was peculiar to him and which won him the wholehearted and enthusiastic affection of the people.

Although but recently arrived in Paris, and living in one of the most deserted streets in the Marais, I was immediately called up for service in the National Guard, thanks to my large size and my moustachios. When I objected to Tallien, who was chairman of the Minimes Section (formally that of the Palais Royal) that I was still two or three years short of the required age, he replied in a most agreeable and flattering manner that—

"*Chez les âmes bien nées*
La vertu n'attend pas le nombre des années,»[1]

and eight days later I found myself standing with fixed bayonet in the ranks of a picket three hundred strong drawn from our section of the National Guard and destined to furnish the King's Guard at the Tuileries.

Usually the honour of being selected for this duty was outweighed by its most immortal boredom, but on this occasion it was quite the other way about. The previous evening

---

1. Gentle birth waits not on years,
Its virtue is its own.

the rumour had been spread that there might be trouble in the Faubourg St. Antoine; to prophesy trouble was a well-known method of creating it and of collecting together those who liked it. A fairly general opinion attributed the project to those who hated the constitutional monarchy; but I heard people who knew better prophesy that it would turn out to be a Royalist *coup d'état* destined to stifle the Revolution. The facts showed that both parties wished to contribute to this mad day's work, although their mutual loathing certainly rendered cooperation impossible. It was learnt that during the morning some hundred men, probably bribed, had entered the Château de Vincennes without difficulty and that they proposed to pull it down in order to prevent the powers that be from converting it into another Bastille. This pretext had been furnished them by the municipality which had, most imprudently, ordered that the château should be repaired and converted into a subsidiary of the Paris prison system. It would have been extremely easy to revoke the order, but then there would have been no riot, and it appears that a great many people were agreed that a riot was necessary. When the voluntary demolition party had got to work they were par-leyed with instead of being given an opportunity to measure the depth of the moat. Naturally they took no notice of the speeches made to them, and the Hôtel de Ville then ordered a battalion of the National Guard to be sent against them. There were sixty from which to choose, and out of this number they chose the only one they should have excepted—that com-manded by Santerre the brewer, a man whose exalted dema-gogy was known to every one. Whether or no he knew which party was provoking the riot, he was certainly of the opinion that a riot was a sound idea, in that it would result in the au-thorities showing their impotence and incapacity. With this object he kept his companies assembled and refused to march in spite of repeated orders. When informed of this, Lafayette ordered two squadrons of the subsidised National Guard to mount, put himself at their head, left at full trot for Vincennes, and dashed through the Faubourg St. Antoine showing an armed force which had no fear of breaking the ranks of the malcontents. When we met this picked troop we gave the general the military honours, but he was so preoccupied that he did not notice us in spite of his invariable politeness.

Our picket eventually arrived at the château and took its post in Princes Court. Other detachments established themselves in the guard-rooms which had been constructed from the ignoble hovels which then formed the centre of the Tuileries and where now stands the Carrousel Gate. These courts were separated by similar barracks and communicated one with the other by carriage gateways in which were small doors served by a porter and guarded by sentries. The outside gates which gave into the Carrousel and faced a labyrinth of little streets were exactly similar. Everything, within and without, was ugly, dirty, and unworthy of a royal residence. The château was but little better, and the Parliament at Rennes was infinitely better housed. When I expressed my astonishment I was told that no repairs had been made to the Palace or its dependencies within living memory.

The Court had been here since its arrival from Versailles and was credited with a desire to return thither as quickly as possible. "It is said to be for tomorrow night," remarked my informant with a laugh. There was in fact a rumour fairly generally believed in Paris, to the effect that one fine morning the guests of the château would be reported missing. The departure of the King's aunts and the attempted departure of Monsieur[2] had lent colour to these incredible stories.

We took over the posts at the Palace; the most important was the guard-room at the entrance to the royal apartments; but it was separated from the latter by a door which was hermetically sealed and a succession of rooms which were inaccessible even to our view. This post was purely honorary and

2. The eldest brother of the King of France.

guarded nothing whatever. The surveillance of the courtyard seemed less fictitious and the day's disturbances rendered it necessary to exercise it strictly. But there also our service was confined to being on the spot. The gateway on to the Carrousel was shut and the wicket therein confided to the care of a porter to whom we were to render assistance in case of need. At nightfall our sentries began to grow uneasy about the number of visitors who were arriving and whose appearance was by no means reassuring. They were men wearing long cloaks and three-cornered hats pressed down low over the eyes. It was remarked that instead of going towards the Pavilion de Flore they went towards a part of the château where the entry was not guarded by our men. It was impossible to see where they entered as they vanished in the dusk, the courtyards at that time being lighted by a few rare lanterns whose rays were better calculated to exaggerate the shadows than to dissipate them. The sentries did their duty resolutely, and after cross-examining the porter, who turned a deaf ear, they informed him that they would arrest the next visitor he introduced and call the guard to have him identified. When they added that the unrest on the faubourgs forbade the admission of unknown people to the Palace, the porter, touched no doubt by their anxiety which vouched for the soundness of their opinions, reassured them by protesting that these mysterious beings were gentlemen.

"But how can you be certain of that?"

"By a card which they show and a password they give me on coming in," was the reply.

My young comrades found these precautions extremely suspicious and recollected that in this manner plots were hatched. Their turn of duty over they informed their commanding officer of what they had seen and heard. In such a critical situation we needed a tried soldier and not a soldier by hazard such as our commander, who was a furniture manufacturer of the Rue St. Antoine; rich and highly esteemed, no doubt, but one from whom it was too much to expect the qualities which go to make a man of war! Nevertheless he extricated himself from this thorny position in an extremely capable manner, and suddenly gave proof of character, activity and intelligence. He called out the guard, ordered them to load and held the drums ready to beat to arms. After a short and inspiring speech he put himself at the head of a strong patrol, visited the posts and questioned the sentries. He made certain from their reports that more than eighty people, apparently disguised, had been admitted to the château; and it was allowed that this figure was doubled or trebled by those who had entered by the Cours des Suisses, thus avoiding all semblance of control. People in the confidence of the Royalists stated the following morning that there were seven hundred men in the apartments.

The patrol was about to return when the clash of arms, shouts, and a heavy fall were heard. Guided by the noise we ran to the scene. It was our sentry at the small door who had been bumped into violently by one of the new guests of the château, who was rushing towards the back staircase. This lack of manners had earned the gentleman a blow with the butt which rolled him over on the pavement, swearing and uttering most imprudent threats the while. When it came to arresting him he resisted furiously, and force had to be applied to bring him to the guard-room. There to our extreme surprise we discovered that under his cloak he was equipped like one of Schiller's brigands in the Black Forest. His court dress, complemented by a belt full of daggers and pistols, gave him a most grotesque appearance, and it was difficult to recognise in him one of those elegant gentlemen, familiars of the Tuileries.

This incident led to an agitation quite impossible to describe. We were all convinced that the adventurers who had already entered the château were now in command of it and that they were about to carry off the King willy-nilly. The fact that they had intended to carry this out under our very eyes roused the calmest among us to a state of fury, and the most violent proposals were made with a view to meting out condign punishment to the conspirators.

At this juncture the gate on the Quai opened and General Lafayette, streaming with sweat and covered in mud, galloped into the courtyard, followed by a few of his staff. We welcomed him with cheers, for it was high time that he arrived. He had come from Vincennes and had crossed Paris with such rapidity that his horse, completely foundered, lay down on its side as soon as he dismounted. The General had arrested some sixty of the demolition party at Vincennes and had sent them to the Conciergerie. On his return journey he had burst his way through the crowds on the Faubourg St. Antoine and his rapidity and courage had so disconcerted his opponents that Santerre had only been able to loose off two or three shots at him. The municipality, which had not only the power but the duty to put fifty battalions on the move to cover him, had given no orders, and its lethargy was such that it was completely ignorant of the danger which menaced the château. Lafayette had been advised by a late despatch, and he was bitterly crestfallen on realising that the riot at Vincennes was merely a ruse to keep him away from the Tuileries and profit by his absence. His first words were to ask after the King, who he supposed had been carried off. Doubtless our commander told him that the people who had intended to do so were still in the château—for the general, in a tone charged with menace, shouted—

"I'll put some order into this," and then, in a tone of command as though he were leading us into battle: "Follow me, Gentlemen."

Immediately we followed on his heels and in a serried mass climbed the stairs of the Pavilion de Flore. After passing through two or three rooms we came to the closed door which marked the entrance to the apartments. This remaining obstinately closed, the general made a sign and it opened as if by magic. The room we entered only contained a group of officers whom I took to be a bodyguard. At the double we reached the door of a very much larger room, and there found ourselves face to face, or rather breast to breast, with the enemy. Fifty or sixty men were there, pressed one against another, all armed to the teeth, wearing court dress and a most unprepossessing expression. The General had entered first and found himself in the middle of them; and recollections of the *forty-five* of Henry III coming to my mind, I thought him a dead man. Without doubt they could have meted out to him the same fate as that of the Duc de Guise at Blois, but they hesitated and the chance was lost. "Disarm them," called the General, and without stopping he pushed his way through, scorning the danger, or rather his opponents of whom he seemed to say—they dare not. While we held off the conspirators at the point of the bayonet and disarmed them the general strolled on to the door at the farther end of the room. I ran after him, certain that he was going to his death and that the next room was full of enemies also. However, at the entry he took his hat off, held us back by a gesture, and found himself in the presence of the King, who was standing alone in the middle of the room. "Sire," he said with emotion but in a tone which indicated his pent-up anger, "whilst the National Guard and myself are doing our utmost for your Majesty, these adventurers, equipped like assassins, are admitted to your Palace, and on their heels will come a raging populace whose vengeance it will be beyond the power of anyone to stop."

Although I was only a few yards from the King I could scarcely hear a word of his reply, so much noise was going on in the next room. The phrase appeared to me to be noncommittal such as: "I know nothing about this"; but I heard the following words quite distinctly: "They are too-zealous servants," he said, "who were under the mistaken impression that I was in danger; do all you can to avoid harm coming to them. I do not wish this to go any further, nor that it should be talked about." These last words of which I only reproduce the sense, were I think much more marked; they were uttered with an obvious intention and with emotion.

The General received a very cold reception at the Tuileries every day, and could scarcely expect a better one when his visit was not only unexpected but undesirable. He was therefore profoundly astonished to hear the King address him with a kindness and a species of confidence which he had not hitherto obtained, even when he most deserved it. His resolution seemed to desert him; he uttered some words of devotion and assured the King that his orders would be carried out. If he believed that he had sufficiently manifested his power and therefore could seize the ascendancy which hitherto had eluded him, he must have been quickly disillusioned by a significant circumstance which followed. He had scarcely quitted the Royal apartments when the door was slammed behind him with the insulting rudeness peculiar to domestics. This incredible expression of hatred might have led to the death of the prisoners awaiting their fate in the ante-rooms. Some lay on the floor bound with the window curtains, others stood against the wall expecting at any moment to be thrown from the balcony to the courtyard pavement. Lafayette, who before the King had seemed to be irresolute, when confronted by a real danger was calm, clever and courageous. His voice was drowned at first under a storm of shouts and curses, but he eventually succeeded in instilling a feeling of pity into this crowd of maniacs. He said that he would never forgive himself if, voluntarily or otherwise, he were involved in any event leading to bloodshed in the King's Palace, and that he would abandon any country whose best citizens preferred vengeance to the merit of forgiveness. He asked, as a reward for his services and a token of the affection which they might bear him, that the prisoners might be spared and that they might be expelled from the château immediately without violence of any kind. The success of this speech was assured by the officers, who led the applause by crying "*Vive le Général,*" an acclamation which must have caused him the more satisfaction in that his enemies heard it and were forced to recognise his power thereby. The prisoners were immediately unbound and pushed out by the scruff of the neck through the door leading on to the Quai *via* the Cour des Princes. There they were freed and left to congratulate themselves on a remarkable escape from death. It has been stated that they were outrageously manhandled, but to my knowledge nothing of the kind occurred. They were certainly not treated with indiscriminate gentleness, and those who affected a certain haughtiness were made to see the error of their ways; but their foolhardy enterprise had laid them open to any reprisal, and those who saw the collection of weapons of which they had been deprived asked themselves whether they had been let loose merely to encourage others to try again—perhaps with better luck.

After the General's departure I saw the relieving pickets arrive. They started searching everywhere, convinced that there were still some of the enemy hidden behind the tapestries. They were right; a large cupboard was discovered which contained a dozen, and there were as many more in a wood-house. It was the general opinion that many more had escaped than had been taken and that they had used secret passages to reach the Cour des Suisses and the Rue St. Nicaise. In the King's apartments I had also remarked several persons standing quietly aside, and asked their names in the hope of discovering among them the man who had shut the door on the general with so much violence. I recognised him at once as being the Comte d'Hervilly, late Colonel of the Rohan-Soubise, who in 1788 had been charged by the Court to round up the members of the Breton Parliament. I remember the occurrence filled my infantile mind with furious indignation at the time. He was a little bilious man, ambitious, and determined to succeed at any price. An extremely good swordsman, he was friendly with all the Paris masters-at-arms, who were famous for their perfection in the art of scientific slaughter, and he had no difficulty in assembling them under his orders in the Tuileries apartments with a view to carrying out the plot which had just gone awry and of which he was probably the author. The following year on the 10th August he had no better luck. Three years later I saw him once more at Quiberon flying before the grenadiers of General Hoche. One of our bullets hit him, and he crawled aboard an English ship to die. The presence of this man at the head of the bravos he commanded left no doubt as to the nature of the designs which had been premeditated, and which were realised four months later by the flight of the King, followed, unhappily, by his arrest at Varennes.

This day's work advantaged no one, and the facts concerning it have remained in a doubtful obscurity, no eyewitness having revealed them until now. It had, however, the gravest consequences; it brought about an open state of war between the three parties who had been spying on one another for so long, and it put an end to the state of affairs which the Federation of 1790 had consolidated.

When I descended to the Cour des Princes I found it filled with National Guards who were arriving at the Tuileries from all directions; and I heard many a curse directed at the heads of those who had let the prisoners go. These newcomers talked easily, but they would probably have acted like us had it come to arresting men who had the courage not to defend themselves. I went to find my commanding officer, who had sent for me. "You have been at my side throughout these events and you know them as well as I do; could you recount them?" On my replying in the affirmative he added in a low voice: "M. de Lafayette has, rightly or wrongly, undertaken a heavy responsibility; I am not inclined to share it, and I wish to do my duty towards my electors by rendering them an account of what has taken place. I wish to give them a written report, but I have not a sufficiently open mind, and I prefer to send you to the Section Committee which is sitting permanently at the moment. You will recount briefly what has happened and they will know what to do."

I accepted this staff job with pleasure; it was the first of all those I have carried out during the last forty years. The commanding officer gave me the password and certain instructions and let me out of the château himself by the gate on the Quai. I found my way to the Minimes, where I discovered all the lights out and the National Guard wrapped in the most profound slumber. But the Committee was awake, and I was introduced immediately the presence of an orderly from the Tuileries was made known. After having given the password to Tallien, who presided, I briefly recounted the events of the night. Undoubtedly so fine a theme would have earned me a legitimate success at the Collège de Rennes, but here my audience was so preoccupied by the subject of my story that they took little notice of its form; they interrupted me a hundred times by angry exclamations, and the President was obliged to intervene in order to get me a hearing, with leave to cross-examine me afterwards.

Tallien was thanking me effusively when a man who stood warming himself at the fire, and who appeared to me to be a stranger to the Committee, approached the table and addressed me with an authority which was apparent not only in his words but in the silence with which he was heard. He was a thickset man with a broad countenance, a high voice and bold piercing eyes.

"Was the National Guard prepared to kill these creatures?" he asked me.

"Undoubtedly, sir," I replied, "had they defended themselves."

"But," he replied with a pitiless logic, "those people were not enemies on a battle-field; they were conspirators, and criminals in consequence. Justice kills criminals—it does not fight against them."

I was careful to make no serious reply to this ferocious argument. "Sir," I said, "had you witnessed the occurrence you would not complain. These particular conspirators were so curious that any country which owned them would make it a duty to preserve them—if only to make sure that a more courageous offspring should not arise from their ashes."

"Well said," he replied with a loud laugh, "but if they come back I will hold you responsible for them!" I bowed

"Who is that gentleman?" I asked when leaving.

"What!" replied the attendant, "don't you know?He's M. Tallien's friend, the excellent M. Danton."

When I found myself in the street at last I was only too pleased to be able to go to sleep in peace after my first—and bloodless—campaign.

CHAPTER 2: 1792

1st Marine Artillery & Civil War

It was the middle of September 1792. France seemed unable to hold out against her enemies. They had resolved her ruin, her servitude, and the partition of her territory. Lille and Valenciennes were besieged, and the Prussians, masters of Longwy and Verdun, were advancing through Champagne to Paris.

I returned to Rennes. One morning when working in class a sound of drums accompanied by the lamentations of many unhappy women disturbed the peace of our studies. The Mayor of Rennes, followed by the Town Council, entered the great court and proceeded to carry out an unpleasant duty. We formed a circle and I still seem to hear the words he spoke:

"Young students, the enemy has invaded France in order to stifle our liberty and destroy our independence. He is already in Champagne, and Paris may be taken at this very moment. The country calls her children to her aid. The Law Schools are prepared to march. Who amongst you will follow their example and leave tomorrow for the army?"

"All! All!" we replied unanimously.

"Good," replied the Mayor, "come and sign your engagement."

Nobody hesitated, and the entire college made ready to march against the enemy. It was an unhappy day for the families in town. It is true that it was promised that we should return home immediately the war was over, but never was human vanity more painfully exposed; the majority of those students perished prematurely and whitened all the battlefields of Europe with their bones. As for me—although death passed me by for some unaccountable reason—I served the flag for forty years and never left it for a single instant.

My dream had been to go to the northern frontier and there repulse the enemy. I was not so lucky; my first experience of war consisted in painful and perilous successes gained over the insurgents of Morbihan in the fields of Brittany. It was during this first campaign that I learnt that civil war is the most appalling scourge that can afflict a nation.

One day there was a fair at Hédé, a small town situated some ten leagues from Rennes. The peasants, who were there in large numbers, were given free drinks and profited by the privilege to get drunk. This was merely the prologue; the play followed quickly after. The *bad hats* rushed the town hall, threw the records out of the window and made a bonfire of them; they then beat the Mayor senseless, drove off the *bourgeois* who came to his rescue, hauled down the tricolour, hoisted the white flag in its place and sounded the alarm to call the neighbouring parishes to insurrection. The inhabitants, who had been literally pitchforked out, arrived at Rennes covered in blood and told us the story. A few hours afterwards a strong column marched on Hédé, formed from the National Guard and some youngsters taken from the mass levy. The honour of having belonged to the Paris militia found me and others a place in this column. On our arrival we were greeted by a lively fire of musketry, which left no doubt as to the insurrection having long been premeditated. But on seeing us charge the peasants gave way, and in spite of the hedges and coppices which favoured their escape many were wounded, killed or made prisoner. The latter were taken to Rennes and thrown into the cells of the Tour le Bat, filthy holes compared to which the dungeons of the Bastille were veritable palaces.

The following morning the neighbourhood of the prison was crowded with the wives and children of these unhappy wretches, tearfully pleading to share their fate. This distressing spectacle made me bitterly regret our ill-fated success. One woman in particular was the very picture of despair; she was trembling so violently that I expected her to collapse at any moment. Her daughter, a child of ten or twelve, was kneeling before her without being able to help her in any way save by reciting the prayers for the dying. I could not get a single coherent word from her which might have enabled me to help them. An old peasant who believed that I was well-intentioned swore on his hope of Paradise that this woman's husband had done nothing and that nobody knew why he had been arrested; he gave me his name, which did not, in fact, figure on the list of prisoners. The poor devil was merely one of the hostages we had taken with us from Rennes; on the way he had been put in a cart with the prisoners and had been mixed up with them on the convoy's return. The mass sentence which was shortly to be pronounced against them was likely to include him also. Félix Mainguy, to whom I had recourse in order to put matters right, gave himself no rest until this fatal error had been corrected and the man restored to his distracted relatives.

I had scarcely time to clean my arms, reflecting bitterly on the less fortunate side of human existence the while, when a dispatch from Vannes announced that the town was surrounded and that skirmishing was going on in the outskirts. It was necessary to despatch another mobile column to relieve it, and I was called on once again. This time it was not a temporary affair but a real campaign. The insurrection had extended to the majority of the parishes of Morbihan and arms and ammunition had been landed by the English. For four months there was a succession of more or less serious engagements. Sometimes merely a night attack on our outposts, at others a demonstration against some important point with a view to drawing us into an ambush. We learned, to our cost, to defend ourselves against such stratagems, and more than once we led the enemy into the traps he had prepared for us.

But, good God! how cruel and hateful those victories were. The conquered were Frenchmen, good, credulous fellows sent to their doom by political adventurers whom our bullets never reached. Besides, pity, confidence, humanity were virtues against which we had to guard ourselves or perish. If you did not finish off a wounded man he crawled after you and shot you whilst you were reloading. On one occasion, in a barn in which we were to pass the night, we found a man amongst the straw, wounded and apparently dying. Instead of killing him we gave him some brandy—the only thing we had. As soon as we were asleep he set the barn alight and loosed off a double-shotted gun at us at the very moment when we were attempting to save him from the flames. But his gun, which he had hidden in anticipation of this ambush, burst in his hands and blew his jaw away. On another occasion, suffering from thirst, I entered a house with a comrade to ask for a drink. A man, who probably had good reason for remaining concealed, was hidden behind the door and cut me over the head with a sabre. On hearing my shout my comrade fired at random and killed him. My thick felt hat was cut clean through and if my skull was not split I owe the fact to the thickness of my hair. I could not prevent the volunteers from burning down the cottage. A sabre cut, a dead man, a burnt house—and all for a cup of water! I bitterly regretted my thirst.

We could not keep the insurrection in check, but to stamp it out we needed ten times the strength ; and the army of the north had no reserves to offer to the army of the west. The National Guards of our column had been allowed to go home a long time since and had been replaced by volunteers from the mass levy. The People's Representative, satisfied with our services, had formed us into free companies and, as the custom then was, we had chosen our own officers. Nowadays those new troops would look more than odd ; they paraded abominably, marched anyhow and had not the least idea of small-arm drill. But when they went against the enemy they sang and dashed to the attack with an irresistible enthusiasm. Recruited from all classes of society, they were gifted with an intelligence far superior to that of the soldiery of former days. I have bivouacked a hundred times with men who spoke Latin like professors, who could turn out charming verse, or who sang like our compatriot Elléviou. The finest *morale* prevailed, and I could cite many instances of it. I will content myself with one. On a fine night the main-guard, of which I was one, was heavily fired on. We replied and advanced, but the enemy's fire having ceased we retired on our positions. All turned in except myself, who was posted as our sole and unique sentry. My job was far from pleasant. At dawn we received without fail a more or less well-directed bullet, and a large oak which marked the limit of my functions carried the traces of some twenty shots which the enemy had consecrated to my predecessors. Listening with all my ears I seemed to hear smothered groans. It might have been one of our wounded, and as the dawn allowed me to pick out details I advanced in order to make certain, taking, to be sure, all the precautions which appeal to a hunter who may at any moment become the hunted. I found something quite different from what I had imagined. In a ditch surrounded by bushes lay a young man, dead or dying, and near him on her knees a fine young girl weeping bitterly.

"Oh, save my poor brother's life," she said, "without help he'll die, and I can do no more for him."

"But," I replied, "won't the danger be just as great if he is carried to the town? We might not be in a position to protect him."

"I daresay," she replied, "but I can only trust in God; so help me carry this poor boy; he has nearly bled to death already and is bound to die if we do nothing."

I did not hesitate, despite the fact that to give aid to a

Chouan leader was a capital offence in those days. I ran to the guard-room, and the sergeant himself came with two or three of our friends and carried the wounded man to one of the neighbouring houses. We gave him a forage cap and a cloak to enable him to pass our sentries, and thanks to this we succeeded in getting him through our lines. One of our surgeons visited him and pronounced his wound to be mainly superficial. This assurance gave the young peasant girl a new lease of life; but the common clothes she wore did not disguise the fact that she was one of the most beautiful and best bred creatures in the country. Without her the brother would have died where he fell. Having failed to find him she beat the heather and eventually discovered him abandoned and apparently dying in a ditch. Happily at that moment I turned up and enlisted the aid of my comrades. The Lord only knows how dearly that act of humanity might have cost us, but happily the secret was never divulged.

If only our adventures had always been as heroic! Unhappily they were usually monotonous and occasionally perilous. When we returned to bivouac the commissariat was usually missing and we had an indefinite fast ahead of us. It is true the bread from the bakeries was commandeered, but it was scarcely sufficient to give us a mouthful apiece. A half-dozen of my young comrades, spurred by a ferocious appetite, organised a marauding expedition. I agreed to join them provided no violence was used. An hour later we were in a village, apparently deserted. Near the church was a house which looked promising. Our appearance in the courtyard was heralded by the hurried departure of a distressed and aged female who returned accompanied by a decent looking man. The latter asked us whether we had come to arrest him. I replied that he had mistaken our profession, but that our own was not particularly attractive, since its followers were condemned to starve for forty-eight hours at a time.

"This compels me to ask you for bread," I remarked.

"With the greatest of pleasure," he replied, "come in."

Touched by these words we left a sentry on the doorstep and walked in. The parson—for it was he in peasant clothing—gave us an excellent meal accompanied by several jugs of cider. We were eating like tigers when our sentry gave the alarm. We had kept our muskets between our knees and in a second were on the doorstep prepared to argue with a dozen well-armed men who had just entered the yard.

"Don't worry," said the parson, coming between us, "my parishioners are very attached to me, and have come to help me under the impression that I am in danger. I will send them away at once."

The deed followed the word, and the peasants retired after having received his blessing and having shown him the most marked respect and affection.

Night having fallen, our host would not hear of our leaving unless he accompanied us to our advanced posts. He probably knew that the road presented considerable danger for such as we. To avoid mistakes he sent his dog ahead carrying a stick in his mouth to which two lanterns were attached; which was the method he used when visiting his flock by night. By an infallible instinct this dog invariably barked at the *Blues* and made much of the *Whites*. Our host had to explain to him that I must be made much of despite the colour of my cloth. The clever animal understood only too well. One day on parade an enormous dog bounded on to the ground, came straight to me and proceeded to welcome me as a friend of the family.

"That dog belongs to the Chouans. How do you come to know him?" asked the People's Representative, who happened to be present on parade. The reply was difficult, as I wished neither to tell the truth nor to lie. A friend came to my aid with a joke.

"The bones they give us daily in the shape of meat have made friends of the two of them," he shouted.

The volunteers, who strongly suspected that the Representative and the Commissariat were not total strangers, burst into loud laughter and called out "*Bien touché.*"

In the meantime the dog had disappeared, and wisely so, since in order to slaughter him legally it was already being alleged that he was a spy and carried information in his collar. Furthermore, as he was not of a character to invite inspection, it was evidently necessary to bash his head in first and declare his innocence afterwards. The foregoing is not an exaggerated example of the judicial methods of the period, and I was remarkably lucky in that the *proconsul* could find no pretext which would permit him to avenge the insult of which he considered me the author.

The war we were waging must not be judged by the examples I have given. Doubtless if one side showed humanity the other side tried to do better; but it only needed new chiefs to be appointed or new orders to be given, for us to fall back into barbarism. We never had a moment's security, repose, or peaceful sleep; the constant alarms did not permit of our quitting our clothes or our arms. If you saw a man's head over a bush you were certain to hear a bullet whistle past your eyes and were only too happy to have come up against an indifferent shot. When a former gamekeeper took a hand one did not escape so lightly.

We were accustomed to danger, but we could not accustom ourselves to the wretchedness of it all, myself in particular. We were considered to be a *corps d'élite* and were posted as an advanced guard in the suburbs, being billeted on the inhabitants, whereas the volunteer battalions were herded into the churches, which were cold, damp and smelt like graveyards. My young comrade having deserted, the first day I was left alone in our billet. My old hostess, although extremely contrary to begin with, took a fancy to me and helped me to live. She made me soup with butter and vegetables but without bread, for I could not bring myself to eat the appalling stuff, which from its colour and its smell resembled anything but what it claimed to be.

Finally we were ordered to leave, after a winter campaign which had lasted five months, which had been murderous and which had resulted in nothing more than forcing the enemy to abandon his intention of capturing the town of Vannes. We proceeded toward Finisterre, partly by sea and partly by land, where it was intended to form a camp destined to cover the port of Brest. This camp was formed at the extremity of the Armorican peninsula, amongst the granite battlements of Finisterre, bathed eternally by the rollers of the Atlantic.

The Breton contingents soon arrived and we set to to give them some military training. It was hard work. The mass levy of 1792 consisted of townsmen already accustomed to the use of arms through their training as National Guardsmen; but the levy of 300,000 men in 1793 brought in peasants who had never touched a musket. Nevertheless such is the inborn aptitude peculiar to the great country which is France, that after three months they manoeuvred like Prussian grenadiers.

The Committee of Public Safety sent us an Inspector-General appointed to brigade the battalions and form the cadres. It was General de Vaux, who was reputed to be a clever organiser. Before splitting up the troops he picked a certain number of men out for the Marine Artillery; he picked me for this arm, although my constitution certainly did not recommend me for it, since physical strength was essential. The following morning I was enrolled in the first Regiment of Marine Artillery (of which but the name remained) together with a few old non-commissioned officers, who told me all about their campaigns in India under Suffren. These stories appealed to me in that they bore a strong resemblance to those of Sinbad the Sailor; but I was soon otherwise occupied. The recruits were told that as soon as they had acquired the knowledge which all good gunners should possess they would be detailed to the outside harbour forts and find themselves confronted with the English warships. This thoroughly awakened my competitive spirit, and although theoretically this apprenticeship needed a whole year, I succeeded in reaching the first class in two months. This distinction should have merited the rank of corporal, and Colonel Cordoran was about to give it to me when it was pointed out that he was, unconsciously, giving way to a spirit of revolution, and that the tradition of the regiment demanded that I should attain to this dignity by the right of seniority only, the fulfilment of which condition would demand at least ten years.

The above would merit no attention did it not emphasize the important facts that firstly, sixty to eighty days sufficed to turn a schoolboy into a soldier, well grounded in the essentials peculiar to the most complicated arm in the service. Secondly that, even in 1793, the fifth year of the Revolution, nothing was changed in the traditional viewpoint of the old regiments, and everything took place as in the good old days of M. de Choiseul.

My instruction completed, I was detached to the coast north of the harbour to aid in its fortification. Fort Minou, where I was in garrison, is situated above the narrows of Brest at the spot where the two banks spring sharply apart to form the immense circular basin known as de Bertheaume and Camaret roadsteads. The anchorage is an open one, and almost daily ships from the enemy squadron entered it in pursuit of our merchantmen or fishing-smacks. The old forts around the neighbouring coast could not put a stop to this audacity, since they had been long neglected and their cannon, lying in the sand and grass, were completely out of service. The greatest exertions were required to haul the heavy pieces and the enormous mortars to their platform eighty feet above sea-level, and this after having brought them more than a league by tracks which only seemed accessible to goats. The difficulty was increased by the necessity of concealing our movements from the enemy. We were obliged to hide our works behind thorn bushes and our threatening gunports behind screens of flowers. More than once when the blockading frigates approached our rock the men were obliged to lie flat on their stomachs to avoid detection.

One of our fears was to see our plans betrayed by some of the fishermen who were frequently in touch with the English squadron, either to sell their fish or possibly to give information. A certain fisherman who was reputed the most daring on the coast had been pointed out to us as following this unpleasant calling. Nobody having found a better means of ensuring his discretion than that of murdering him in cold blood, the poor devil without knowing it was in danger of a violent death, when I suggested a more Christian course. The commander of Fort Montbarrey sent for him to mend some nets, and kept him there, half by force and half by goodwill, attracting him with wine and brandy; he succeeded so well that when he wished to let him go his pensioner only acquiesced with considerable reluctance.

I had at last the satisfaction to see completed a battery of eight thirty-six-pounders and two fifteen-inch mortars. That very evening an English ship accompanied by a frigate chased an unfortunate merchantman under the guns of the fort; she had already started to lower her boats when we opened fire with red-hot shot and sent over two enormous shells, which cut up her rigging and brought down her top-mast. The pirates paid no further attention to their victim, but got out of range as quickly as possible in order to repair their damages. The following night they sent in boats to attempt a landing in a small bay whence they could attack our battery from the rear; but we had anticipated this. Two old guns retrieved from a ditch had been so mounted as to enfilade the landing-place. One discharge sufficed to make the enemy retire, and the loss he suffered on this occasion effectually damped any enthusiasm for further undertakings of the sort.

The success of the Fort Minou battery having acquired us a certain distinction, our detachment was ordered to Conquet to repeat the operation ; the latter is a little port situated at the very end of the granite peninsula of Finisterre, and one which Providence has planted amidst the most dangerous reefs in order to give sailors some small chance of safety. Several attempts had already been made by the English fleet to reconnoitre this important post, and it will be remembered that in a previous war they had had the hardihood to capture it. The moment seemed to favour a repetition of this exploit, for although the Revolution was in its fifth year it had not yet penetrated to this remote and savage corner. Disquieting rumours were abroad, and our old soldiers were convinced that relations existed between our hosts and the English cruisers. I refused to countenance these stories, and persisted in the assumption that the number of fools, madmen, and evildoers in this world is greatly exaggerated. I must admit that this opinion, to which I still adhere, was most singularly unjustified on this occasion.

Where we were the newspapers, the post, and the highroad were unknown. At Conquet we lived in a cheerful security, ignorant of the terrible events which menaced the very existence of our country. One morning, however, some gunners who had gone to Brest on leave returned with the most alarming rumours. A plot had been discovered to enter the port *via* Penfelds and burn the shipping and the stores. A false attack was to be made on the Porte de Récouvrance by an English column, supported by peasants, bribed sailors, and *emigrés* landed in the neighbourhood. Soldiers capable of appreciating this project found it sound, and the proof is that for the last fifty years works have constantly been constructed in order to render its success impracticable.

That same evening, the post on the coast having been doubled, those most exposed to danger, namely the gunners whose works were completed, were ordered to return to Brest. One of them, a fine young fellow who had shown me a lot of affection, seemed very upset at the idea of our imminent departure. His feelings getting the better of him, he told me that he had had the good fortune to appeal to a beauteous young lady who lived in a half-ruined manor-house some half a league from Conquet and situated in a spot rejoicing, if I am not mistaken, in the barbarous name of Trébabu.

He had arrived at the stage where oaths of fidelity, proposals of marriage, and plans for elopement were cheerfully intermingled; and a few hours later a pitiless order forced him to depart, probably for ever! He begged me to bear him company to his rendezvous to keep his courage up. The idea did not appeal to me at all; but I was obliged to agree, flattering myself that on the way I should be able to dissuade him from an interview the consequences of which I feared and which threatened to lead him to desertion.

In the evening, being off duty, we launched out on the barren and deserted heath whose rocky paths eventually led us to a deep-cut valley. There lay an old granite building, part of which was tumbling into ruin; in front was a large courtyard surrounded by walls sufficiently high to prevent a view of the doors and windows on the ground floor. A mean thatched farm adjoined this manor worthy of the art of Salvator Rosa. I tried once more to dissuade my young friend from embarking on a visit which might be lengthy, and would in that case lead to a return in darkness and the consequent risk of nocturnal aggression. All I could obtain was a promise from him to cut his visit short and to rejoin me in half an hour. As might have been expected, I awaited his return in vain, and I departed very discontented with the role of confidant which I had assumed despite myself. Fearing to lose my way on the heath, I took a path which led towards the shore and carried on to Conquet by the cliffs. From this height I looked over the sea, and noticed the fishing smacks which had caused so much suspicion. On one of them which seemed deserted there were, nevertheless, two braziers from which smoke arose in two columns. Happening to turn my head towards the lonely house, I was surprised to see two columns of smoke rising from that. Despite my inexperience I could not fail to recognise that these were signals, and that they probably portended something lawless. Was it contraband or counter-revolution? I had no notion; but I was convinced that my young comrade had fallen on a wasps' nest and that his life was in danger. I was not reassured by the apparition of a suspicious-looking individual who, bareheaded and apparently panic-stricken, was hurrying along a narrow path at the foot of the cliffs which led to the old manor by a track cut among the rocks. I lost sight of him and went my way in a very uneasy frame of mind.

It was dusk when one of our sentries challenged me; on his whistle a corporal came up and asked me if I had met a pedlar. He told me that an hour before his picket had captured on a track in the middle of the broom a man leading a horse whose panniers seemed stuffed with merchandise. The load seemed very heavy, and the volunteers decided to inspect it; they found that it consisted of ball cartridge. By the time they thought of arresting the driver he had disappeared in the bush; they were about to pursue when two shots were fired at them to stop them. The person responsible was a decent-looking man in sporting dress, carrying a double-barrelled gun. As he was about to disappear into the wood the corporal fired and shot him dead. The papers found on him and the captured horse were sent back to the rear and a hasty report gave the details to the commanding officer.

The corporal could not forgive himself for the escape of the alleged pedlar, and when I told him that I knew where he was he would have gone after him with the greatest pleasure, in spite of the darkness. We discussed the best methods of investing the lonely house, catching the fugitive and delivering my young friend—if it was not too late. These measures we put into execution immediately. A beacon, previously prepared, was lighted, and thereby gave the signal to the main-guard to come up in support for reasons of extreme gravity. The corporal remained in order to give all information to the commanding officer and to serve him as guide; meanwhile, accompanied by two volunteers, I went forward to reconnoitre the enemy. For this service they gave me the late sportsman's gun, which I charged heavily with split shot. We acted so quickly that within half an hour we were beneath the walls of the lonely house. It was not easy to find the way in the darkness, but I already possessed to a certain degree that species of second sight which enables geologists and staff officers to sum up a terrain.

I did not share my overconfident companions' opinion that the house would prove to be deserted, but I was nevertheless astounded to hear the noise that came therefrom, which heralded a garrison not only numerous but truculent and determined.

As we were examining the gate of the paddock and had assured ourselves that it was strongly barricaded, we saw outlined on a nearby hillock the figure of a man who was stealthily advancing. It was the pedlar returning to roost after an unprofitable day. He passed quite close to our hiding-place without seeing us, and I had great difficulty in stopping my companions from attacking him. I hoped he would show us the way to get into the house. In fact, after inspecting the door, he proceeded to climb the wall at the spot which he knew to be easiest, whence he slid down the roof of a lean-to on the other side and so jumped into the courtyard.

Hitherto we had only heard rough and angry voices, but when the newcomer opened the door of the hall where these gentry were assembled I caught the sound of a pitiful moaning, a prayer for mercy, and I could no longer doubt but that my young friend was there in the midst of those wretches and exposed to all the fury of their cruelty. Powerless to save him, we were nevertheless led to try by an instinctive impulse which exposed us to the greatest risk. Young and fit as we were, we were soon on the top of the wall; one remained there as sentry, but chiefly to act as guide for the help we expected; a delay of a few seconds and all might be over with us. Followed by the other I walked along the top of the lean-to towards a high window, dimly lit, from whence the noise of the ground floor came to me most distinctly. We passed through and found ourselves in a vast loft full of straw, which extended the entire length of the hall in which such terrible things were taking place. The planking was pierced in many places, and a large gap at our feet would have let a man through. Keeping back in the shadow we could see the whole horrible scene through this loophole. Around a long table covered with pots and bottles some twenty men were gathered, armed with muskets, pistols and hunting knives, and clad, some as country gentlemen, others as sailors. Excepting three or four who ate and drank without worrying about what was going on, the whole crowd seemed convulsed with fury. The object of their anger was my unhappy young friend who, surprised during his rendezvous by their sudden entry, had been unable to leave the house and had taken refuge in the loft. The old planking had given way under his weight, and the conspirators had seen fall into their midst a volunteer who must evidently have surprised their secret. He had been immediately seized and pinioned, and the poor lad was lying there, more dead than alive, merely awaiting the particular form of torture which would prelude his extinction.

"He's a spy!" cried furious voices, "he should have his throat cut."

"No! No!" cried others, "no bloodshed; better strangle him, Jean will throw him from the cliffs into the sea at high tide."

"Yes, yes," shrieked every one, "it's carried. Bring a rope, a rope at once!"

Immediately a man whom we recognised as the pedlar produced one, which he placed round our unfortunate friend's neck, dragging him towards a hook in the wall from which he intended to hang him.

I forgot that we were face to face with an enemy ten times our strength and that our friend's fate was the only reward that awaited us. I drew a bead on the executioner and killed him with my first barrel; the second hit his assistants and put the lamp out. Curses and cries of rage and pain rose from the darkness with such violence that I remained appalled, and it needed a reminder from my companion before we reloaded, if not to save our lives at any rate to sell them as dearly as possible. In any case it could only be a question of minutes before we were discovered, pulled out, and torn to pieces. But at this moment of dire peril the door of the hall opened and a strident voice, which dominated all the others, shouted:

"The house is surrounded. The walls are carried. Each for himself!" At the same time we heard the "Forward!" of the volunteers which announced their welcome arrival.

The hall was suddenly emptied by means of secret passages, which, however, did not assure the safe retreat of the conspirators, for the sound of a volley told me that our people were at grips with them. A dozen were made prisoner and half as many again shot dead. Descending by the gap in the planking, my comrade and I were the first to arrive in the deserted hall. Relit with straw the fire dissipated the obscurity and showed, besides two or three corpses, the body of the imprudent young man who had ventured into this den of cut-throats. I had stopped his hanging by killing his executioner, but the rope they had passed round his neck was already so tightly tied that he was completely asphyxiated. I was in despair. All our efforts to revive him were in vain, but the volunteers called up one of their comrades who was reputed a very clever surgeon, and in effect, by means of bleeding or something of the kind, he restored my poor companion to life, and although somewhat dilapidated he was sufficiently recovered to be transported to Conquet at dawn.

The same evening I left for Brest. I found the town in an uproar, forming mobile columns to beat the countryside and rope in the flying conspirators. A considerable number were discovered hiding amongst the rocky caverns of the coast. The arrest of the leaders led to the failure of the plot and was a salutary lesson to those who might have been tempted to follow their example.

But—without the garrison love-story, which was the cause of their discovery, they might have obtained the same success as at Toulon the year after.

The following day I received orders to join a ship which was about to set sail.

Sydney Smith & Toulon

The brig-of-war *Papillon,* in which I made my first sea campaign, was reputed to be the fastest sailer in the Brest fleet. Her captain belonged to the old navy; that is to say, he was a gentleman and a royalist, but a fine man and much beloved. The other officers were recruits, in other words, auxiliaries borrowed from the merchant marine; they were republicans, but this difference did not lessen the esteem and devotion in which they held their chief. The crew was well-assorted, well led and very happy. It was a family of brave men devoted to their duty and doing it gaily, as at a party. I was kindly received by every one. The lieutenant and the captain questioned me; and, although merely a gunner I was appointed master-at-arms. Soon I was given charge of the ship's accounts, complicated work which I feared to be beyond my powers; but success showed me the opportunities which are the reward of will and perseverance. These were the first official statistics confided to me; I was then sixteen years of age.

The brig's mission was to visit the ports of the Levant and convey fresh instructions to the French Consuls there, and I was enchanted at the prospect of visiting so many places hallowed by antiquity. My hopes were cruelly deceived, for it had been written that none of our beliefs, reasonable as they were, should be justified in fact. Thus when we sailed we expected to find ourselves faced by the enemy squadron, then blockading Brest. Not a single English vessel did we see there or elsewhere, not even at the landfalls off Ushant and Finisterre, where at this period there was a regular patrol covering the entrance from the Atlantic and the exit from the Channel. I hoped to see the celebrated straits of Gibraltar, which for so long had passed as the gates of the world; my hopes were dashed once more. We made this celebrated passage one dark night, and only a few vague lights showed us that we were in view of Europe on one side and Africa on the other. We entered the Mediterranean without being sighted; we were as solitary as if we sailed the Ocean. Astounded at this monotony I complained bitterly, but the old sailors told me that it was often thus; that there were men who had sailed for fifty years without having seen a single bad storm, and others who had served the ten campaigns of the American War without having seen a single naval battle. Among the various misfortunes of my existence at least I cannot include those two!

One evening at sundown, when the brig, with a soft breeze astern and a sea like glass, was making rapid progress, showing no trace of her passing but her wake, the lookout signalled land on the port bow, and a moment afterwards we made out a fleet ahead which appeared to be rapidly increasing in numbers. Immediately books, guitars, and backgammon-boards were thrown aside, and all telescopes were requisitioned. Was it the Toulon squadron? Was it not more probably the enemy? In the meantime night drew a veil across the horizon and the vision vanished. The commander's orders were to put into Toulon to collect his last despatches; the brig therefore was headed for Toulon in all haste, and the following morning at dawn we dropped anchor in the harbour. Unwittingly we had strayed into an inferno.

We had scarcely anchored when two boats came alongside; one brought us an order from Admiral Trogoff to join the battleships under his command, which were in full revolt against the Convention; the other directed us, in the name of

Admiral Saint-Julien, to remain faithful to the Republic and to join the ships of his squadron, the crews of which were devoted to him.

The two parties started by nearly fighting among themselves, and finally turned on us because we did not agree to their proposals with sufficient promptitude, and because we exhibited more astonishment than ardour when listening to their vehement speeches, rendered triply unintelligible by the Toulon accent, southern volubility, and the exaltation of passions entirely out of control.

We were in a hopeless dilemma. To leave the harbour meant falling in with the enemy squadron, for their ships of the line blockaded it closely and left us no chance of escape. To join the republican party in the hour of its ruin meant adding one ship more to those which France was about to lose. To obey the orders of Admiral Trogoff meant compounding with infamy and treason.

To get us out of this labyrinth our captain had recourse to a stratagem the secret of which he kept to himself. The vessel sprang a bad leak. The pumps being unable to overcome it, it became necessary to careen the ship. To this effect a pontoon was anchored in a deserted corner of the port, and the brig, having been towed there and lightened of her guns and ballast, was put on her side to admit of an inspection. The prevailing disorder rendered it impossible for the administration to send us dockyard workmen, and we were thrown back on our own resources to carry out the work; this meant prolonging its execution almost indefinitely, which was exactly what the captain wanted.

Our isolation from the centre of disturbance re-established calm on board; but one night several officers of the Republic came aboard and told us of the Royalists' intention to deliver the squadron to the English. The effect of this news on the crew was such that the captain felt convinced that at the first opportunity they would seize the ship and join Admiral

Saint-Julien. To put a stop to this he arranged with the town authorities to requisition a detachment from our seamen and gunners, destined to be employed on guard or on the fortifications. The advantages attached to this mission disguised its real object, and the brig, disarmed, was left to the keeping of those of the crew unfit for duty.

In the midst of this eruption the captain found time to think of me. He gave me a nomination as artillery guard in charge of an arms and powder magazine destined to supply the ramparts. When leaving he advised me to act with the greatest discretion; a wise counsel which I would have done better to have followed more literally.

Alone in my new post I tasted of a tranquillity which contrasted strangely with the appalling scenes of tumult common to the neighbourhood. Knowing nobody I learnt nothing, whatever may have been the urgent necessity that I should be enlightened; but by a sheer chance I was soon in a position to dispose of the most extensive information. Owing to its close proximity I had taken *pension* in a large hostel which from time immemorial had been the haunt of captains in the foreign trade. Commercial prosperity in the Levant during the last reign had afforded these people an opulence which forbade my messing with them. I had therefore no alternative but to come to an arrangement with my young hostess, despite my instinctive aversion to money matters. She assured me that she would look after my interests and limit my expenses to what I could afford, and I must admit that never have the finances of a country been administered by a chancellor of the exchequer as efficiently as were mine. The chancellor in this instance was a young widow, nineteen years old, whose portrait can be seen by any visitor to the Louvre in the shape of the Venus of Aries. The disinterested courage shown by this daughter of the people merits the reader's attention. Her name was Petrona, and she was of the pure Greek type. My evident interest in current events led her to

45

make daily enquiries as to what was happening or likely to happen. She succeeded with the connivance of some twenty merchant captains, who were only too willing to prove their zeal and devotion in return for a smile from Petrona.

During the Revolution I had often seen the people give free rein to their anger; but it resembled the anger of a lion in that its very power gave it grandeur. Here men seemed possessed by a sort of hydrophobia, like hyenas or jackals. Toulon was a prey to the terror. Admiral Trogoff, who had already used all his influence as commander of the fleet to corrupt its crews, came ashore to discuss with the municipality a proposal to call in the enemy fleet and hand over the port. Rear-Admiral Saint-Julien thereupon rejoined the ships which remained faithful, and formed them in line at the entrance to the bay so as to bar the passage to the English. But the insurgents were masters of the forts and were preparing to bombard our ships with red-hot shot. *La Perle,* frigate, commanded by Lieutenant Van Kempen, was the first to desert; she left our fleet and came to anchor under the walls of the town; Trogoff boarded her, hoisted his flag, and sent emissaries to the Republican ships to preach treason. He succeeded in this unworthy purpose; certain ships lifted anchor and came over to him, and Saint-Julien was left with some six ships in all. In desperation he lifted anchor that night, put to sea, and succeeded in passing the enemy's fleet. He eventually reached Brest, with his ships and crews, where they were welcomed as their fidelity deserved.

Meanwhile the leaders of the insurrection sent two representatives, Barallier and d'Imbert, on board the English fleet, which was cruising between Marseilles and Toulon. The conditions they proposed are unknown; we only know that they offered Admiral Hood free entry into the harbour and as guarantee the *Grosse Tour* and *Fort Lamalgue.* The plot which had been hatching so many months had at last attained its object. On the 23rd of August King Louis XVII was proclaimed,

and four days later the English fleet, followed by the Spanish squadron, entered the harbour without firing a shot. Thus
treachery delivered to the enemy the key to southern France,
and with it our Mediterranean fleet.

The Convention outlawed Toulon.

That unhappy town was the lions' den into which I had
fallen, and where I ran the risk of being torn to pieces, together with my friends. How imminent the danger was can
be judged by the following occurrence.

All communications were cut; one could neither leave the
town nor receive news from without which might lead us
to hope for relief. I was terribly worried. One day I met a
sergeant of Marines, by name Lambert, a bold and intelligent
man who had proved his devotion to the Republic on many
occasions. He was of the opinion that existence in the midst
of our mortal enemies would shortly become impossible, and
that we must get out of the town somehow; he had two hundred resolute men upon whom he could count. I joined in
with him and went to the rendezvous fixed for the following
night. As is always the case when it comes to carrying out a
dangerous plan, half our promised supporters were missing.
We proceeded in absolute silence to a postern gate of which
Lambert had the keys. The door opened without difficulty,
and for a moment we thought we had succeeded; but the
outlet of the tunnel which gave on the moat was closed by a
door which we found it impossible to open. Whilst endeavouring to do so we heard a noise from the direction of the
postern, and a portcullis fell, cutting off the retreat of the men
who had entered the tunnel. Happily several succeeded in
getting clear before the trap fell, but three remained behind,
and Lambert was one of them.

We had no sooner realised that we had fallen into a trap
than we were fired on from the ramparts. A few of us replied,
and even proposed to attack the enemy with the bayonet, in
spite of their obvious superiority in numbers. This example,

however, failed to raise the courage of our men, who dispersed almost immediately. I had so little knowledge of the town that I was likely to experience great difficulty in finding my road, when suddenly a child's voice said: "It is this way." It was a little girl of ten years, Petrona's servant, who had followed me by her orders without worrying about the firing. She warned me to return immediately if I wished to get back before the visiting-rounds and so conceal my absence, and in fact, shortly after my return, an officer, evidently acting under orders, visited my post and inspected my arms and equipment. Nothing gave me away and his report established my alibi. Otherwise I should have been arrested, condemned and hanged. It was the first time I had run that risk, and I remember that I was considerably upset thereby.

Our three unfortunate comrades were condemned to death, and although every possible precaution was taken during their journey to the scaffold, the indignation of the populace nearly brought about their escape. In the Rue des Chaudronniers their escort was fired on from the windows and put to flight, but as their orders were to kill the prisoners in the event of any attempt at rescue, they fired on them. One was killed outright and the other two dangerously wounded. Lambert, nevertheless, had taken refuge in a neighbouring house, and having already changed his clothes was hoping to escape; but his enemies tracked him to his hiding place by his trail of bloodstains. They bound him and his companion, and after beating them brutally dragged them to the gibbet.

Meanwhile General Carteaux, who commanded the Republican army, had secured Marseilles and was marching upon Toulon. His movements were desperately slow at first, probably by reason of the numberless difficulties created by the state of want in which he found his troops. However, the orders of the Convention and the presence of young Robespierre and Fréron hastened up the march of the army, which took position around the town and harbour and entrenched. From then on there were daily actions of varying intensity, designed to tighten up the investment and harden the new troops and national guards of which the majority of the besieging force was composed. All the neighbouring villages, which had been fortified by the English engineers, were captured one by one. Ollioule, which was held by sectionaries, Spaniards and Irish, was stormed, and from the ships in the harbour the French columns could be seen debouching on the Toulon road and establishing themselves there.

The attacks were not always so fortunate. On the 1st October the defile known as the Pas-de-Laydet was forced by a column which marched straight on to Fort Faron without securing its retreat. The enemy cut it off and attacked with infantry in mass. Our young soldiers, their backs to the cliff, threw themselves into the sea rather than surrender.

When General Dugommier took over the command in the middle of October the war assumed a different aspect. He took Seyne village, which the English defended most obstinately, and repulsed General O'Hara, who attempted to surprise the battery on the Arènes.

In the town meanwhile the terror was rampant, and no one dared speak openly of the progress made by our arms. In addition the enemy employed every possible strategy to hide it; they spread false news of pretended successes, and their detachments invariably returned covered with laurels, although their exploits were certainly nothing to boast about. But towards the middle of December these political falsehoods became frankly impossible; the fighting took place within view of the ramparts, and our troops were invariably successful. Finally General Lapoype and Representative Barras carried the heights which command the city. There they mounted guns which took the batteries below in reverse. General Dundas, commanding the English troops, gave the order to retreat, and the enemy shipping slipped their moorings, fearing artillery fire from the west side of the harbour, where the French had just made good their positions. On the 17th December the forts commanded by the batteries which Major Bonaparte had constructed during the night were precipitately evacuated. Some eleven thousand English troops re-entered the town, and there were certainly five thousand in hospital. Attempts to dissimulate this retreat under the pretext of a change of position were useless. As soon as it was known that the town was to be abandoned to the terrible vengeance of the Convention, terror, tumult, and confusion broke loose everywhere. A maddened crowd filled the roads which led to the port, carrying everything they hoped to save and imploring the English boats to afford them a refuge which they could not possibly give to more than one in a hundred. It was impossible to reach the beach, which was covered with baggage, women, and children. Any attempt to make a way through this mob for the sick and wounded was hopeless, and they were abandoned without means either to live or to die. I had already witnessed the scenes of disorder which accompany defeat, but I had never seen anything which approached the spectacle of this terrified population throwing itself into the sea to escape from an invisible enemy about to pounce and tear it.

The merchant shipping had left that morning, and the enemy fleet had hauled off to an anchorage beyond the *Grosse Tour*; in consequence the loaded boats had a desperately long distance to cover. Several were overloaded and turned turtle, and all their passengers were drowned. The fishing-boats which had taken off certain rich families at incredible prices were said to have thrown their passengers overboard in order to return and profit by the market which the circumstances offered. A detachment of Neapolitan troops fired on the receding boats in order to force them to return and take them aboard. The French were expected at any moment, and no words can express how we longed for their appearance; had they arrived a day earlier many a calamity might have been avoided.

We did all we could to hasten their approach, but none

of our men could get through; all we could do was to make certain that the guns in the batteries would not be turned against them, and at dusk, on the pretext of inspecting the primings, we spiked all the pieces which could be trained on our columns. After this dangerous and difficult operation we renewed our efforts to get into touch with the exterior; their failure decided us to return to the harbour, following the crowd which was flowing in that direction. The English troops had already embarked, but we soon fell in with a detachment of Spanish or Neapolitan troops with torches, who were making for the basin where the *Perle* was lying. We decided to attack them, and in spite of our inferiority in numbers we boarded at the moment when the fire was taking hold. The action scarcely lasted a minute; in the twinkling of an eye there was not a live enemy left in the frigate, and with the aid of a troop of galley-slaves we extinguished the fire and succeeded in saving one of the best ships in the fleet.

Early in the evening the convicts had broken gaol and armed themselves. These men, rendered outcasts by the questionable justice of the period, manifested an unshaken fidelity to their country at a time when disaffection was rampant in every grade of life. I would also add that this example was accompanied by discipline and military courage. I am qualified to speak, since it fell to my lot to lead these fearless rascals during several murderous actions before the night was out.

Three other frigates had also been fired, and we saved them too; furthermore, we repulsed the Spanish troops sent by Admiral Gravina to burn the six ships remaining in the basin. But we soon found ourselves faced by much heavier metal, against which some six hundred convicts and one hundred and fifty marine artillerymen were hard put to it, when it came to saving France's second seaport from destruction.

England had commissioned a man to destroy the French shipping who was destined one day to outshine Napoleon's star at Jaffa: his name was Sidney Smith. The first part of his mission was already terminated; the *Commerce de Marseille,* one hundred and twenty guns, and the *Pompée,* eighty, were already added to the English fleet, but twenty ships of the line remained in the harbour; they could not put to sea, and Admiral Parker was determined to burn them. In the evening Sidney Smith with a picked body of men had attempted to enter the port, but his reception was such that he had not tried to force the gates. He retired and called up the gunboats which always accompanied the English squadrons to such good purpose. He embarked his men, and, skirting the quays at dusk, turned our positions. Deceived by his supposed retirement, we had posted our advanced guards and taken up position in the principal harbour buildings; we thought the drama finished, when it was only about to commence.

In the meantime the enemy had occupied buildings in our rear, and when the gunboats summoned us to surrender they opened fire on us from the bakery. We were taken aback by this sudden attack, but soon plucked up courage, posted sharpshooters amongst the stacks of goods which littered the ground, and dislodged the English sailors with considerable loss by means of four field guns. In retiring the enemy set fire to the buildings they had occupied. The light thus afforded was fatal to us, since it enabled the gunboats to fire without fear of missing, and our losses were so severe that we had to give up the struggle in this quarter. Some twenty artillerymen thereupon occupied a large storehouse, barricaded the place and resisted for half an hour against a large body of sailors commanded by Sidney Smith in person. But we had to deal with an opponent as intelligent as he was stubborn. Whilst he held our attention by this attack he was pouring tar over the stacks of wood next to us. He set fire to these, and the flames caught the roof of our building before we were aware of it. Sidney Smith ceased firing and summoned us to surrender before the roof fell in. Under these circumstances we had to come out into the open. The Commodore was astonished at the smallness of our numbers and complimented us in French; he also promised to recommend us, and in spite of all he had to do he kept his word. This kindly sentiment, however, did not prevent our being sent singly and separately on board the gunboats.

I was desperate, and expected to be thrown into the hold, as was usually the case with prisoners. It turned out otherwise. The captain told me off to join the crew who, officers included, were anxiously hauling the boat off from a large black ship in tow of several English barges. Every detail of the scene was as clear as in daylight for the whole shore was aflame; every storehouse was a furnace which baffled all obscurity.

In the meantime the ship which had passed us had entered the arsenal, where the ships of the line were anchored and the towing boats were returning hurriedly. I asked a sailor the name of this vessel. He replied with a leer that it was the *Vulcan*. I was in no state to appreciate mythological allusions and this name meant no more to me than any other. At this moment an appalling clamour arose and a sinister flickering was seen on the doomed ship. It was the lighting of the fuse. Immediately a succession of explosions launched a shower of flaming tar barrels among the shipping in the immediate neighbourhood. In a few moments the squadron was ablaze and became one immense furnace, vomiting flames and smoke which blotted out the horizon.

The catastrophe was so terrible that even the English were appalled. They asked for nothing better than to quit, and it was obviously only Sidney Smith's order to embark the landing-parties which kept them alongside. Their situation was not to be envied, since they were distributed among a number of boats moored abreast and covered with fugitives who looked upon the English as the primary cause of their misfortunes. Suddenly silence fell like a pall, followed by a shriek of terror. It was a dreadful moment. The frightened mob dashed from ship to ship in an effort to reach the shore, overran the gunboat, and carried the crew with them in their panic. This appalling mix-up ended my captivity, but the price was heavy. I was scarcely ashore when a terrible explosion took me off my feet and a shower of burning debris filled the air. It was the powder-ship *Iris,* which a Spanish admiral had blown up. Apparently another powder-ship suffered the same fate at the same time, but I was too stunned to notice it. All I know is that when I got to my feet everything was on fire. I was lucky enough to meet an old sailor whose acquaintance I had made at Petrona's, and with his aid I rejoined the brig, which was ready to put to sea.

We had two problems to face—to pass the forts and to pass the enemy. We hoisted the tri-colour and were hailed by Fort Lamalgue. I do not remember what we answered, but we were through before they fired a shot. The greater danger was ahead, for once past the forts we were in the midst of the enemy fleet. Happily we were favoured by a thick December night and the general confusion. We were faster than they, and all we could see of them at dawn was their top-gallant sails on the horizon. Thenceforward we were safe, and within the week we dropped anchor in Brest harbour, where we were welcomed as becomes those who have been given up for lost.

During this first naval campaign I saw nothing of the Levant; instead, I witnessed civil war in all its horror.

Forty years later, at the funeral of Casimir Périer, I met Sir Sidney Smith, the most distinguished of our opponents, both for character and courage. We discussed what had happened at Toulon, and despite my respect for his brilliant career I could not avoid saying:

"Admiral, that was a bad business."

"God forgive me," he replied, "it certainly was."

CHAPTER 4

Sea Battle of the 'Glorious' 1st of June

Certain years seem accursed. The year 1794 was one. Blood ran everywhere, even in the ocean. To defend her new-found liberty France was fighting to the death on her frontiers and at home. At sea she was faced by the formidable fleets of England, eager to avenge the lost American colonies. To the misery of a hard winter was added the scourge of famine. The price of corn was prohibitive and the bread was uneatable. To remedy matters the Convention decided to import grain from America, and Admiral Vanstabel was ordered to convoy two hundred American corn-ships destined to relieve the public want.

The English government, which put to profit our internal dissensions, thought rightly that famine would further its aims, and at once took measures to intercept this convoy. To find an historic parallel it would probably be necessary to turn to the wars of the Italian Republic, where possibly a similar conception may have seen the light in the mind of some Italian freebooter.

What opposition could France offer to the enemy fleet? Her only hope lay in the Brest squadron, and God knows that was feeble enough. The squadron was fifty per cent, below strength, partly disarmed, and chiefly composed of ships which had served in Italy and India and were from fifteen to twenty years old. Amongst these ships were some which had lain in port since 1783, whose worm-eaten hulls were covered with barnacles. They were only kept afloat by their pumps. All these vessels were hastily repaired, scraped, cleaned, and brightly painted. They were armed with rusty cannon dating from the epoch of de Tourville and Duquesne, and sent to reinforce the fleet. The old sailors called them the "drowners."

This does not mean that the squadron did not comprise some magnificent ships, such as the *Tigre* and the *Sans-Pareil,* a testimony to the genius of my old friend Sané, who outclassed anything ever attempted by the shipbuilders of England. But one unhandy ship can wreck a line of battle and put the finest ships on earth at the mercy of an enemy.

The state of our navy was reflected in its personnel. The crews consisted of young conscripts knowing nothing of the sea, or else of fisherfolk who had never seen a battleship. The army furnished the garrisons, and the Marine Artillery had already furnished all the gunners possible. Few officers could boast more than two years' experience and chiefly owed their commissions to the necessity of finding substitutes for the King's officers who had emigrated. Our best captains were said to be the old helmsmen. They were rough and uneducated, but they were extremely brave; they could sail their ships and they hated the English most heartily, for they knew them of old.

Brest was a cross between a workshop and a taproom. At the morning gun the port bore a close resemblance to an anthill. Here a ship was being masted; there provisions were being stowed; further on were guns and powder. Barges were embarking troops, others were carrying shot; storehouses discharged biscuit, sails, cables; convicts strained on a windlass to step a topmast; topmen wrestled with a yard; gunners were at practice; ships were being towed towards the chain which closed the entrance to the port. All this resulted in endless noise and movement and had one single object—to fit the fleet to take the sea and fight the enemy.

The evening offered an entirely different spectacle. At the sound of the bell some twelve to fifteen thousand men dashed through the gates like schoolboys. They wished to profit by their existence while they were sure of it and before they found themselves at sea, on an unstable deck, faced by the guns of an English three-decker. This unpleasant prospect did not depress them; on the contrary I have never seen a more cheerful crowd. In a flash the town became one enormous pot-house, the cafés were crammed, and drinkers lined the streets; outside the gates the distractions were less innocent, dances were held, and the dancers were fixed in purpose and indecent in appearance.

One day three cannon shots were heard. The bottles were put aside, the dances ceased, the syrens wept aloud: the *Montaigne,* flagship, had given the signal to weigh anchor. At once a long procession of sailors, soldiers and gunners took the road to the port and the boats which were waiting to take them aboard. All glasses were directed on the *Montaigne.* On her poop two men could be seen in conversation. One was Jean-Bon Saint-André, the People's Representative sent by the Committee of Public Safety; the other was Admiral Villaret-Joyeuse, an old officer of the Royal Navy who had served in Indian waters under Suffren.

The *Montaigne* began to move, and after her all the fleet got under way and with a favourable wind passed the channel of Brest without incident.

Where was I in all this uproar? On the signal to the fleet to put to sea two companies of marine artillery had been sent on board the *Colon,* an old guardship which it had been decided to man. Although renamed, repaired and heavily painted, she was absolutely rotten, and infested by a smell of must which made any stay in her not only unpleasant but unhealthy. Luckily it became evident that she could not be got ready in time,

57

and her crew was distributed among other ships which were short. I fell to the lot of the *Jemmapes,* 74, whose name seemed of good omen.[1] Had it not been that the events of the campaign tried my stamina rather too highly I should never have had cause to regret the time I spent in her.

The weather was beautiful, almost too beautiful, for the light spring breeze was scarcely strong enough to move these massive vessels. It followed that not only was progress slow but manoeuvring was difficult. One noticed then that every ship had her different character, just like men. Some always lagged, even under a full spread of canvas, whilst others invariably led even under little sail, and we could estimate what each might be expected to do in action.

We were so impatient to meet the American convoy that we expected to sight it at any minute; we were, however, considerably off the mark, and many things were destined to happen before our hopes were fulfilled. On the 28th May the sun came up in a cloudless sky. The sea was practically a flat calm. At eight in the morning, as the bells sounded for breakfast, signals were perceived from our frigates astern, and shortly after our lookouts sighted the masts of line-of-battle ships on the horizon. We soon realised that we had to do with the English Channel fleet, commanded by Admiral Howe and consisting of thirty-six sail of the line, of which eight were three-deckers. We had only twenty-six, of which three were of one hundred and twenty guns. We were seven to ten, but this superiority in numbers worried nobody. On the contrary, when the immense line of the enemy fleet could be seen on the horizon a cry of "*Vive la République*" arose from our ships and carried to the English a challenge and a proof of our devotion to the cause we were about to defend. I have long regretted that we did not attack at this moment, when Admiral Howe's fleet was not yet assembled and when our crews were fired with such enthusiasm. Whatever the result might have been the English

1. Victory gained by the French under Dumouriez over the Austrians in 1792.

ships were scattered and could not have hindered the passage of the convoy, and we had an excellent chance of victory. Five days later fortune's wheel had turned. Certain that we had missed our chance I had the temerity to say to Admiral Villaret himself, ten years later, that in my opinion had we attacked on the 28th May we would have completely defeated the enemy. Employing his favourite phrase he replied: "Doubtless, but I was tied by my instructions." Whether he should have followed them is another matter, but that problem could scarcely be threshed out by an *aide-de-camp.*

The attitude of our crews convinced the English Admiral that he could not rely on his numerical superiority alone, but that he would need all his tried experience. Instead of passing us he manoeuvred all day to get the wind of us. It is common knowledge that the man who gets to windward is master of his movements, and can attack or retreat as he pleases. That very evening his skill caused us a reverse. The *Républicain,* three-decker, a bad sailer badly commanded, had fallen to leeward, and although the fleet was under half sail she had parted company. Perceiving this Admiral Howe sent some half a dozen ships to engage her. It seemed that such a force would oblige her to surrender; but although her captain was killed and the ship dismasted she continued to fight until her assailants were called off by signals from their Admiral. Instead of allotting to the frigates the task of taking her to the nearest port, a ship, the *Audacieux,* left the line and escorted her to Rochefort; a peculiar attention which deprived us of a second battleship at a moment when the enemy strength was being constantly increased.

The men having been piped to quarters in the morning and the hammocks stowed, we slept on deck beside our guns. That day and the days following we existed on cheese and biscuit because the kitchens were closed down when we cleared for action. It is asking a lot to expect men who have fasted for a week to fight to the death when called upon. Although this regime should have had a sedative effect, there was nevertheless considerable excitement in evidence that evening. The abandonment of the *Républicain* was blamed, and it was claimed that it was not by temporising that we should clear a passage for the convoy, and furthermore that such a policy was impossible, because no two fleets of so great a size and so combative a spirit could help fighting, whatever the orders might be to the contrary. The truth of these assertions was very shortly to be proved by the events.

When I went on deck the following morning I was literally astounded by the magnificent spectacle offered by the two fleets sailing on the same course, as though in concert, and almost abreast of one another. One saw there sixty line-of-battle ships in line ahead with colours flying and the guns showing through the open ports, accompanied by as many frigates and a swarm of brigs and dispatch boats. I asked myself why, instead of this scene representing the prelude to a battle between the two greatest nations in Europe, it was not a crusade undertaken mutually to deliver other peoples from slavery. Anchored before the Neva or the Golden Horn, near St. Petersburg or Constantinople, this unparalleled fleet would by its very presence have restored Poland to her own and given liberty to Greece, Egypt and Asia Minor. I was brought back to reality by the sound of cannon.

The English squadron, whose previous movement had served to mask its real objective, attacked our rearguard with its rear division, and breaking our line with several of their best ships cut off the *Tyrannicide* and the *Indomptable* who, attacked on both sides, were badly knocked about and partially dismasted. The *Montaigne* immediately gave the order to put about and go to their rescue. It can only be supposed that the signal was misunderstood, for the head of the line continued on its course as though determined to abandon these two ships, like the *Républicain* the day before. Thereupon Admiral Villaret threw off his customary indecision and by some happy and honourable impulse threw himself into the fight, hoisting the signal: "Who loves me follows me."

The power of the example was irresistible. Those furthest off obeyed so promptly that they arrived in time to form at close intervals within half gunshot of the enemy. Heavy gunfire was opened, and continued without interruption for an hour or more. At our approach the English ships surrounding our two hauled off to take up their battle stations, so that their attack can be said to have failed completely. Although the engagement lasted long enough to be murderous, it had in fact no great consequence, since the English being under sail we had to imitate them, and the constant movement of the ships resulted in few shots reaching their target. We received some twenty aboard the *Jemmapes*, without counting those through our canvas; and in the evening those among us whose first experience of a naval engagement this was spoke extremely scornfully of naval warfare, and considered the sunken roads of Brittany and the brushwood of the Vendée a great deal more dangerous. Experience acquired twenty-four hours later caused us to alter this opinion.

During the two long days of the 30th and 31st May (11th and 12th Prairial) an unforeseen phenomenon forced a truce on both fleets. A thick white fog came off the Atlantic, and we could scarcely distinguish either the bowsprit of our next astern or the side of the ship abreast of us. Signals were forbidden, as they would have betrayed our presence to the enemy. During the strange isolation which the fog-curtain imposed upon us we set about repairing the damages sustained in the last engagement and preparing for another one. But was this all we could do? Were we doing our utmost for our cause in steering blindly through the fog, ignoring both the position of the enemy and that of the convoy we were destined to defend? Is it permissible in war to pass forty-eight hours within gunshot of a fleet one is bound to fight and nevertheless undertake no operation either defensive or otherwise? Would a battle in the fog, split up into individual actions, have been more risky than any other, particularly for a fleet inferior in numbers? Is it absolutely necessary in naval warfare to have the enemy's entire fleet in sight? Cannot they be beaten one by one in the obscurity, as one attacks fortresses, profiting by darkness, tempest, or fog?

The proof that inaction was fatal is that it weighed heavily on everybody. It got on our nerves beyond expression, and when at last on the 1st of June (13th Prairial), a cloudless day, we saw the English fleet, there was a shout of joy; it seemed as though we had been delivered from the captivity in which the fog had held us idle without giving us an opportunity to offer our lives for our country. The sentiment must have been deep-rooted, since it was not stifled by two unfortunate facts which might have shown us the futility of our devotion. The enemy fleet had been reinforced by several ships, and, what was still worse, he had profited by the two days' fog to get to windward of us.

The two fleets kept on the same tack for a long while; they then approached one another and were soon within gunshot. We could see the open battery ports and the gaping muzzles of the guns. We saw the riflemen in the tops ready to pick off the officers or the admiral on his quarterdeck. Great nets were spread above the deck to protect the men from falling blocks and tackle. We saw flying from the mast of our Admiral's ship the square three-coloured flag which as yet knew neither victory nor the ocean, but which this day was to be consecrated immemorially by our blood. On the other side floated the banner of St. George, proud of its ancient renown and the swarm of experienced officers over whom it flew, whereas those whom we might have opposed to them had deserted their country and now conspired with her implacable enemies against her.

At about nine o'clock in the morning, when we were finishing a frugal and hurried breakfast, the English line broke, and whereas the head continued to hold us in check the remainder suddenly changed direction and rapidly, impulsively, under full sail attacked between the centre of our line and the rear division. A magnificent three-decker, the *Queen Charlotte,* followed by the *Bellerophon,* the *Leviathan* and many others, carried out this bold movement with equal accuracy and courage. Their line, bowsprit to poop, crashed into ours and cut it at right angles astern of our flagship, the *Montaigne.* It was a solemn moment. Fire not having been opened the scene was free from smoke and could be clearly taken in. Everybody understood the consequences of this decisive act, and the most hearty curses were heaped on the head of the captain who had allowed the line to be broken ahead of his ship. The *Queen Charlotte,* and after her all the ships which followed her through the passage she had opened, poured their broadsides into the two vessels which they separated. These broadsides, raking them from stem to stern and meeting nothing to obstruct the passage of the shot, were murderous, and dismounted the guns in their batteries. Once through the gap the English ships turned on the other tack along the length of our line, and cannonaded it from one side, whilst it was attacked from the other by a second column which had been held in reserve for the purpose, thus putting our rearguard between two fires and opposing two ships to one; that is, one hundred and forty-eight, or even one hundred and ninety-four, guns against seventy-four. This naval manoeuvre corresponds to the oblique attack in vogue during the Seven Years' War; its object is to smash an inferior force by a surprise attack carried out by one considerably superior. Simple as it is and simple as the means may be by which it may be countered, it has constantly succeeded for England, and its success has raised to the rank of genius certain admirals who, brave as they doubtless were, possessed no great talent either as navigators or tacticians.

Admiral Villaret no sooner perceived the extreme peril in

which our rearguard was placed by this manoeuvre than he put the *Montaigne* about and ordered the head of the squadron to follow him and imitate his movements. He did not wait for his signal to be acted upon but threw himself straight into the fight. We came into it at about the same time, and although I was serving at the quarterdeck guns and at one time even those on the poop, I could see no distance at all; a thick smoke covered the whole battle area and only permitted us to distinguish such enemy ships as came to attack us at point-blank range.

The cloud which enveloped us was produced by the burning of a hundred thousand barrels of gunpowder; it did not in any way resemble the sea fog of previous days; instead of a uniform grey colour it varied not only in tint but in intensity according to the circumstances. Sometimes it was a thick sooty black, gleaming with sparks and suddenly stabbed with ruddy flame; then again it was transparent, giving to the light of day the appearance of moonlight and blotting out objects by a fantastic sort of mirage. It was frequently sown with brownish circles floating upwards horizontally, which recalled those traced by medieval painters above the heads of saints. This peculiar phenomenon, which has never been satisfactorily explained, is one of the effects produced by the explosion of even the best powders.

When the cloud split, some enemy ship, girdled with its double or triple band of red or yellow, loomed up, her side bristling with guns ready to crush us with their thunder. Soon this floating fortress, gathering the feeble breeze in its immense spread of canvas, came nearer and seemed to cover itself in flame. An appalling explosion was heard and a hail of enormous cannon-shot crashed through the wooden walls which served us for a parapet. Often we forestalled this murderous discharge by that of all our guns and when, through the smoke wreaths, we could see that we had brought down a mast or a yard, or stove in a bulwark and made a large breach in the enemy's battery, then a cry of triumph arose which raised the courage of our companions less favoured by the fortune of war. These terrible occurrences were constantly renewed. Generally an English ship came alongside and opened a furious fire of guns and musketry in the hope of making us strike our flag; deceived by the strength of our resistance, she would haul off and depart to seek an easier prey elsewhere. But even more perilous encounters awaited us toward the end of the day.

Whilst we were replying to a seventy-four, a second came to attack us on our other side. We were pounded by them for more than an hour. Our foremast was shot away close to the deck; the mainmast broke in half, and the fall of one brought down the other. The shock was so violent that in the lower battery we all thought the ship was splitting in two. As a matter of fact our situation was little better. The masts with their yards, sails, and tackle hung alongside, half in the water, and weighing on the ship gave her such a list that she seemed about to turn turtle. We all ran to close the ports. It was high time; the water was already coming into the lower batteries and we were going under. The crew, headed by the most active among the officers, armed themselves with sharp axes and set about cutting away all shrouds and rigging which attached the wrecked masts to the ship. We were certainly lost had the enemy continued to fire on the exposed parties engaged in this work, but a fire having broken out in his battery he was obliged to look to his own safety, and in fact it caused him such loss that he hauled off without adding further to our misfortunes.

Without sails or the means to use them we were nailed to the spot unable to defend ourselves. Realising our desperate situation a three-decker placed herself across our stern. The admiral commanding her appeared on her poop, high and embattlemented like the tower of some old castle, and called to our officers:

"Gentlemen, I trust you have struck."

"Not at all, sir," replied our captain; and calling a signalman he said, "My lad, go aloft and show our colours to the admiral."

The boy sprang up the ratlines of the mizzen shrouds, and seizing a corner of the flag which was hanging for lack of wind, spread it out full length and held it so in defiance of the enemy. The English admiral sent us to the devil with an oath and gave the order to open fire. It was really equivalent to hitting a man when he was down, murdering the wounded and mutilating the dead. In the position in which we were none of our guns would bear, and we had no alternative but to allow ourselves to be shot to bits without resistance. It is true that the shortness of the range prevented the enemy from using all his guns, but half of them sufficed to produce an appalling slaughter and sink the *Jemmapes* under our feet.

In fact, the first discharge from his three batteries swept our decks, dismounted our heavy guns, and sent shot down into the hold where they finished off our wounded. Our loss would have been even greater had not our officers ordered the gunners to lie flat when they saw the English take up their port-fires. Nevertheless a second discharge would undoubtedly have finished us, and our fate seemed sealed when a happy chance delivered us. The enemy admiral was shot by four young marines posted in the mizzen top, the one mast which remained to us in our distress. This event disordered the attack, held up the fire of which were the destined victims, and gave time to the *Montaigne* to come to our help. The English ship in danger of finding herself in the same position as ourselves, that is being attacked by the poop, hastened to rejoin her friends. Our end had seemed so imminent that we could scarcely believe in our safety.

The *Montaigne* came up and we cheered her loudly. Admiral Villaret and the Commissary to the Convention examined our unhappy ship with interest; her last mast had fallen and she was left as flat as a pontoon. They stood on the taffrail and baring their heads cried: "Bravo the *Jemmapes* and her captain," words which were enthusiastically repeated by the ship's company of the *Montaigne*. This latter ship was always the first in and the last out of a fight; she had been hit three hundred times in her hull or on the water line and had had three hundred officers and men killed or wounded. Her Captain, M. Basire, lost his life, and she could only muster five lieutenants or ensigns fit for service after the battle. She had engaged twelve or fifteen enemy ships, and had opposed a magnificent resistance to seven who attacked her simultaneously.

Our captain, who had behaved so bravely during this long and trying day, was quite overcome when he heard the cheering. A moment before I had witnessed another example of the queerness of human nature. The young volunteers in the mizzen top, who had fought like heroes, were called down on deck as the mast threatened to fall; but when it came to descending from that height their courage failed them, and we had to send topmen to give them a hand; which provided a little comedy in our tragedy.

The sound of cannon which had deafened us for the last seven hours was now feeble and distant. The English ships had evidently quitted the field in accordance with an order of recall. It was a sign of our success; but on looking about us, it seemed unlikely we should live long enough to see its results. Our situation became worse every minute. The hold was full, and the water would soon be over the orlop deck. The forward biscuit-room was already flooded, and when we listened at the hatchways we could hear the sea washing in through the shot-holes on the water-line and cascading into the body of the ship. The chief warrant officer reported four and a half feet of water in the well, and that pumps were helpless against it. In this extremity we called all hands to the pumps, even the wounded and the officers. The caulkers descended as far as they could into the hold to find the leaks and plug them provisionally with tarpaulins fixed in place by wooden cross pieces. The carpenters carried on the work from without and succeeded in plugging one hundred and fifty shot-holes on or above the waterline. This hard and dangerous work was rewarded. The captain himself admitted that we had gained two feet in clearance and in continuing with the pumps we had a certain feeling of security provided nothing vital carried away. This was to be feared owing to the riddled state of the vessel and the loss of bolts and ironwork.

All these circumstances merely meant that we were in danger of death, and habit dulls that impression; but I was filled with a sense of horror which no amount of reasoning could conquer, at the aspect of the charnel-house which once had been the lower battery. To start with it had been necessary to put the wounded there, for whom there was no room in the hospital on the orlop deck; then, when the orlop deck had to be abandoned owing to the water, we had to haul up these wretched creatures, mostly dangerously or even mortally wounded, and put them side by side in two lines in the battery. The luckiest were those who had a friend or brother to give them what little attention our appalling situation permitted. They at least got something to drink, whereas the others vainly prayed or cursed for water, for it was very difficult to find anything to drink, all the stores having been carried away. Many, it is true, soon found deliverance from the miseries of this life, and by their departure left more room for the survivors. I remember the following morning hearing a lot of splashing alongside and asking a quartermaster the reason of it. "It's *père* Simon," he replied, "a shipmate of thirty years standing; we have just thrown him overboard, and the sharks are fighting over his body." These terrible creatures swam alongside in veritable flocks waiting for the bodies to be thrown over; they counted on this to such an extent that they did not leave us until we were off Ushant.

Without being actually wounded I was little better off; my limbs and body were covered with painful bruises and bleeding scratches. The detonation of the thirty-six pounders a few inches from my ears had made me deaf, and my arms were practically dislocated by the enormous weight of the heavy calibre sponge and rammer which I had had to manipulate during the battle; I thought at one time I had been badly wounded in the face by splinters which a shot threw up close by me; but I was quit with a number of scratches, except for a sliver of wood four inches long which had lodged in my right cheek below the eye, without penetrating very deeply. When I went to find the surgeon to rid me of this tiresome visitor I was unpleasantly surprised to see him get out his knives, all bloody and splintered by the work to which he had been putting them, in order to open my face. I thanked him for his kind intentions but refused to accept his services; it will be seen later on that it was just as well I did.

Night had come and silence reigned where six thousand cannon had thundered all the day. Nothing was heard except the sound of the pumps and the hammers of the caulkers, who struggled to prevent the sea from swallowing both conqueror and conquered and distributing them impartially to the sharks. Having exhausted what little strength remained to me in working in the batteries, I fled from between decks, where there was a terrible stench of carnage, and sought comfort with an old helmsman with whom on ordinary occasions I used to talk hydrography. This worthy man rolled me in a flag and made me lie down in a corner of the poop, the only spot where I could get a little rest. I was devoured by thirst; but in a ship shot about like ours it was impossible to find a drop of water, and my comrade advised me to resign myself. A moment later someone approached and in a low voice told me to sit up. It was the captain, the captain himself, who had come to bring me water. I was so touched by this kindness that I could not say a word and burst into tears. This kind-hearted man had been one of the heroes of the battle, whilst I, whom he treated with such fatherly kindness, was only a poor lad whom he could scarcely have noticed in the fury of the fight, Nowadays it is doubtful whether a sub-lieutenant fresh from school would condescend to such an action, but then, throughout the service, kindness was much less of a rarity. I remember with gratitude that during the return of the squadron my comrades, seeing that I was absolutely exhausted, went to the lieutenant without saying a word to me, and asked that I should be exempted from keeping watch, offering one of their number to take my place each night. The officers were persuaded that it was from lack of food that I was gradually becoming weaker, and they ordered that food should be sent me daily from their table. To overcome my objections they pretended it was an order, and that I had no right to do as I wished. Such, in their intimacy, were those Frenchmen of 1790, who for half a century Europe, and even their own countrymen, condemned in mass as bloody murderers.

We awaited the dawn with terrible impatience; it would show us whether we or the enemy were victorious, and it would explain why the night had passed without news of our fleet. At dawn, to our great disappointment, we found ourselves surrounded by a thick fog, as before the battle. From out this mist came plaintive cries, which greatly disturbed our men, who put them down to the super-natural and were under the impression that they emanated from the souls of our departed comrades. After many conjectures and a long wait we finally discovered a poor devil who had been floating about in the sea all night attached to a hen-coop. He was one of the crew of the *Vengeur*. This ship, attacked by three of the enemy, had refused to surrender; dismasted and hard pressed, she had continued to defend herself until the sea invaded her batteries; and already half-submerged still flew her flag. When she disappeared her crew, reduced by half by the action and the sea, could still be heard shouting: "*Vive la République!*"

A few men were saved by the enemy, and the others, like the man we picked up, had drifted away on the wreckage with the prospect of dying by hunger or the sharks unless they found help among the solitudes of the ocean.

When the fog lifted we were filled with surprise. The two fleets, ours and that of the enemy, were at least half a league away from us; the first to leeward and the second with the weather gauge; they were well together and at that distance seemed in tolerably good trim. At the same time there was generally something missing, yards, topmasts, mizzen gaffs or other things more or less indispensable; but these damages were nothing compared to those of the ships which had remained on the scene of action, incapable of leaving it. Around us there were fifteen or sixteen ships of the line completely disabled, of which not one had masts, and in consequence neither sails nor tackle. Having nothing from which to fly a flag it was hard to say whether they were French or English; after examination there seemed to be about equal numbers of each. Our men who knew the lines of each ship made out the *Tempétueux,* the *Achille,* the *Juste,* the *Amérique,* the *Northumberland,* and the *Sans-Pareil,* all of seventy-four guns except the last, which was an eighty-four. We learnt in the evening that the *Jacobin* had sunk, since she was not included in the number.

We supposed at first that our fleet would return to pick us up and take possession of the enemy ships which, being defenceless, could have been taken without firing a shot, as were ours the following day. But we had our doubts, since our fleet was to leeward. How had we fallen into this disadvantageous position? We could not tell; only later were we told that the advance guard, which had shown signs of indecision from the very beginning, had found itself far to leeward when the battle was over. Admiral Villaret, who had remained with one division, had been forced to rally his main squadron to leeward, hoping to bring it back to the scene of action, and if necessary renew the fight. This generous design could not be realised, and fifteen years afterwards when discussing the events of this unhappy day, the admiral told me they had broken his heart and that he would never get over it.

We, on the other hand, did not know what was taking place in the fleet, and we were looking forward to the capture of seven or eight English ships which were lying disabled amongst our own pending the time when one of the two admirals should come and take them.

In this manner the day passed, full of hope deferred which gradually turned to exasperation. Towards evening a light brig, the *Papillon,* eight guns, came towards us, passing quite close to the disabled English ships. By good luck she gave the *Jemmapes* the preference and offered our captain a tow. A line was immediately thrown aboard her to which a hawser was attached, and following our feeble comrade we started off. We had rigged a jury-mast with considerable difficulty, and on this we hoisted a sail, which lightened the tow and enabled us to rejoin the fleet. It was like getting home again. We were ordered by signal to continue our course, and thanks to fresh sails and four jury-masts which we had managed to rig we followed the fleet for eight days and anchored with it in the Bay of Bertheaume, at the entrance of Brest Channel, on the 10th June or the 22nd Prairial. Five ships were in tow out of nineteen.

Reduced even to the state in which it was the fleet had nevertheless succeeded in its object, but it must most humbly be confessed that it was more by good luck than good judgement. In order to cut off the American convoy the English Admiralty had not only despatched the fleet of thirty-six ships which we had just fought but had sent another squadron of twelve ships to await its land fall off Ushant. This force had already made itself felt by driving back a squadron of six ships which had left Brest to join our fleet. Had the convoy gained four days on its crossing from New York, it would have met the blockading squadron and been lost. By chance the enemy had come far in to the Bay of Bertheaume when our fleet was sighted on the horizon. Not knowing whether we were victorious, and being badly placed between us and the land, they turned about and steered before the wind into the Channel. Their retreat opened a free passage to the convoy, which anchored forty-eight hours later to the number of two hundred sail and with the corn it brought relieved the public want. Its arrival without the loss of a single ship completely frustrated the plans of the English Government and rendered without object the manning of two fleets.

It is true that the battle of the 1st of June brought great fame to Admiral Howe; but the actual advantages were not so great as they appeared, or were said to be. With the exception of the *Sans-Pareil* the ships captured were nothing better than hulks and only fit to make pontoons, and as a matter of fact this was all the English could do with them. In spite of a crushing superiority in number, the English could neither capture by boarding nor cause a single vessel of ours to strike her colours. The ships which fell into her hands were picked up twenty-four hours later like wounded on the field of battle. A badly equipped squadron, suffering from a dearth of experienced officers and men, had given battle during an entire day to a much more powerful squadron, well commanded and manned by picked crews. Our young ratings, fighting for the first time at sea, had equalled in courage and tenacity the old Royal Navy of England, and they had left behind them the example of a ship whose crew preferred to die rather than to strike.

Injustice it must be admitted that the enemy manoeuvred with superior skill and constantly took advantage of the wind. He showed great resolution in attacking our line and consummate prudence in hauling off and taking up the station which gave him the initiative. Let us add with equal impartiality, that he exhibited kindness and humanity when the *Vengeur* sank, and did his utmost to save the men who had not been sucked down when that vessel disappeared.

When we anchored in Brest harbour the division which

we found at Bertheaume almost made good the losses in the battle, and we found ourselves with approximately the same number of ships as at our departure; but this was a delusion. All the ships which had been engaged were riddled with shot; two or three of their ports had been blown into one, the divisions between them having disappeared. The sails showed hundreds of holes; the shrouds were split, the rigging cut, and the masts replaced by any piece of wood which could be requisitioned for service. Their magazines were empty and the stocks in the arsenal exhausted. Finally, and this was the most serious, our most experienced sailors and gunners were missing, and half of those who remained were incapacitated by wounds. During four days the roads leading to the Hospital of St. Louis saw a long succession of stretchers carrying our unhappy wounded to what, for the majority of them, was to be their last resting place. Amongst these crowded cases gangrene had set in, and the mortality was terrible.

On disembarking from the *Jemmapes* I had, in spite of my repugnance, to go to the Naval Hospital to be operated on. I presented myself to the chief surgeon, who was famous not only for his skill but for his eccentricity. There were some hundred people there awaiting his verdict and trembling for the safety of their persons. A young student obtained me a special pass on the pretext that I was a rare case. The learned man examined my damaged cheek and with a turn of the pincers succeeded in extracting, comparatively painlessly, a long piece of wood which he exhibited in triumph to the spectators, who were astounded at his dexterity.

"You might have been blinded," he remarked, and added, with the freedom of language which he usually affected: "Don't worry, my lad. You will still be a mirror for some whores."

I was greatly shocked at this suggestion, but I had no time to blush. Two orderlies took charge of me and covered my face with bandages. Thus equipped I was presented to the doctor-in-chief, M. Billiard, who told me that I could not safely remain in hospital owing to the increase of gangrene amongst the wounded. I left with a party for Pontanezen, a branch of the St. Louis hospital situated half a league outside Brest and usually reserved for convalescents. Everything was full, and we had to continue as far as Lesneven, a small town whose hospital was well reputed amongst sailors. On arrival I fainted, on coming to I became delirious, and for a week my condition was desperate. I had caught typhus. My youth, and above all the devoted care of M. Després, the house-doctor, saved my life. I owed much also to the Sisters of Charity, who treated me with true motherly care. I remembered this throughout all the vicissitudes of my existence, and when, twenty-three years later M. Portal, Naval and Colonial Minister, consulted me as to the means to diminish the mortality in Guiana, I laid special stress on the necessity of confiding the management of the hospitals to the Sisters of Charity. Ten of them were sent to Cayenne and rendered invaluable service; but an epidemic broke out and they all fell victims to their devotion; so, by a cruel chance, my gratitude became the indirect cause of their death.

The great naval battle of the 13th Prairial is, in the opinion of sailor-men, the hardest fought and the bloodiest of any witnessed in the eighteenth century. It was lost, if one takes count of the ships which fell into the hands of the enemy; but it was also won, in that it gained its object and prevented the English fleet from intercepting the American convoy, which was the prize of victory and which entered Brest in triumph.

The Battle of Quiberon Bay

The fleet of the Republic, considerably diminished by the losses suffered in the great battle of the 13th Prairial the previous year, was at anchor in Brest harbour under the command of Admiral Villaret. Amongst its units was the *Alexandre,* a seventy-four which we had taken from the English, which was about the only title to recommendation she possessed.

The day I boarded her as Master-at-Arms the signal was given for the fleet to put to sea, and we left without waiting for the ratings on shore-leave.

The rumour spread that the division commanded by Rear-Admiral Vence had met with superior English forces and had taken refuge in the passages without issue which lie behind the Iles de Ré and d'Oléron; our sortie was intended to relieve them.

We sailed along the French coast toward the Bay of Biscay, and doubtless we were intended to surprise the enemy; but his cruisers warned him of our approach and he sought safety in the open sea. We had lost time assembling our ships and in forming line, and the luck which had hitherto been with us had abandoned us.

Returning towards the North, we had already sighted the coast of Finistère, and it only remained to double the great promontory known as the Bec-du-Raz in order to make Brest passage, when the wind suddenly changed and became contrary; several violent gusts followed, accompanied by claps of thunder. The storm was all the more dangerous in that we were partly surrounded by rocks, on which the sea was breaking furiously. In this extremity the Admiral signalled the squadron to take refuge in the Bay of Audierne, a vast semi-circle carved by the waves out of the granite coast of old Armorica. We anchored there in disorder and we, in the *Alexandre,* set to work to repair the damage caused by the gale. While this was going on the captain recollected that the men he had been forced to leave on shore must have been picked up by the *Semillante,* frigate, which had been detailed for this purpose. The frigate being at anchor in the Bay, he ordered me to collect our men; but as he could not lower a boat he stopped a small coaster which he requisitioned to turn the men over. The confidence with which the owner of this boat inspired me being somewhat mediocre, I armed myself with boarding pistols, and under their protection I reached the frigate. I was careful to tie up the boat and to confide it to the care of the gangway sentry, with the order to shoot at the first attempt to slip away. It was not easy to assemble my men who, preferring to stay in the frigate, deferred as long as possible the disagreeable necessity of quitting her. When finally I was ready to embark them I was informed that the boat had disappeared. The owner had profited by a momentary inattention on the part of the sentry to cut the rope and get away under all sail. Bitterly disappointed I exposed our case to the captain, who was sympathetic, and promised me two boats instead of one for the following morning at dawn; the sea being too high and the hour too late to permit of his doing so at the moment.

Seeing that I accepted this solution with an ill grace, he remarked kindly that sailors must not grumble at fate, which was often kinder than it seemed to be. He gave orders that I was to be well looked after, and so in fact I was.

When I went on deck the following morning to ask the

Captain to redeem his promise its execution had become impossible. The *Montaigne* was sending up rockets and hoisting red, yellow, and blue pennants, all of which meant something.

The *Semillante* immediately made sail and left the Bay to reconnoitre the horizon, while the squadron got under way.

But a thick fog carried in by the breeze covered the sea and hid the sky. We were soon enveloped, and the fleet with us, and when the sun rose its rays were not powerful enough to pierce it. Our state of blindness filled me with anxiety, and I could not stay still. I went on the poop to see whether the fog gave any sign of lifting. There seemed no hope of this, and it was with difficulty that one could make out even the nearest objects. Nevertheless, when glancing towards the stern and searching for some break in the heavy cloud which lay on the sea, I saw, looming up unexpectedly at a height of some hundred feet, the truck of the masts of some big ship. Astounded at this apparition I pointed it out to the first lieutenant. The captain needed but a glance to realise the danger of our position. He took charge himself and manoeuvred to change direction and increase speed. When we were at a certain distance he fired three guns, which informed our squadron that we were in touch with the enemy. In effect, as the mist lifted, we saw that we had nearly run foul of an English three-decker and that all their fleet was ahead of us preparing for action.

Our inferiority in numbers putting resistance out of the question, Admiral Villaret's first care was to facilitate the retreat of the squadron by preventing the enemy from forcing us back on the coast, which would have deprived us of any chance of salvation; he hastened, therefore, to profit by the opening left by the English ships, which were endeavouring to surround us, and our whole fleet bore to the South in good order, followed at a distance by the enemy, who had not expected this move. But when night had fallen we turned about and resumed our course towards the North, in order to make the harbour of Lorient which was close by. At day-break on the 23rd June it seemed that this plan had been completely successful. The English squadron, in the ardour of pursuit had not learned of our manoeuvre until fairly late, and his scattered vessels were unable to prevent us reaching the Ile de Groix, which lies almost opposite the fortifications of Port Louis, at the entrance to the port of Lorient.

But an unlucky hazard often upsets the best laid plans, even when their success seems certain. The rapid progress of our squadron had been followed with difficulty by the *Alexandre,* whose rigging had been damaged in the storm, and the faster sailers amongst the enemy caught her up and obliged her to surrender. The *Formidable* appeared to be out of danger when she suddenly caught fire, and whilst the crew were doing their utmost to extinguish the flames she was attacked by several English ships, who took her. An even more grievous loss was that of the *Tigre,* one of the finest ships in the Brest squadron. She at least resisted with a courage worthy of a better fate, and only succumbed to the attacks of three ships, of which one was a three-decker; and Captain Bedout who commanded her proved himself to be as good an officer as he was intrepid a sailor.

The squadron anchored at Lorient and our frigate dropped anchor in front of the town.

By unheard of luck I had escaped the terrible hulks of England, but all I possessed was on its way to Portsmouth in the *Alexandre,* and the only clothes I had were those I stood up in.

Above all I regretted my notebooks and a few tattered volumes, English and Italian, which used to console me during my few moments of leisure. The officers of the *Semillante* learnt of my plight and plundered their library in order to give me some consolation. The captain got out what was best from the linen in the storeroom, and when I refused it, greatly touched at so much kindness, he himself chose out for me what he thought would be most useful.

During those far-off days, now stigmatised as barbarous by the historians of Europe, I never found myself in peril or in trouble without coming across someone kind who helped me, sharing with me his purse, his food, his clothes, although I was a stranger and he might never see me again; or else someone who risked his life for mine with no other motive than to do good. I wish I could be persuaded that it is the same today.

When I left the frigate which had been so lucky for once, I proposed to return to Brest to rejoin my half-brigade. I thought the campaign was over so far as I was concerned; I little thought that the major half remained for me to do, or, rather, that I should have to start another one immediately. I took shelter at Lorient in the naval quarters, where the adjutant, who knew of my sea adventures, lodged me like a prince; I slept in a bed which seemed to me the best on earth, and where at any rate I avoided the motion of the sea. I was suddenly awakened by shots. I dressed in haste and joined the troops where they were assembling. It was hard to know what was the cause of this sudden alarm. I only gathered that the enemy had landed and had already seized several positions of considerable importance.

As soon as a boat was ready as many men as possible were piled into her and sent to Port-Louis, the fort which defended Lorient roadstead and which was then called Port-Liberté. This was the departure point of the detachment for the coast army, whose head-quarters were at Vannes; but the communications with the latter were cut by land and sea, the Chouans occupied all the issues inland, the enemy landing-parties held all the passages along the coast, and the English fleet anchored in the Bay of Quiberon intercepted all craft putting out from the neighbouring ports.

When I got into the place I found everything in confusion, and one could have imagined that the enemy was at the foot of the *glacis*.

The commander complained that he had not sufficient gunners to man the pieces commanding the menaced front; and, having made up his mind to keep those he had, he fixed on me to take charge of an ammunition convoy which was causing him considerable anxiety, because he had already delayed its departure on his own responsibility; this latter fact was serious in view of the military commissioners existing at that epoch, who were empowered to carry out summary justice. To escort this convoy he gave me a dozen hard cases from the colonial depôt commanded by a sergeant who was drunk; the teams were supplied by horses levied by force from the peasants as stubborn as their owners. I had a lively recollection of the master at Audierne who had got away with his boat under the very eyes of a sentry, and I took my precautions in order to avoid being duped a second time by these sullen but cunning mystics. I put each carter between two soldiers, their muskets slung but their bayonets in their hand, with orders to use them at the first sign of treachery. I formed an advanced guard in case of ambush, with muskets ready for immediate action.

Everything went off excellently so long as the night was clear and the roads easy; but after an hour or so the darkness became profound and the road extremely bad. The horses could only move at a walk; their drivers seemed overcome with sleep; the harassed soldiers relaxed their vigilance and, in spite of all my efforts, the escort was overcome by the sort of sleeping coma peculiar to exhausted men, particularly just before dawn. We were rudely awakened by the sharp, hoarse cries which the Chouans use to signal and which came from a rock commanding one side of the road. The drivers immediately replied with a similar call, turned their horses violently into a side track and went off at a gallop. The movement was so rapid that it bowled over the soldiers on the left flank of the convoy. At the same moment I gave the order to fire. We hit one of the traitors and wounded a trace-horse, which leapt in the air and pulled the first limber across the track, blocking the road for the second. Nevertheless, the remaining carter found time to cut the traces and get away with the other horses. We could do little to stop him, since at that moment we were fired on from the hedge bordering the sunken road in which we were. We replied, taking cover behind our limbers, which were riddled with bullets. The action lasted till dawn, and we were expecting to be exposed to a considerably more effective fire when the Chouans suddenly abandoned their position. A company of grenadiers in the neighbourhood, having heard the firing, had come into action at the double, and their appearance on the scene had sufficed to put the enemy to flight.

These good fellows were delighted at having rescued us; they helped us pull our limbers out of the sunken road into which our cursed drivers had led them, and they commandeered new teams from a neighbouring farmstead. After I had explained matters the captain took charge of the convoy and sent back the escort to Port-Louis; he then insisted kindly that I should remain with him as a volunteer.

"Here we are on the coast," he said, "it is almost sea service that we have to do, and we know next to nothing about it; with your experience you could help us tremendously. In return we can offer you a fine campaign in good company, from which the Republic will come out the winner. You will serve under the first soldier in France—General Hoche—who loves us like his own children and who has certainly not brought us here for nothing."

It was more than sufficient to decide me. I agreed to stay with the grenadiers, and received as token of my application the famous horse's tail, the red plume which when spread out covered our hats and the sight of which undermined the courage of the enemy.

We arrived at the camp of Sainte-Barbe and took up position there. It was out there that I could learn with certainty the course which events had taken and what was expected for the future.

As a consequence of the naval battle of the Ile de Groix the English fleet, being the absolute mistress of the sea, had collected an enormous number of transports and had escorted them into the Bay of Quiberon, a vast basin in the coast of Brittany formed by the great salient of Saint-Gildas and the long peninsula of sand and rock which gives the anchorage its name. The spot was excellently chosen, being near the Morbihan, where the Chouans swarmed, and the two banks of the Loire, which the Vendeans covered by their armies.

Ten thousand *émigrés,* forming five regiments and several free corps, were put ashore by the English boats on the 27th June on Karnac beach, at the bottom of Quiberon Bay, between Vannes and Lorient.

The army, instead of following up this movement and advancing on Vannes, which could not have resisted, entered the peninsula of Quiberon and advanced up it as far as Fort Penthièvre, which bars it at its narrowest part. This fortress, which should have been able to put up an effective resistance, surrendered at the first summons, its garrison having been suborned a long time previously. Its defence was confided to a picked corps of *émigrés,* and in order to render it more formidable they retired the guns from the batteries bearing on the sea and used them to support entrenchments destined to repulse attacks coming from the land. This position was extremely strong, and might even having been considered impregnable, for it was flanked on the right by a flotilla of enemy gunboats and on the left by the English fleet, which, in addition, was constantly in communication with the little harbours on the peninsula.

Despite these advantages it was nevertheless a military operation of a crass stupidity to start an invasion by shutting up one's best troops in a fortress instead of taking the offensive with them on the spot.

At the moment of the enemy's appearance the army of the west was scattered throughout Brittany employed in suppressing the local risings which were breaking out; furthermore it was very weak in numbers; but at its head was General Hoche, one of the best men and greatest captains which France possessed during the Revolution, fertile though that period was in military genius. On being informed of the *émigrés* landing the Convention did not lose a moment in supporting the General commanding by all the means with which the Revolution had endowed it. Two of its members, Blad and Tallien, were sent off immediately, and arrived at Vannes on the 1st July. From the coast of Morbihan these representatives could follow all the movements and undertakings of the enemy, from the point of Saint-Gildas, where lie the ruins of the monastery once ruled by Abelard, to the thousand stones of Karnac, where, it is said, the camp of Caesar stood two thousand years ago. In the immense basin of Quiberon, between these two extremities, the English fleet lay at anchor, and sent its boats or transports in all directions loaded with troops, artillery, provisions and ammunition, destined to fan the flame of civil war in our unhappy provinces.

As soon as our troops were concentrated, Hoche put himself at their head and marched on the town of Auray, which was taken by storm. Karnac and Landevan were evacuated by the enemy, who also abandoned the village of Sainte-Barbe, a key position at the entry to Quiberon peninsula, commanding its communications with the coast. The General-in-Chief had realised its advantages with that eagle glance which characterised him. He had just given the order to entrench there when the grenadiers to whom I belonged arrived on the scene. Five redoubts were to be constructed, and that on the right flank fell to our lot. It closed the road which, skirting the northern shore of the peninsula, led to Fort Penthièvre, whose rocky summits covered with fortifications would be seen about a league and a half away. The white flag had replaced the tricolour there.

The captain charged me with the construction of the redoubt, of which an officer of engineers had merely traced the outline. We worked so hard that it was finished by evening, despite a considerable obstacle: the lack of earth and turf. Around us was nothing but sea sand, which fell away whenever we endeavoured to pack it and make a parapet. The idea came to me that if we mixed it with manure it would hold together, and there being any amount of this commodity in the villages of Lower Brittany I succeeded in running up the revetments of our redoubt. Without this invention we should have had to take earth from the only two places where it could be found: the cemetery and the curé's garden; an operation which did not appeal to us and which would have caused us to pass as unbelievers in the eyes of the inhabitants.

The curé, who hid his tonsure under a blue cloth cap and was clad like all the other peasants, heard about our respect for his church and came to thank the captain, remarking that our action would bring luck to our arms. This prophecy was borne out by the facts.

The enemy perceived eventually that our camp at Sainte-Barbe shut him in the peninsula and that he was blockaded there. They decided to make a combined attack, and one dark night three columns commanded by d'Hervilly, du Puysaie, and Tinteniac, advanced against our position, without, however, having previously reconnoitred it. The last of these columns, being obliged to follow tracks in the sand, lost its way and arrived too late. The two others attacked our redoubts with impetuosity, but were repulsed and put to flight by the fire from our guns and by our musketry. Three hundred men remained on the *glacis,* and the ground was littered with packs, muskets, and accoutrement. We brought in four field pieces with their limbers. The defeat would have been even more complete had our pursuit not been held up by the fire of five English gunboats, anchored broadside on to our left flank near the shore.

The fight at Sainte-Barbe should have convinced the enemy leaders that an invasion of France was a dream and that they possessed neither the strength nor the intelligence needed for success. But men under the influence of an evil fate are inevitably vowed to destruction. It is worthy of remark that the unworthy means employed to ensure the success of this invasion were those which brought about disaster; and this is how this bloody reckoning came about.

It is common knowledge that for twenty-five years the prisoners of war in England had been crowded into old hulks, called *pontoons*, and that their sufferings in these appalling prisons were beyond anything hitherto experienced. When the Quiberon expedition was being prepared the rank and file were recruited from amongst these desperate men. Many flatly refused to serve against their country; others accepted, with the secret resolve to change their flag when the opportunity offered. Among the latter was a gunner, David Goujon by name. Enlisted in a regiment of the royalist army he was landed at Quiberon and detailed to the garrison of Fort Penthièvre; he studied the lie of the ground, and profiting by the confusion after the fight at Sainte-Barbe he slipped out of the fortress and after considerable difficulty reached our outposts. Led to the grenadiers' redoubt he recognised me, having met me during the siege of Toulon, and begged me to lead him to our captain.

The latter listened attentively to the story of his escape; and General Debelle, who was in Hoche's confidence, and who had come to visit us, discussed the story of his escape at length and in considerable detail. Our deserter was shortly ordered to headquarters and took leave of me as though he never expected to meet me again. It turned out quite differently. Forty-eight hours later, on the 2nd Thermidor (20th July 1795) at nightfall, he returned to the redoubt, accompanied by a sergeant who never left him and who appeared to be his mentor. I did not pay much attention, since his arrival coincided with our orders to move. Although our movements were carried out at night and in the strictest silence, certain facts led me to suppose that we were about to attack the enemy positions. Our troops were massed at three points; on the left General Humbert assembled five or six hundred men in the neighbourhood of the village of Saint-Clément, at the commencement of the route leading to Fort Penthièvre following the shore of Quiberon bay. This route was under short-range fire from the English gunboats anchored broadside on to defend its access. A strong detachment led by General Vateau was posted at the head of a track leading across the highest ground on the peninsula and at about an equal distance from its northern shore. Finally our column, consisting of two hundred grenadiers under the orders of General Ménage, bivouacked across the road which, following the sea along the north side of the peninsula, ended at the cliff on whose summit was the fortress.

Our three corps were at a quarter league distance one from another; but since the ground narrowed to some sixty metres on approaching the fort we were bound to come together as we advanced and finally to make our junction. That, however, was some time ahead, for we had to cover a distance of a league and a half, during which our two flanks were exposed to the fire of the English ships and we were within point-blank range of the guns and various outworks of the fortress.

For a moment at sunset General Hoche faced the unpleasant prospect of a clear night. He wished to judge for himself the position of the troops and the general lie of the land. A natural observatory was afforded him by one of the rocks which stand up out of the sand to a considerable height and which on the coast of Morbihan take the form of a tower or a Gothic steeple. The peculiar formation of this rock had earned it the name of the *Roche aux Fées*. The general climbed to the top and it was from there he surveyed the field of battle. His plume was no sooner seen than the army showed its affection for its heroic leader by a salvo of applause, which spread from column to column to the outskirts of the camp. Never since Caesar had that countryside witnessed such a spontaneous outburst of affection from an army to its chief.

Like the theatre, military life has its intervals of appalling boredom. Seeing no end to the preliminaries of the evening's entertainment I lay down in the sand and slept soundly beside our piled arms. When I awoke, with a start, the scene had entirely changed. The rising tide had brought with it a change of weather; a cold, piercing wind flung the waves upon the rocks and the night was so dark that a platoon could not see the one ahead of it. We formed up by divisions and left at midnight, following the sea shore, which served us as right marker. Our commander, General Ménage, ordered absolute silence, and was particularly strict in regard to the *quolibets* and repartee which are peculiar to the French soldier when going into danger. Never was an order more necessary or better followed. The obstacles increased at every moment. The road, as it advanced into the peninsula, gradually narrowed and became a mere track lying between the sea and the rocks.

We marched by sections and finally in file, which caused us to cover a long stretch of route and weakened us in the event of attack. A storm was raging, and waves were breaking on the flank of our column, which was likely to be broken or carried off by the waves. The whistling of the wind and the noise of the shingle deafened us and made it impossible to hear a thing. This circumstance saved us, for our presence would certainly have been betrayed to the shore sentinels or the inshore gunboats if the noise of our arms on the rocks had not been stifled by the fury of the storm.

During a short halt the general commanding came to inspect and encourage our column, which was slightly in advance of that on the left. I learnt then that David Goujon, accompanied by the sergeant whom we called his *shadow*, was at the head of the first platoon and was guiding it.

New orders passed from mouth to mouth gave us to understand that we had reached the base of the rocky escarpment which surrounded the fortress. We redoubled our precautions and slipped along the narrow space between the sea and the foot of this obstacle. We left our packs in a cave, and after passing several rocky spurs dominating a raging sea we commenced painfully to clamber over a mass of stones which I took to be *débris* from the side of the cliff. The escarpment which we had to climb then appeared before us, and we were near to the success or failure of our undertaking. The moment was a solemn one, and on seeing the enemy above our heads and the gulf beneath our feet, our young grenadiers started to cross themselves.

The face of the rock, which is appallingly high, is not flat as it would appear at first sight; it consists of a series of terraces one above the other which leave a narrow path at the base of each.

These species of steps are missing in many places, and there progress is impossible, but if one searches to the left or the right of the path one is on, another terrace can always be found above.

God alone knows how we reached the top of this escarpment, for it was too dark to see anything, and our individual knowledge was confined entirely to our own actions. I imagine that on at least a dozen occasions the grenadiers beside me lifted me on to the terrace above, and as often those already there pulled me up to them. My musket followed the same route and I rendered to others the same assistance that I received. The terraces were some five feet high and eighteen inches broad.

At the summit of the escarpment was a wall giving on to the *terre-plein* of the fortress, and which served as parapet to a large battery *à barbette* trained against an enemy approaching from the extremity of the peninsula. We climbed this wall, which was not high, and dashed into the battery to the shout of "*Vive la République!*" The Guard, which had doubtless taken shelter from the storm, ran to the parapet, but were taken in the rear and hurled over the cliff. A body of enemy troops, rallied by a Colonel named Folmont, tried to defend the important post which they had allowed to be surprised. Instead of replying to their fire we attacked with the bayonet and put them to flight. Their commander and many other *émigrés* fell, the remainder sought refuge, in a lower part of the fortress known as the *retranchement*. There the fight was furious; the garrison was in force, and we had to turn them out of the barracks, which were carried by storm with terrible slaughter.

At the moment when, masters of the platform of the citadel, we attacked the citadel itself, the enemy troops who occupied it had so little conception of the peril of their situation that they opened the fire of their batteries on General Humbert's column, which was being attacked simultaneously by the English gunboats anchored on its left bank in the bay of Quiberon. At dawn this column, which was advancing along the shore, had been discovered by the gunboats and the fortress and was exposed to their fire. These two fires made it appear evident that the right column had failed in its object and that the grenadiers must be lost. Under this impression the commander ordered a retreat, which had already commenced when the tricolour was perceived flying from Fort Penthièvre.

Never did a country's colours cause more surprise or joy. The army, scattered amongst the sands of the peninsula, greeted them with cheers, and General Hoche, despite his usual calm, gave the example to his men. We replied from the walls which we had just captured, and the sound of this enthusiasm was carried to the enemy fleet as a convincing testimony to our devotion to France and our illustrious commander.

It was now within our power to chastise the English gunboats which had fired upon our infantry. There before us were the long-range mortars which had been loaded by the enemy when the fortress was in his possession. It sufficed to change their bearing slightly, and the bursting of heavy projectiles amongst these gunboats sufficed to apprise their crews that fortune's wheel had turned against them. When they cut their cables to avoid our shells an immense shout of laughter rose from the bank and pitilessly followed them.

General Hoche came to visit the rock we had climbed, and thanked the grenadiers for their fine feat of arms, which had decided the fate of the campaign and confounded the enemies of France. A trait characteristic of those times is that none amongst the grenadiers received promotion. Nobody ever thought of such a thing; every one conceived that he had merely done his duty.

The fortress taken, the enemy which it had protected were now uncovered. We did not lose a moment, and the army in columns of attack advanced to the further side of Fort Penthièvre. It is hard to imagine why an invading army should, of a set purpose, have established itself in a position without water, of no military value, surrounded by the sea and lacking even a suitable site for embarkation. We could not understand why, instead of covering the fortress and defending its approaches supported by its heavy guns, the commanders of the royalist troops had taken position behind the fortress, which could neither protect them nor be protected by them. These commanders were undoubtedly men of honour and courage; but they served their cause badly and waged war in the manner of Minden or Rosbach. Their principal position lay among the sands of the peninsula a league from the fort. It was a wretched village called Kervadis, or some similar name; it was surrounded by stone walls which served as entrenchments ; more than three thousand men were there, under the orders of M. de Puysaie. A cloud of skirmishers advanced resolutely enough, but when our men recognised them as Chouans, an enemy they hated bitterly, they charged them without firing a single shot.

This movement sufficed to make them disappear entirely; and shortly our advanced guards informed us that the garrison of the village was evacuating it by a sunken road or ravine which had served them for a rifle pit. We could only reach these stragglers, who paid for all the others.

In this village the houses were full of baggage, munitions, and arms of all kinds. We promptly advanced and marched on Saint-Julien, another village situated a league farther on, where the Comte de Sombreuil had his headquarters. The enemy were still nine thousand strong, but were so demoralised that they were flying in all directions. The Comte de Puysaie set the example. He jumped into a boat in order, so he said, to inform the English admiral of the defeat, a piece of information which the admiral could have dispensed with, since he had seen the tricolour floating over the fortress since dawn and had observed our advance along the shores of the peninsula.

During their rout the enemy halted at the Port d'Aliguen. Forced to abandon it, they retired to Fort Saint-Pierre, situated above the sea on a rock. An English frigate and several brigs swept the two beaches leading to this fort with their artillery, and while their fire kept our troops in check their boats took off the fugitives.

The embarkation, carried out amongst the rocks, was extremely dangerous. Prisoners informed us that evening that it was there that MM. de Damas, de Rohan, de Contade, de Vauban and d'Hevilly made their escape. The latter died; but a crowd of others lost their lives there. The English sailors, fearing that their over-loaded boats would be swamped, thrust off pitilessly all those who were hanging on and made them loose hold with strokes from their cutlasses. Two pieces of field artillery which we placed in position cut these communications. Thereupon the enemy, summoned to lay down their arms by General Ménage, surrendered at discretion. Amongst these unhappy prisoners were the Comte Charles de Sombreuil, who, I think, was commanding in chief, the Bishop of Dol, MM. de Rieux, de Soulange, de Broglie, and many others bearing historic names or honourably known.

Since the English ships continued obstinately firing after the surrender I foresaw the moment when their kind offices would become fatal to their *protégés*.

This terrible day, if I make no mistake, was the 29th July, twenty-four days after the capture of Fort Penthièvre by the enemy.

The army destroyed there was twenty thousand strong, *i.e.,* ten thousand *émigrés,* two thousand Chouans, four thousand French prisoners recruited from the hulks, and some three thousand sailors and marines belonging to the English fleet.

The long column of prisoners marching to their death was a sad and moving spectacle. There were to be found priests, generals, naval officers, gamekeepers, peasants. Women with their children followed weeping; they were allowed to remain with them at each halt. Like many others I took charge of a child whose mother could no longer carry it, and the captain fully approved my action. I had several opportunities to speak to the prisoners, and I was forced to admit that the majority, despite their unhappy situation, were possessed by a sort of infatuation which rendered their fate inevitable. They had been forced to surrender at discretion, but they nevertheless considered themselves as prisoners of war ; they were not aware of the decree which had put them beyond the pale of the law, and they expected to be set free sooner or later by the insurrection in the Vendée. During the night some three thousand succeeded in escaping to the coast where the English ships were anchored. The others, shut up in the church of Saint-Esprit at Auray, were brought immediately before a military commission. The terrible massacre which the condemnation of so many men would render necessary appalled the judges. They declared themselves incompetent. It was merely a respite for the prisoners. Another commission, formed by the orders of the Convention, did not hesitate, and eight hundred prisoners were shot, at the rate of sixty a day, in a field close by the gates of the town. One hundred and eighty-seven others were condemned at Vannes and executed. M. Charles de Sombreuil and the Bishop of Dol were amongst them.

I was not a witness to this bloody business, thank God! I had returned to Fort Penthièvre late in the evening. It was full of troops engaged in celebrating the victory with the aid of the excellent English beer and port wine brought in abundance by the English fleet for the use of the Royalist army and its allies in Morbihan. Never had the means to render an invasion popular been so lavishly bestowed. In every village there was an astounding profusion of stores of all kinds, and had we reckoned the enemy by their store-houses we should have expected them to number at least one hundred thousand.

It was with the greatest difficulty that I could find a place in Fort Penthièvre to pass the night. Half the army was holding a triumphal orgy there. Republican frugality had been unable to resist the temptation of an evening's carousal, and the citadel had been converted into an enormous hostelry; where, in a hundred improvised fire-places, between two guns, an innumerable quantity of hams from Cork and sides of salt beef, the best in Ireland, were being cooked.

The guests, arranged in a circle around a barrel of strong beer, drew on it by turns whilst awaiting their succulent repast, and outshone one another in singing the hymns of the Republic in a thousand different keys. All this noisy gaiety saddened me. Seeing me, the officers of the grenadiers called me to share their good fortune; they were going to drink some coffee! One cannot imagine nowadays what a rarity coffee was then; there were some youngsters there who had heard it spoken of but had never seen it. The English, who then had all the coffee in the world, had embarked bales of it on board their fleet, and we had captured an enormous quantity. We did what we could with it under the circumstances.

The troops left at daybreak, and I took leave of my good friends the grenadiers.

I reached a little port on the northern coast whence a ship was leaving for Lorient.

On board there were some twenty peasants in their best clothes, also two soldiers going on leave, under pretext of I know not what illness, and whose equipment made it evident that they had assisted in the rout of the royalist army. When making sail a prayer was said in common, as was the custom in Brittany when about to confront the perils of the sea. I followed the example without hesitation and thus obliged the two soldiers to imitate me, which they did with sufficiently bad grace. We were still kneeling when the person next to me got up and made a speech in Gaelic of which I did not understand a single word, but which he uttered with an emotion which was heartily shared by his audience. When finishing he said a few words of which I was evidently the object, for when they arose the women turned towards me and curtseyed and the men shook me cordially by the hand. Whilst I did my best to reply to these courtesies, all the more remarkable as coming from people noted for their ferocity, I saw the two soldiers turn pale and retire fore-ward behind the foremast where they remained during the entire crossing without speaking a word to anybody. On sitting down my neighbour turned to me and said in excellent French:

"Sir, we are already old acquaintances and even, I am sure, old friends. I am the *curé* of Sainte-Barbe. You saved the garden of my presbytery from destruction and what is better, the holy ground of my parishioners' cemetery. I have just informed the people present of this fact, and they ask me to express to you their gratitude. You have justly earned it, and mine as well. I could have wished that that had been the only duty which I had to fulfil, but seeing those two men bearing the spoils of civil war and clad in the garments of their victims, I had to anathematise so cruel a disregard of the rights of humanity and of the dead, and my parishioners have joined their voices to mine in reproving this criminal action and in praying God to receive in his bosom those poor wretches who perished yesterday. As soon as you came on board," he added, "these peasants remarked that you had taken no part in that odious pillage, and they have judged you a man after their own heart."

I was surprised and touched to find, amongst the savage inhabitants of a sandy village in Armorica, such high sentiments, such virtuous indignation, such courageous piety; they recalled to my mind a beautiful and generous thought of the Roman historian: "The victories of civil war (says Tacitus) call not for trophies but for tears and expiation."

CHAPTER 6: 1796

The Irish Insurgency

Those who have lived beside the ocean are aware that winter is not announced by frosts but by storms. As the solstice approaches the hurricanes redouble in violence and the sea becomes so heavy that vessels are often disabled, their boats carried away, and their bulwarks often stove in as by a cannon shot.

In certain years, for unknown reasons, these hurricanes spread and seem endowed with an increased power of destruction. In the autumn of 1796 there were signs that one of these terrible epochs might be expected. In calm weather the sea was surly and agitated; foreign birds sought shelter amongst the rocks on the coast, and shoals of fish, urged by instinct, mounted the rivers of Brittany to find a haven.

In Brest at that moment were thirty battleships with troops on board. The objective of this expedition gave rise to all kinds of conjecture; some supposed it destined to ravage the English Antilles, others that it was to succour the Irish insurgents. But it was the general opinion that it could no longer set sail, seeing that the constant delays had given time for winter and the west winds to set in, which rendered the narrow channel unmanageable. It was also obvious that some of our ships, old and badly equipped, could not keep the sea during this redoubtable season without running the gravest risks.

We were still discussing this question in the *Coquille* frigate, in which I was master-at-arms, when the *Immortalité* frigate, flying the flag of Vice-Admiral Bouvet, hoisted flags and fired signal guns to get under way.

The squadron, consisting of fifteen sail of the line and a dozen frigates, was soon under sail, driven by a violent wind which inspired but little confidence in the minds of experienced seamen.

Detailed to collect the last orders which were awaited from Paris, we could only get under way towards evening, long after our ships had disappeared from sight, and it was night when, having disembogued, we arrived at Berthaume, a vast semi-circular bay which, with that of Cameret, forms the entrance to the magnificent basin of Brest harbours. A dispatch vessel which awaited us and had made out our lights transmitted us an extremely unexpected order. At the close of day the frigates which were scouting ahead of the squadron had discovered off the Isle of Ushant an English fleet of thirty ships or frigates ready to dispute our passage. Our admiral, determined at all costs to attain the object of the expedition, had immediately signalled the squadron to avoid an action and to pass by the Rag, a dangerous open passage through the rocks of Finisterre and the reefs surrounding the Isle of Sein. Our ships had observed this dangerous passage immediately, and it was by the same route that we were to rejoin them if we succeeded in escaping from the perils which menaced us from all quarters in the darkness.

Our captain was one of those tried men for whom duty is a religion. He took command of the frigate from the quarter-deck, and with admirable calm gave the orders which were most likely to afford us a chance of safety. The boats were cleared; picked men were stationed at the halliards in order to lower sail the moment ordered; carpenters with axes took post by the masts in order to cut them away at the first signal; officers, with the lead, were posted in the chains; topmen were stationed on the bowsprit and the fore-yard to signal breakers; gunners, cutlass in hand, stood guard over the hatch-ways to stop the men leaving the deck and to prevent useless hands from coming there. The bearings of the coast lights were taken continuously in order to determine our position and that of the entrance to the Rag; the slightest error would have led us to miserable disaster. Then, summoning the senior warrant officer, the captain handed him boarding pistols with orders to shoot the first man who broke the silence which he had ordered in the common interest. These same orders were welcomed with tacit approval, everybody realising that it is only with a well-disciplined crew that a ship sailing in the midst of reefs can hope to escape disaster.

At this moment a man appeared on deck of whose presence in the frigate we were ignorant. His appearance made a peculiar impression. He was a short man whose square shoulders, muscular legs and hairy chest gave evidence of great physical strength. I recognised in him one of those Gauls who inhabited Armorica some two thousand years ago and who have retained, since Julius Caesar, their features, their language, and even their costume. His long black hair escaped from under a blue linen cap and floated in the wind. Instead of the trousers which characterise modern civilisation he was wearing those ludicrous breeches, the appearance of which so struck the Romans that they named the country after this strange garment.[1]

He inspected the frigate's sail with a sneer, made certain alterations, and caused screens to be placed over the helms-men's lanterns, whose light incommoded him. He took his place beside the captain, who used his authority to carry out the orders he prescribed. This man, whose commands domi-nated us like destiny, was a pilot from lower Brittany, the type of sailor that can neither read nor write but has inherited the experience transmitted from father to son in each family since the boatmen of the Veneti guided the fleets of Rome

1. Bracata Gallia.

some twenty centuries ago. A peculiarity which struck our men and gave rise to superstition was the fact that this pilot could see in the darkest night, and that he consulted the deepest shadow when steering the frigate amongst the reefs; and it was a fact that his eyes remained fixed on points of the horizon where we could not discover the slightest glimmer, and seemed to find there the elements necessary to guide us. I often thought that some distant light must serve him as a guide; but none among us could make out anything of the kind, and the crew came to the conclusion that the pilot was endowed with second sight. In the dangerous situation we were in we had considerable need of supernatural assistance.

We had doubtless been engaged in this terrible passage but a short while, although it seemed hours to us, when a flash was seen in the midst of the night, followed almost immediately by a loud detonation. It was a distress signal from a ship about to perish. Every succeeding signal made the most courageous of us humble. The force of the wind gave great pace to the frigate and brought her immediately to the scene of the disaster, almost touching the wrecked vessel. She was the *Séduisant*, 74, having twelve hundred soldiers and sailors on board. A heavy sea had thrown her off her course and piled her up on the great Tevennec, a formidable rock on which she was impaled. Her bows, battered by the breakers, were already submerged and going to pieces, while the stern, where the crew had taken refuge, was grinding on the rock and making water at every moment. Her battle-lanterns lit this scene of desolation.

Clinging to her lower masts we could see those who remained upright, a crowd of men struck dumb with terror at the sight of the waves which broke upon the deck and carried away each time a few unhappy souls. The old sailors had lashed themselves together in order to resist the force of the sea better and were making a raft from spars and topmasts. When the frigate swept past like an arrow the shipwrecked men thought themselves saved and blessed us; but when they saw they were abandoned they shouted with rage and cursed us. Our pitiless resolution was similar to that of a grenadier who when mounting to the attack kicks aside the body of his fallen comrade. A cry of pity was heard from our deck. A young midshipman, recognising his brother among the shipwrecked, leaped on the hammock netting, crying that he wished to share his fate; he narrowly escaped death at the hands of the warrant officer detailed to see that silence was observed, and he owed his life to an officer who carried him below like a child.

Two minutes later the spectacle of this terrible catastrophe had passed from our sight like a dream, and the frigate, driven by the storm, continued her route in darkness, lightened only by the phosphorescent glow of the breakers. Finally we reached the end of the channel; the swell from seaward, which caught us broadside on, told us that we were out of that terrible labyrinth wherein so many sailor-men had met their end during the two thousand years that man had known of its existence.

Day came, dull and foggy, lighting a dark horizon and showing us a black and choppy sea. Towards midday a break in the clouds enabled us to make out our squadron, scattered and badly knocked about. We joined the Rochefort division, commanded by Admiral Richery; and we then found a fleet of sixteen sail of the line, with a dozen frigates and corvettes and several transports. Several were still missing, and we searched in vain for the frigate *Fraternité,* which carried Vice-Admiral Morand de Gallés and his Major-General Bruix, whom we regarded as the soul of the expedition. General Hoche, commanding the expeditionary force, was also on board this frigate. By a chance which has no parallel in the history of the navy, the *Fraternité* had gone astray in the fog and left the squadron and the troops without instructions. It was nevertheless impossible to find two other leaders to compare with Hoche and Bruix.

On the 21st of December, on the sixteenth day out from Brest, we sighted the coast of Ireland. Soon, despite a contrary wind and a heavy sea, we beheld Bantry Bay, a large open harbour on the west coast of the island capable of holding all the fleets of Europe. Looking about us we did not experience the joy which the storm-tossed sailor is supposed to feel at the sight of land; nothing on earth could have been more desolate or depressing than the country we saw before us. It appeared to be uninhabited; we saw neither landmarks, villages nor any trace of cultivation or human life. The hills which rose abruptly at a certain distance from the beach were covered with brushwood; but the plain was bare, save for a few snowdrifts tormented by the wind. The coast was bordered by rocks forming islands or high promontories. Everywhere the sea foamed against these inhospitable shores, grinding the shingle of which the beach was formed. The prospects of remaining in the bay where we had anchored, or of disembarking, were equally unpleasant.

The waves from the open sea rendered communication between the ships difficult and dangerous, and the violence of the wind threatened to make our vessels drag their anchors and drift ashore. We were a prey to another anxiety: the enemy squadron might attack us in our critical position, and the absence of our leaders paralysed our movements. The rumour spread that a council of war had been held in the *Immortalité* and that General Grouchy wished to be put ashore with the six thousand troops we had on board. In the meantime the *Coquille* was instructed by signal to reconnoitre, with the object of getting into touch with the insurgents who were supposed to be masters of this part of Ireland. The longboat was manned and took on board a dozen men commanded by a lieutenant.

I was not told off for this expedition, but the captain, noticing that I was examining the coast curiously said: "Go along too, if you want to." I was so eager to take advantage of this permission that I jumped into the boat unarmed save for my cutlass. An officer had boarding pistols sent to me, which I attached to my belt.

We were no sooner landed than our commander marched us ahead with as much confidence as though we were going to some cheery fair in a village in Lower Brittany. This confidence increased when, on a plateau situated behind the opening of a valley, we made out some Irish peasants who waved to us to join them. At least that was the interpretation which our commander placed upon their actions, which could more rationally have been considered as meaning exactly the opposite, since these men could have simply run towards us had there not existed some reason for not doing so. I was making the remark when a body of cavalry, in ambush behind a hill, suddenly dashed into the plain and charged us at full gallop. Taken by surprise our detachment, instead of reserving their fire until point-blank range, fired at random and broke for the boat. I judged the distance to be too great to avoid our retreat being cut by the enemy, which would have left us to face the alternative of being saved or taken prisoner.

Instead of imitating my comrades and running for the sea I dashed ahead toward the mountains, where I hoped to get beyond the reach of cavalry. One trooper had attached himself to my heels, and fired his pistols at me without hitting me. I replied, and doubtless hit his horse, for he stopped, and when I had reached the top of the hill in safety I could see him returning on foot. Looking towards the plain I made out the detachment which I had so fortunately quitted advancing towards the interior, surrounded by yeomanry, who escorted them to Dublin, where they were exhibited as a glorious trophy, captured from the French Republic.

My situation was certainly not an enviable one. I was abandoned and alone, without resources, on enemy territory, in a wild country, sterile, beaten by the gale and destined shortly to vanish in the darkness of a winter's night.

Nevertheless I considered myself lucky to be free instead of sleeping like my comrades on show in some filthy gaol in the company of felons, or trying to sleep in a hammock, listening to ejaculations such as: "The frigate's dragging her anchor; she's drifting, we are going to strike, we are lost!" and other remarks which do not lull one to sleep. Undoubtedly I was faced with the prospect of an uncomfortable bed on mother earth, nothing to eat, and the icy temperature of December. But the insurgents in the field faced all that I, a Frenchman of the Revolution, could do as much. I had but to find our friends the Irish, to whom we had come through the storm to bring them freedom. I thereupon set out to find them; it was high time, for night was falling.

The steep hill which I had climbed and which had saved me from the cavalry stretched on its reverse slope down to a deep bay. I descended in this direction, convinced that a road must follow the coast, and in effect I found one parallel to the cliffs which stretch their wall against the waves of the Atlantic. This road should of necessity lead to some habitation: a village, some fishermen's huts, a pilot's cabin. I was delighted at this discovery and pursued my way, taking all possible precautions against unpleasant surprises. I walked for several hours, but only by the uncertain glimmer of the breakers. There was no sound but the whistling of the wind and the thunder of the surf. Finally the road passed over a rocky crest and descended to the level of the sea, and I saw that it was crossed by a stream, fordable by means of large stones placed across its bed. This was the first sign of man that I had seen in a country where nowadays they have more inhabitants than they know what to do with. Convinced that I was about to become acquainted with hosts more or less inclined to welcome me, I ascended one bank of the stream and, sure enough, I arrived at a hamlet consisting of some thirty cabins ranged in a circle about a valley overlooked by high cliffs. I knocked at several doors; nobody answered, not a dog barked and, although it was midnight, not a cock crowed. I came to the conclusion that the village was uninhabited. Tired as I was I decided to go no farther, at least for the moment, and discovering a stack of hay I made a hole in the top and thrust myself in it up to the neck. An instant after I was fast asleep.

I was awakened by the mewing of a cat; I thought I was dreaming, but had to admit the evidence of my eyes. A young girl was there, four paces away, feeding a thin and famished cat. She was a child some fourteen or fifteen years old, tall, thin, with blue eyes whose glance was sad but kind. Her only garment was a poor smock of blue cloth which left her neck and arms free. Her whole appearance gave an impression of suffering and unhappiness which filled me with pity. It was difficult for me to show myself without frightening her, and I could not talk to her since neither of us knew a word of the other's language. I must admit, to the shame of my intelligence, that the only expedient I could improvise was to imitate the mewing of her cat. It was infantile, but it served the purpose. She immediately lifted her eyes to mine; surprise and fear were depicted on her features when she saw I was a soldier; but when, by a happy inspiration, I showed her my cockade she started to smile, as though she had at once understood how I came to be there, and with a gesture she pointed out the position of the French squadron, to show me that she well knew where I came from.

Adversity brings humans together. This child, eager to help me, ran to her house and brought me back some hot potatoes, cooked under the cinders like chestnuts; she peeled them whilst I ate them burning hot to satisfy my ferocious appetite. I did not at first understand how she came to be alone in the hamlet. She gave me the story of her misfortunes in a mixture of Gaelic and Carthaginian entirely unintelligible to me and which, despite the softness of her voice, sounded as barbarous as the harshest dialect of Morbihan. Nevertheless her gestures were so expressive that with the knowledge I already possessed I was able to put her sad story together. All this part of Munster was allied to the Irish insurgents by ties of religion. The defection of the peasants had been provoked by the excesses which the Hanoverians in the pay of England committed with impunity. These soldiers, a collection of adventurers recruited on the continent, were known collectively as Saxons; their barbarous conduct had made their name a byword for brigandage and butchery. More interested in plunder than in guarding the coast, they had allowed a French brig to land a cargo of arms and ammunition near Bantry, which cargo had been carried into the interior and had disappeared as if by magic.

During the subsequent inquiry it had been discovered that young Mary's brother had rescued a French sailor from drowning. His complicity was taken for granted; he was condemned by the provost-marshal and shot on the spot. The other inhabitants, threatened with the same fate, made up their minds without hesitation; the men left to join the insurgents, the women and children went to Cork to beg for their living. The village was abandoned. Mary alone remained to look after her grandmother, who was paralysed.

Although not absolutely sure I was fairly certain that my young hostess knew where I could find the insurgents. When I asked her she pretended not to understand, and took on the air of a person charged with a state secret. I judged, rightly, that she was sworn to silence by an oath upon which her safety depended. I therefore told her that I was determined to start at once to find the camp of the United Irishmen. She took fright at this and did her utmost to dissuade me, pointing out that those of the inhabitants who could guide me would not dare to, and that in any case it would be courting death to roam about in plain daylight when the Hanoverians were beating the country. She invited me to her cottage to pass the day, since she was obliged to go away. She gave me to understand that she would be back before nightfall and that then she might be able to give me some interesting news. I allowed myself to be guided by this child, not without marvelling at the mature judgement with which misfortune had endowed her. After making sure that we were not watched she led me to her cabin. The door had been barricaded, and to get in we had to follow a long circuitous corridor along the palisades. When my eyes were accustomed to the darkness I made out, stretched on a bed, an old woman, who seemed to be dead. Her grand-daughter knelt before her and spoke to her. Then from this apparent corpse a voice arose. It was, I think, a prayer to God in my favour and a supplication for the deliverance of her land. At the request of the sick woman Mary fetched a blue coat riddled with holes and placed it in the hands whose paralysed fingers struggled to hold it. It was the garment her son had worn when they shot him.

The butchers had sold it to this unhappy mother, who had it brought to her every day and soaked it with her tears.

Before leaving, Mary put me in the loft, which was reached by means of a ladder easily withdrawn. A skylight in the roof offered a means of exit to the open country.

Between the rocks against which the village was built and the village itself was a space some ten feet wide forming a sort of ditch. A plank stretched across this permitted of a prompt retreat into the neighbouring marshes.

Faithful to my military habits, which forbade my settling down until I had explored the immediate neighbourhood, I did some reconnoitring during my young hostess's absence, hoping to learn something of use to the expedition when the troops eventually landed. This event, upon which I was counting, seemed somewhat remote when on reaching the shore I got sight of our squadron. The storm, which was raging with redoubled fury, had handled our vessels so sorely that they had hauled off from the coast and struck their yards and topmasts. Some new ones had arrived; but on the other hand it seemed that others had departed. It was evident that no attempt to land troops could be made before the weather changed, and no such change seemed probable. I could therefore join the insurgents, and I had plenty of time in which to do so.

Although a considerable stretch of country was open to my view I saw no one except some twenty soldiers or customs officers in green uniforms; they disappeared in the opposite direction and I paid no attention to them.

When Mary returned she told me, as I expected, that she was authorised to lead me to the insurgents' camp. Her relations with them made me think that she could probably find me some cartridges for my pistols; in my hurried departure from the frigate I had taken none, and the cavalryman who had pursued me had led to my using the only two I had in self-defence. The girl immediately supplied this urgent need with the same intelligence of which she had already given such conclusive proof. Leaving the house by the loft we circled part of the hamlet and arrived at a dilapidated chapel. The door was walled up to prevent profanation by a heretic soldiery, and we had to get in by the window. Mary fell on her knees and prayed fervently. She then passed behind the altar and opened the door of a burial vault which served as a magazine; it contained several barrels of powder and a case of cartridges, the remains of a cargo landed from some French ship which the insurgents had been unable to carry away in its entirety. On leaving the church the girl showed me a young elm planted in front of the door. It was the only tree on this desolate coast, and in happy times there was dancing in its shade. Other souvenirs were destined to attach themselves to this ill-omened tree.

After a frugal meal I kissed this worthy little girl good night and mounted to my attic, full of hope, to sleep on a truss of straw.

Long before dawn my young guide came to meet me, and I was ready as promptly as in bivouac. We left the loft by means of the plank, which we carefully removed after our passage. We then followed narrow paths across an immense marsh, followed the crests of many barren hills and arrived at a river flowing between high reed-covered banks. We crossed it by a ford. Here the country changed and became a mass of thickets formed of some thorny plant. This formation was ideal for an ambush and reminded me of Brittany; I concluded that it was the head-quarters of the insurgents. In effect, following certain signals from Mary, two large men suddenly appeared from behind a thicket, armed to the teeth, but in a state of rags and tatters impossible to describe. They welcomed us kindly and led us into their fastness. The best comparison that I can imagine would be that of King Alfred's camp in the Avon marshes. The enormous space which it occupied within its natural fortifications formed a species of archipelago whose islands, covered in briar, gorse and broom, were separated by deep bogs, muddy or flooded. These were impassable save at certain points, which were strongly guarded. In many instances the passage was only practicable by means of hurdles, which were immediately removed.

When we had passed from one to another of many islands in this manner I arrived at that occupied by headquarters, which consisted of some half a dozen cabins. The commander, who came to meet me, was a fine young man some twenty-five to twenty-eight years old, tall, good-looking and with a distinguished manner. He spoke perfect French and some of his officers who had been at the college of St. Omer talked to me as easily as if their entire life had been passed in Paris.

An excellent dinner was followed by a council of war at which I assisted; we settled the final details of a daring plan which had for object to gain some signal advantage in profiting by the panic which the arrival of the French squadron had caused. It was proposed also to prevent the English troops from marching on the coast by making demonstrations against the various positions they were guarding.

I insisted on taking part in this expedition and the commander, who was known simply as the Laird, or the Lord, very courteously told me I might accompany him. He gave me a fine double-barrelled gun, adding that he was sure I should use it for the good of the cause.

The start took place in the evening, by detachments and by different routes; the camp was entirely deserted when we left it. Horses awaited us a short distance away and scouts were posted along our route. Long before night was over we halted in an old manor-house, where we remained all day. We left it at dusk, hoping to be in touch with the enemy at midnight. The insurgents were masters of the country. The object of our expedition was the town of Cork. Doubtless it was not within our power to attack it seriously, but it had been decided to insult and intimidate the garrison, encourage the partisans to revolt, and finally to make a military reconnaissance which would open the way to the French troops when they landed. In consequence two false attacks had been prepared in order to distract the enemy's attention whilst we attempted to take one of his principal posts by storm. The post in question was a fortified barracks which covered a suburb and was defended by a body of infantry, who were accused of having on several occasions slaughtered the prisoners which had fallen into their hands. The approaches to this post had been cleared to prevent surprise, and advanced sentries formed a cordon at the foot of the *glacis*. Nevertheless our men, cleverly guided, had succeeded in hiding themselves within almost point-blank range of the sentries and less than two hundred yards from the barracks.

Our first platoons had reached this position by crawling, and they remained there flat on their stomachs awaiting the signal to attack. The commander, his *aides-de-camp*, and myself were led up to the line by a young man who was remarkably brave and intelligent; his name was Sheill. He placed us in the interval between two enemy sentries, who must have heard us but for the wind.

From this stage-box nothing escaped our notice. The lights

within the barracks enabled us not only to make out the entrance, but even the loophole in the walls flanking it. There lay my worry; at the council I had suggested blowing open the door which, according to our spies, was strong and well guarded ; but we had to abandon the idea because we lacked all means to put it into practice. We had to fall back on the simpler but more dangerous plan of breaking down the door with axes; and men had been chosen from volunteers who had presented themselves for this perilous service.

Messengers who passed from one column to another with extraordinary speed had already informed the commander that everything was ready for the attack, and he had raised his arm to fire the pistol shot which was the agreed signal, when the door of the barracks opened to give passage to the visiting round. The lantern carried by the drummer shed a bright light ahead, but left the officer who was marching behind in complete obscurity. We could nevertheless estimate the distance at which he was when he replied to the challenge of a sentry. The line he was following led him straight towards us, and he could not fail to discover us and fire the alarm if we hesitated for an instant in stopping him.

"Carry on, gentlemen," said the commander; and immediately a shot killed the officer.

A reflection from the light on his gorget had furnished the target for the bullet which hit him. A ferocious cheer rose suddenly from the thickets and dominated the storm like the growling of wild beasts. Recognising the war cry of Ireland the sentries and the rounds dashed towards the barracks to take refuge there. But we were on their heels and arrived there with them. The gate which was open to receive them could not be shut because it was blocked with corpses. The insurgents, without replying to the firing, dashed into the interior and killed the garrison to a man. The building was set alight and utterly destroyed by the exploding ammunition which was stored there.

During this bloody business skirmishers had operated against two different quarters of the town and had held the garrison in check. By this means they had rendered possible a reconnaissance which left no doubt as to the possibility of carrying the place when the French troops gave their support to the insurrection.

We had just remounted when a strange scene attracted my attention. From a nearby paddock came the cries of a mass of animals who replied to the calls of human voices which were no less harsh and raucous. On the one side was a summons, an incitement; on the other the furious impatience of an enormous number of horses, bullocks and cows beating the ground with their hooves and hurling themselves against the fence which penned them in. A part of these animals had been seized to pay overdue taxes; others to pay the rent of some wretched hovel; the majority in order to pay the *dime* to the Anglican church. They had been parked inside the town with a view to selling them by auction on the morrow. To carry them off had been one of the objects of our expedition, and if it had not been realised it was because the officer detailed for the undertaking had been unable to resist joining in the attack on the barracks, which seemed to him more promising of glory. The military being absent, a crowd of women and children had collected in an endeavour to recover their animals. They dared not approach for fear of the enemy, and therefore carried on the noises and passionate communication with them which had aroused my curiosity. Recognising the voices of those who had fed them, all these animals had given tongue for joy; but seeing that there was delay in setting them free they turned wild, and dashing against the boarding which held them captive they beat it down and poured through the break in mass bellowing savagely, and making the earth tremble under their weight. A few hours after, with that wonderful instinct peculiar to animals, they had all found the houses where they were born.

Back in the insurgents' camp, I settled down in one of the huts, thinking to find there the deep sleep which is heralded by utter fatigue; but haunted by the image of the events through which I had passed I saw again in my dreams the attack on the barracks and the massacre of the garrison; I heard the piteous cries of the men we had slaughtered, and the impression was so vivid that I awoke. When I opened my eyes I could still hear them. Instead of an illusion it was a sad reality. A few paces away lay a man, trussed like a pig about to be stuck, uttering heart-rending cries. His red hair told me that he belonged to that Saxon race so loathed in Ireland. No wound justified his appeals, and it appeared that he had remained silent since he had been brought into camp; but he had just noticed some insurgents nearby, engaged in splitting some old planks of pitch pine in order to make faggots, and with a terrible intuition of the fate they held in store for him he had immediately realised that they intended to roast him alive over a slow fire. Perceiving my cockade he had had a glimmer of hope, and in spite of the cords which trussed him had dragged himself to my feet to ask me in English either to save his life or at least to ensure him a death without torture. I thought at first that fear had turned the poor fellow's brain and that he was exaggerating the danger of his position. I was undeceived by an officer who told me that the man had been condemned to death for his crimes by a secret tribunal and was destined to die by the fire.

"In any case," he added, "were this brute to die a thousand times by torture he would never expiate the evil he has brought upon this country. But," he added, seeing the look of horror in my face, "you evidently know nothing about this filthy swine. He is a man vowed to treason and to plunder, who has caused more tears than he has blood in his veins. A nobleman's overseer, he persuaded his master to put under pasture an immense acreage which from time immemorial had been hired out to the peasants, and six hundred persons were evicted in midwinter from the ground they had cultivated with their sweat; they saw their trees torn up, their gardens levelled, their houses destroyed, and they were not left even the consolation of dying in their ruins ; they were driven out like wild beasts. Highly recommended for this inhuman action, this man was appointed tax collector; a position which gave him the power of all evil. To despoil us he could bring into play the forces of law and order. To make a better job of it he dug out all the old registers. He called in forgotten debts, and to pay them seized the cow whose milk nourished some child. The child died of want and the mother of sorrow. It was thus he had confiscated the herd of animals which we recovered yesterday. He worked for himself in the same fashion. He bought up old debts for a song and suddenly laid claim to the house or the field which we had inherited from our fathers. Having no money either to pay or to go to law, many families were evicted by this brigand, who became rich in consequence."

Despite these details and many others the vengeance they were about to take appeared horrible to me, and I went to find the Laird to point out to him that civilised men fighting for the cause of liberty could not tarnish their glory and their names by practising the cruelty of the most odious tyrants. I spoke to him freely, with enthusiasm, and perhaps the eloquence of conviction. He listened to me coldly, took his stand upon the sentence already passed, and informed me that he could not even change the method by which the man was to be put to death. My mind was made up in a moment; I said goodbye to him and left. I sent him back the carbine he had given me. He refused absolutely to accept it and offered to give me an escort to the coast, which I refused in my turn. The officers of the camp insisted affectionately that I should stay with them, and accompanied me as far as their outposts, expressing the opinion that we should meet again shortly, when the present subject of discussion was forgotten.

When I quitted the rebel camp night was falling. I took advantage of the remaining daylight to fix my position. I succeeded without great difficulty. I left the thickets with the greatest precaution, ready to shoot at sight. I recrossed the river and reached the hill path without trouble. The storm had not ceased, but there were occasional lulls in the wind, and I hoped that tomorrow communication might be established between our squadron and the shore; I wished to approach the anchorage in order to take advantage of this and await my opportunity, either in the village, if I met Mary, or in some hiding-place I might find amongst the rocks.

After walking many hours I was warned of the neighbourhood of the coast by the sound of breakers. I could not be far from the hamlet, but could distinguish nothing in the darkness. Looking along the level of the ground in order to make out more clearly any object in relief, I seemed to hear a faint noise towards my right. I advanced in this direction, and my doubts were soon at rest. What I heard was the sound of human voices, and as I got nearer I could distinguish cries of pain, dominated by sounds of oaths and curses. A few paces further and I was on the edge of the cliff at the foot of which the houses extended in a circle. There was no light save in the house from which came the cries, and I recognised with horror that it was the one where I had received hospitality. Without stopping to think I took a leap through the skylight and from the loft fell anyhow into the room below. I cannot adequately picture the revolting spectacle I saw.

Very late in the evening two soldiers of the foreign legion who had come to the village looking for loot, having doubtless heard Mary's grandmother saying her prayers, naturally thought that this one inhabited house would be better worth plundering than the others. Unable to gain admission they got in by making a hole in the wall. One can imagine in the meantime what must have been the slow agony of the two unhappy women, whom each falling stone brought nearer to the mercy of those devouring wolves. The old woman, who could not move, begged her grand-daughter to save herself whilst there was yet time, but the latter, who in her ignorance supposed that all she had to fear was death, refused to leave her grandmother. On entering the soldiers found one on her knees and the other on her bed clutching the cross of her rosary, both imploring aid from God. They started by asking for food and drink, and because there was no whiskey they became threatening. It was a sort of prologue prepared by them for the drama to follow, and for which this little hut was to be the stage. Hungering for loot the elder approached the old woman and tore away her beads, whose little silver medals had excited his cupidity. She must have money hidden somewhere, he remarked, and swore that she should show it him or be killed. The other brute had turned on the young girl and, finding her deaf to his persuasions, had thrown himself on her like a wild beast, flinging her to the floor. But the child resisted tooth and nail, and he was obliged to call his companion to hold her. No sooner was the old woman freed from the latter than, realising the horror of her grand-daughter's plight, and in a state of frenzy, she recovered her lost faculties and rose from her bed endowed with the strength of a mad woman. She seized the throat of the man holding the child's arms, and forcing him to defend himself rolled with him to the ground.

When from a height of fifteen feet I fell into the midst of this scene, the young girl's strength was almost exhausted, and her cries were no more than a death rattle. The soldier who had thrown down the grandmother held her beneath him but could not make her lose hold; he wrestled vainly with the wrinkled hand which clutched his neck and throttled him. Furious at his inability to free himself he seized his bayonet and plunged it several times into the body of the old woman, who died immediately.

The justice of Heaven was not long in coming. The murderer rose, covered with the blood of his victim and was about to attack me when I shot him dead at my feet. His comrade, who had abandoned his prey with a growl of rage, threw himself upon me, plying his sabre with both skill and vigour. I was reduced to defending myself with my gun, for in leaping from the ladder with more impetuosity than prudence the shock had fired one of my barrels, and the cartridge I had fired was the only one that remained to me. I could not have recourse to my other weapons because the slightest movement to take hold of them would have uncovered me and undoubtedly brought about my death.

Happily the fire of broom burning in the hearth threw its light on my opponent and enabled me to parry his blows; he noticed this and made a leap to change his place; but at the moment when he came towards me with his sabre lifted his arm fell powerless to his side. He had been struck by a scythe blade with which the girl had armed herself when she saw the unequal struggle in which I was engaged in her defence, and which looked like having a fatal issue for the two of us. Before I realised what had arrested the blow which was destined for me, this fight to the death had been finished by a bullet from one of my pistols.

Mary and I had succeeded in saving our lives, but to preserve them we had to escape from the perils surrounding us. The brigands had made a breach to get into the house. The first thing to do was to fill it up, for their comrades, attracted by the firing and guided by the light, might discover us at any moment; furthermore, they might see us through the hole and shoot us at leisure like rabbits in a warren. It would have been better to abandon the place immediately, but the girl could not bring herself to do so until she had given the final proofs of the love she bore her grandmother. She gave her all the care to which the dead have right, and having wrapped her in the best sheet the cottage afforded laid her on the bed, her arms crossed on her chest and consecrated boxwood in her hands. We had next to see to the bodies of the two soldiers, which, if discovered, would have infallibly brought about the burning of the village. My repugnance to touching them was all the greater in that their hideous faces still bore the traces of their evil passions, and it seemed to me that in order to visit upon these men its inexorable justice Heaven had appointed me their executioner.

Finally, having barricaded the doors and eliminated all trace of the dead, we left the house. We took the cliff road before daylight, and one hour's walk sufficed to lead us to a cave giving on the sea which had already afforded shelter to Mary's family in the days of persecution. Many exits and hiding places made it a sure refuge. From it I could have seen the whole of Bantry Bay had the weather not been misty; but I could easily make out our ships rolling at anchor in a heavy sea, which left no hope of a landing for today. Giving way to my fatigue I fell asleep. When I woke, Mary—who had been praying fervently—told me that she regretted having left her grandmother's body unburied, that she feared some outrage if the house was broken into again, and that she wished to put it beyond the reach of heretics by moving it to a cave in the cliffs, the entrance to which was difficult to discover. I objected strongly to this plan, which seemed foolhardy, but she persisted, urged probably by religious scruples which made her regard as a profanation the possibility that the good woman's body should fall into the hands of criminals. I insisted on accompanying her; she refused, because, she said, by leaving at once she had nothing to fear from marauders who waited for darkness before beating the country. She promised to be back long before dusk, and departed, leaving me in the greatest anxiety in spite of all she had said. It can be imagined what my anxiety became when the slow progress of the hours brought evening and then night without my seeing her return. Ten times I went to meet her and then came back, in the hope that she had taken some other track. Eventually I had to give up this illusion, and it was with the darkest forebodings that I walked rapidly towards the abandoned village.

The previous night I had already taken this road, but I had been so agitated at the time that I had not taken any note of it. I was therefore walking at random when I saw a reddish light on the horizon. I had no doubt that it was the village and its burning huts. Guided by this sinister illumination, I advanced to the top of the cliff against which the cabins of the hamlet were built. As I approached I had reason to believe that my first conjecture was wrong, for the burning village would have given a continually increasing glare, whereas this remained always more or less the same and did not seem to be in proportion to the cause I had assigned to it. In effect, as soon as I had reached the summit of the hill which dominated the village, I saw that the light was caused by a bivouac fire lighted at the foot of the rock near the church and quite close to the tree which had been piously protected for so many generations. Round this fire were half a dozen soldiers, their arms piled and guarded by a single sentry posted at the crossroads near the sea. It was probably a patrol of Hanoverians which instead of guarding the coast had settled down here to get drunk on whiskey stolen from the peasantry and warm themselves with wood taken from the neighbouring houses. The songs, the brawls, the oaths and the the noise informed me that the orgy was in full swing and had probably started some time since. I glanced at these marauders and followed a circuitous route to the cliff behind Mary's cottage. The state in which I found it would tell me whether she had visited it. I crawled round the rock to find the plank by which we reached the skylight in the loft. To my surprise I discovered that instead of being withdrawn it had been left in place. Mary had evidently come to this dangerous spot to carry out the task she had set herself; but had she the daring to carry it out almost under the eyes of these brigands, or had she left the house at their approach without time to cover her tracks? I was determined to settle this point, even at the risk of descending into the room. What was my astonishment when I saw that the interior was lit up! The light from the bivouac fire filtered through the break which we had closed, and which had been reopened and enlarged. The soldiers had ransacked everything; they had even taken the old woman's shroud, and her naked body lay face down on the ground. They had demolished a part of the roof where we had hidden the muskets belonging to the two marauders killed the previous night; and by this evidence they had learnt the fate of their owners. But what had happened to Mary? Had they caught her in the cottage beside her grandmother's body? In that case the child must be their prisoner; and if so what fate was reserved for her if, as I imagined, they resembled the two brutes from whom she had been so miraculously delivered yesterday?

The thought filled me with a dreadful anguish and I left the cottage immediately, determined to get a nearer view of this orgy, where I expected to discover the terrible truth.

I had just left the cottage and reached the top of the cliff when the soldiers started shouting, and I thought they must have seen me. But they were only calling in their sentry to take a share in the banquet. I kept under cover of the hill at a distance, so that its crest covered me up to the point nearest the enemy bivouac. From there, crawling up to the edge of the cliff, I saw these scoundrels, some forty or fifty feet below me, sitting or lying round a large fire, drinking and shouting and bawling the refrain of a waltz, whilst one of them, seated on a barrel, was prodding some object hanging from the old elm in front of the church and causing it to revolve. I could not at first make out what it was. Suddenly my eyes filled with tears and I was shaken by stifled sobs; attached to the branches I had recognised a corpse, whose face betrayed a violent death after appalling suffering. It was poor Mary, that innocent child, whom these barbarians had foully and brutally murdered.

My tears dried quickly. I was filled with a fury which at first deprived me of all judgement. I accused myself of the death of this young girl, who but yesterday had saved my life. I had come too late to save her life, I could at least avenge her. Many schemes flashed into my mind, but none satisfied me, because it was difficult to find one which in execution would include all these butchers without exception. In this dilemma, I called up all my war experience and suddenly the demon of murder gave me inspiration. I ran to the church; I ferreted in the burial vault behind the altar which I had visited eight days before; I dragged up a barrel of powder; I shouldered it despite its weight and returning rapidly to the edge of the cliff, I threw it into the middle of the bivouac fire around which the murderers sat. The explosion was immediate and terrible; it reached me, enveloped me in a sheet of flame and hurled me twenty paces into a muddy bog. Had the cartridges which I was carrying exploded I was a dead man. My soaking extinguished my burning clothing, but my hair, face and hands were burnt. When I succeeded in getting out of the mud I was in a piteous state. I nevertheless managed to drag myself to the edge of the cliff and looked over. All was dark and silent, nothing remained.

At daybreak I had succeeded painfully in reaching the rocks beside the shore, and was endeavouring to find the cave which had already given me shelter when I heard a hail from seaward. It was a boat from the brig *Affronteur,* which had come ashore to try and pick up an Irish pilot. The officer in charge, so he told me, had taken me for some local savage, and in the condition in which I was, blackened by powder, covered in mud from head to foot, it was certainly difficult to divine who I might be. He picked me up and took me on board, where I was kindly treated. We lifted anchor the same evening and left for Brest in company with several other vessels. The storm which had surprised us at the start and which had lasted continuously during the eight days I had spent ashore redoubled in fury immediately we set sail. It followed us to port and was the cause of fresh disasters to the fleet as grievous as those which marked our passage through the Straits of Raz. The *Scevola* sank with all hands; the frigate *Impatiente* was driven on the rocks off Cape Clear; the transport *Fils-Unique* fell into the hands of the enemy; the *Résolue* lost her masts in a collision and was saved by the *Pégase,* who took her in tow; several ships battered by the storm were forced to take refuge in the Shannon; the majority of the ships only succeeded in quitting Bantry Bay by cutting their cables and leaving their anchors; finally the storm was so violent that when Admiral Lindris re-entered Brest, he was able to drive his way through the English squadron without its being within the power of the latter to bring him to battle.

If the twenty-five thousand men of which the expedition consisted could have been landed, or if only General Grouchy's division of six thousand men could have been disembarked as he desired, Ireland would infallibly have escaped from the domination of England.

Some time after our return to Brest I was at the Marine Commandant's house whilst the enquiry was taking place. Admiral Bruix asked for me; I found him accompanied by a personage from Paris—it was, I think, Hugues Maret.

"My lad," said the Admiral, "you were at Bantry; tell me what you saw there."

I told him verbally the story I have just written, omitting the personal touches. When I mentioned the chief of the insurgents, the Admiral made me describe him and exclaimed:

"It's Fitz-Gerald. Really, I pity the beauteous Pamela, her favourite will end badly."

In effect this Irish nobleman was captured and taken to Dublin Castle, where he was found strangled. He was said to have committed suicide.

"But," asked the Admiral, "how the devil did you come to be there?"

I told him that my captain had given me the chance and that I had hastened to profit by it.

"Ah," replied the Admiral, "you are another one out of step; it would not surprise me if it turns out more success-fully for you than for me, but we can both congratulate our-selves that it has not turned out worse."

Admiral Bruix was often kind enough to remember me and when there was some case of military injustice forward he would send for me. But despite the kindly terms on which he was good enough to place himself with me it never occurred to him that my heroism had plunged me into very consider-able embarrassment. I had burnt my uniform in the explosion at Bantry and the brigade quartermaster wished to make me pay for it, stating that according to his books I was not due for a new one for another year. I consoled myself by reflecting that the proud descendants of the Carthaginians, the lieutenants of Lord Fitz-Gerald, were even more ragged than I.

Royal Navy Mutiny

The course of human existence in those days was sub-ject to terrible upheavals. The sailor, the soldier, the politician daily risked his life, liberty and honour in war or civil war on our territory or that of our neighbours. The man who rose cheerful and full of hope was languishing at night in a captiv-ity from which death was the only issue. Herewith an exam-ple of these vicissitudes: the first scene is comic opera; the last is at the foot of the scaffold.

It was the spring of 1797. I was at the theatre in Brest, where they were playing some charming pieces of which now no one has the slightest recollection. A decent-looking man sat down next to me, and in the intervals, which, if pos-sible, were even longer then than now, we discussed dramatic art, literature, and other subjects which were scarcely in the order of the day. When we parted he asked my name politely, and on learning it told me that he hoped to see me again, which I took as mere politeness.

The following day I was ordered to embark as master-gun-ner in the cutter *Agile.*

Arriving on board I was extremely surprised to find that the commander was my acquaintance of the previous evening who, after having satisfied himself as to my sea service, had asked for me from headquarters. It was my knowledge of the drama which had first attracted his attention and which was to cause me to fall into the most terrible wasps' nest that I have ever been in in all my life.

The *Agile* was a smart boat and a fine sailer but was nevertheless taken or retaken every time she put to sea; for it so happened that she was always given some dangerous or desperate mission which infallibly led her crew either to the English pontoons, if she had been manned in France, or to the dungeons of Brest castle, if she had sailed from an English port. In consequence, although one was comfortable on board, there was no competition whatever to join her for fear of sharing her bad luck. The appalling stories which were told me on the subject had no effect upon me, although I must admit that some of them were most peculiar and guaranteed to shake the strongest confidence.

Within twenty-four hours the boat was at the harbour chain, already half prepared to put to sea; the following day she was in the channel anchored opposite Linon, a sort of dilapidated hamlet lying outside the fortifications at the foot of the rocks on which the Faubourg de Reconvenance is built. Such rapidity gave rise to the wildest conjectures as to our destination, and the captain's silence seemed to confirm the worst of them. In this state of mind the sailors interpreted the most insignificant occurrences as omens. For example, a large black cat having suddenly appeared on deck without anyone being able to explain how it got there, its presence became an event of the greatest importance. The captain, to whom the fact was related, merely gave orders to throw the untimely visitor overboard; but the crew raised respectful objections to this cavalier proceeding, and at their earnest request a boat was manned and the tom-cat was placed on board with great civility and respect, and rowed ashore as became a personage of the highest rank.

The men believed they had conjured away the fatal effects of this visit; but their anxiety was soon reawakened by another omen! A screech-owl, which had left the hovels of

Linon at dusk, perched in our rigging and made the welkin ring with its lugubrious hoots until the moment when a boat came alongside. Everybody ran to the side to examine the newcomers and see whether their appearance justified this unfavourable augury. Mounting precipitately, the passenger nearly fell into the sea and lost his hat, which was carried away by the stream before it could be picked up. This, an old sailor told me, was an undoubted proof that the devil had come aboard. "He is going to put the master on his muster-roll, and you can be sure he'll soon come to claim him."

This superstition reminded me that I had already seen, on another occasion, sailors threaten a cook because he had thrown eggshells overboard without breaking them, as the most rudimentary prudence demanded; for without this pre-caution the shells furnish a boat for the devil, who always seizes the opportunity to put to sea to the ultimate discomfort of seafarers.

Despite these evil omens we set sail with a favourable breeze and passed rapidly down Brest Channel. At daylight we had already disembogued by the Iroise and had escaped the English blockading squadron, which, having hauled off during the night, returned to its position too late to bar our exit.

Nevertheless, in order to deceive them, our commander set a course by the north of Finistère, trusting to his knowledge of the coast to save us from the rocks which guard it, and he made use of their shadow to conceal our presence from the enemy. We followed the coast of Brittany as far as the mouth of the Channel. The weather was perfect, the sea calm, and the wind favourable; our voyage resembled a pleasure trip. We profited by it to alter the vessel's rig and general appearance for a purpose which I did not understand. I asked the reason for these changes; I was told that the object was to give us the semblance of an English cutter. I was not greatly edified by this Anglomania, which seemed to hide some *ruse de guerre*. Subsequent events confirmed my conclusions.

The person who had come aboard at the moment of our departure had fully justified the crew's suspicions. It is extraordinary what a gift for observation these men have despite their rough exterior; they divine the character and capacities of their superiors and sum them up as accurately as they would atmospherical phenomena. In spite of the importance with which he invested himself our passenger received no consideration from them; everything about him displeased them; his clothes, his hair, his dog's ears, his noisy trinkets, and above all his manner; sometimes stiff and formal, at others vulgarly familiar. Their only name for him was "the commissary," which, in their minds, might mean tax-collector, excise-man, or executioner, but which collectively might be summed up as *rogue.* I was more reserved in my judgement, but was convinced that he was an adventurer, or at the least a parvenu. I had no idea that he was a police agent, and I did not suppose that such a thing existed in France as yet. We were still in the fifth year of the Republic.

The commissary who, with perfect reciprocity, paid not the slightest attention to an underling like myself, became after a few days most astonishingly polite and kindly. The captain gave me the reason. He had brought on board a collection of the latest London newspapers and he was burning to know what was in them; although he spoke English fluently he could not read it. He had asked the captain whether anyone could do this for him, giving as a pretext to cover his ignorance the fatigue which the English printed characters caused him. He had certainly learnt the language by committing to memory and repeating the phrases he had heard, as children do; but the pronunciation and the orthography being very different, he no longer recognised the words he knew when he saw them in print. I agreed to see him out of his difficulty, in the hope that the contents of those newspapers might be extremely intriguing.

In effect, my hopes were realised and I found in those old newspapers a mass of news of the greatest interest.

The aristocratic[1] government of Great Britain had sys-
tematically stifled, by means violent or otherwise, the spirit
of the French Revolution which had taken root amongst the
population of the United Kingdom; in the flush of its success
it had overlooked the fact that justice is not only the first
duty of a power but is also its best policy. It had maintained
the despotic traditions of the Stuarts in all their rigour, and
did nothing to alleviate the yoke imposed long since by that
fatal dynasty.

Whilst the traces of barbarism were disappearing from all
the codes of Europe, it continued to kill its soldiers by the
lash and its sailors by that terrible instrument of torture the
cat-o'-nine-tails. Cruelly treated as they were, these men had
nevertheless saved their ungrateful government by their victories; for there is not a shadow of doubt that had we won the
great naval battle of the 13th Prairial the French fleet would
have entered the Thames and England would have become a
Republic for the second time.

Fresh injustices had worn out the patience of the sailors
manning the Portsmouth squadron commanded by Admiral
Bridport. In the month of April they, by a common accord,
addressed petitions to Parliament in which they complained
bitterly of the harsh treatment and brutal punishments to
which they were subjected; they called attention to the inad-
equacy of their rations and the bad quality of the food, and
finally to the miserable insufficiency of their pay, which had
not been increased since the days of Charles II.

Three admirals, sent on board the *Queen Charlotte* to con-
fer with the men's delegates, tried to intimidate them, and
one of them, Gardner, swore on his soul that every fifth man
would be hanged. These threats had an entirely opposite result to what was expected; the men became angry in their
turn and nearly manhandled the admirals. The *Royal George*
hoisted the red flag in sign of mutiny and called a meeting

1. This must be taken in the *revolutionary* sense of the word.

of delegates throughout the fleet, who landed their officers, refusing to recognise their authority any longer.

The details of these counts, which I have abridged, were already known to the commissary, but their official confirmation caused him great satisfaction; and his exclamations left me in no doubt but that he had been instructed to get into touch with the mutineers and make them proposals in conformity with their situation. It was the revenge for Quiberon. But the newspapers which had appeared after his departure from Paris announced an unexpected turn in the situation. Whilst Fox and Whitehead, in the House of Commons, accused the minister Pitt of being the cause of the revolt and forced him, despite his indomitable will, to enter into negotiations, the Board of Admiralty had gone to Portsmouth and had used the personal influence wielded by their senior member, old Admiral Howe, to bring the mutineers to a more reasonable frame of mind.

Without him Parliament would have granted their demands to no purpose, and it was only the respect and affection in which this famous sailor was held by the fleet which caused it to return to duty. The delegates came ashore to fetch the Admiral, and since he was seventy-two years of age and gouty, they carried him on their shoulders aboard each ship. He was accompanied by his wife. Order was immediately established, the red flag hauled down, and the squadron prepared to put to sea to fight the French.

This astounding ending to a formidable mutiny which suddenly died down at the sight of an old man and an old woman, coupled with a faith in a certain number of illusory promises, seemed to me one of the most extraordinary aberrations of the human mind recorded in all history. The commissary was completely taken aback. I consoled him by reading a short article which stated that grave fears were entertained regarding the Thames squadron anchored at the Nore, many signs of mutiny having been reported amongst its crews.

It appeared that the captain and his passengers were bound by their instructions to persist in the object of our expedition, at least up to a certain point, for we continued our course and sailed up the Channel as far as Havre; we then crossed towards the English coast as though we intended to go to Newhaven.

It was a dangerous voyage. We met a number of small coasting vessels, but each was attending to his business, and we seemed far too small and inoffensive to attract attention. Besides, our landing was calculated to take place at night. When towards nightfall we reached the waters which bathe the cliffs of Sussex the captain searched carefully for some object which should have been in view. I thought at first that he wished to get into touch with one of the villages whose lights we saw, and whose inhabitants chiefly consist of smugglers. His purpose became plain when with his telescope he picked out a vessel anchored at the opening of a bay. He immediately manoeuvred to approach it and burnt a blue flare, which was answered by a yellow one. The commissary was delighted and made no secret of it; he was impatient to go on board this vessel; but unhappily the breeze had fallen completely, and our boat, instead of advancing, had great difficulty in keeping its position, the Channel current tending to throw her back. A quarter of an hour passed without progress; the captain and the commissary were on tenterhooks; the former because the situation of his ship was extremely dangerous, the latter because he had almost attained his objective without being able to reach it, and because the appearance of a coastguard cutter might force us to haul off without profiting by information from which he was obviously expecting much. There was one means to put an end to this anxiety; this was to launch a boat and row to the vessel which had replied to our signals; but the captain refused, and it was sorely against his will that he eventually agreed. The gig was prepared and manned by two picked men to handle the oars; the commissary asked that I should command it, and took his place beside me. Although he was not to let us out of his sight, the captain gave me my instructions and recommended the greatest prudence; he personally inspected our arms and, in addition, had two loaded blunderbusses placed in the boat. Every one knows that these are short muskets with a bell-mouthed barrel holding a charge of some fifteen bullets.

The moonlight permitted me to examine the vessel which we were going aboard. She was a large schooner, well equipped, and appeared to have four men on board. This number did not worry us, since our forces were great. On coming alongside we were welcomed in French by the words "*Messieurs, soyez les bienvenus.*" They were the exact words destined to assure the commissary that he was among friends; he was invited on board as well as ourselves, and, doubtless to aid us to make up our minds, a bowl of punch was announced I remained deaf to these compliments, but the commissary went on deck and entered into close conversation with the captain of the schooner.

So far nothing had disclosed the existence of a trap, only the insistence upon our coming aboard to take part in a friendly drink had aroused distrustful suspicions.

Following my orders the sailor in the bows of the gig was watching the English schooner's foredeck whilst the other sailor and myself paid our undivided attention to her quarter-deck.

He came and whispered in my ear that several men appeared to be hidden under some sails thrown on the deck near the bowsprit. Considering the distance at which we were from our own ship, which was unable to come to our aid, we were evidently lost. I seized a blunderbuss, and the first seaman, who had orders to imitate me in everything, did the same. At this moment the commissary raised his voice, either refusing to do something, such as to go between decks, for example, or else to call us on board. The sound of scuffling was heard, then a shot, and the fall of a body on the deck.

Simultaneously along the schooner's side above our heads appeared not four men but double that number, who treated us to a discharge from pistols and muskets.

We replied immediately by a crossfire which carried thirty bullets along the line of our enemies, bowled them over, and opened us the way to board. When we reached the deck, cutlass in hand, only two men remained on their feet; they fled towards the bows, threw themselves into a boat, cut the rope and made off. The sailor who was supporting me advanced quickly to the schooner's side and fired his pistols at them; they replied by a random shot which hit him in the head and killed him. It was then that I realised that I was alone, the remaining sailor doubtless having been hit when boarding and fallen into the sea. Convinced that the fugitives would return in force, I cut the anchor cable and hoisted the standing jib to bring her about and give her the direction of the open sea instead of that of the coast. To complete this manoeuvre it was necessary to unfurl the mainsail and haul it aft. Whilst returning to the after-deck to carry out this operation I received a pistol shot from a man who was lying on the deck amongst the corpses, but who was only wounded. It was a warning which made me think that amongst the supposed dead there might be more than one living, and that the winner stood the risk of being slaughtered by the losers. In my desperate plight I could not pick or choose ; in the twinkling of an eye I cleared the deck and turned the ship into a solitude. To accomplish this task I had need of all my courage, spurred by the pain my wound was causing me. When we are losing our own blood we are less sensible to the sight of others losing theirs. Besides, it must be remembered that only a plank stands between sailors and the bottomless pit—if that plank fails they disappear from this world's stage for ever.

In this bloody boarding the enemy had lost six men and we three; but one of ours had been assassinated. The three who escaped from the struggle were, I think, all wounded.

This murderous action had been directed entirely by chance, which so often brings men's plans to naught.

Nothing took place as either of the two parties had premeditated. The commissary imagined he was going to a conference with men with whom he had been in communication, and he fell into an ambush into which he dragged us also. The Admiralty had discovered the relations established by certain mutineers with France and had prepared a trap instead of a rendezvous; and a corvette had been posted a short distance away to surprise our ship when attracted by the false signals. But the calm which had hindered our approach to the schooner had also immobilised the corvette. It was only after the fight, when a wind got up, that our ship could come to my help, and then the enemy ship left the shadows and advanced under full canvas to capture the *Agile*; thereupon the latter, perceiving the formidable adversary with which she had to deal, left me to my fate and took to the open sea with all possible speed.

As soon as I made out this further complication through the gloom I fled before the wind by setting all the sail I had. Alone in the schooner in the middle of the Channel, followed by a squall which seemed likely to become a storm, wounded, covered in my blood and that of others, I was still better off than if I had been in the cutter, for her crew had but a thin chance of escaping an English prison, pursued as they were by a more powerful ship. In that case I should once more lose everything; my kit, my books and even my service papers would be considered good prize by the enemy.

It was true that as master of the schooner, a windfall which I had certainly well earned, I might perhaps avenge myself; I installed myself as lawful owner and exchanged my soiled clothing, the smell of which was nauseating, for a suit of smart and comfortable clothes which gave me the appearance of a gentleman sailing his own yacht for his own pleasure. I could find no trace of the punch which had been held out as a bait for us, but I found some excellent contraband brandy, which was useful to wash my wound; to bandage it I had no hesitation in using some of the smugglers' finest linen.

I would, however, have given all this luxury in exchange for an essential instrument which I could not find on board—a compass. I vainly searched for the hiding-place where without doubt it had been stowed. I was forced to confide the ship's course to the grace of God and guess vaguely the direction of the wind.

As a matter of fact the sure knowledge of maritime science would not have helped me much. The calm which had been the origin of all our mishaps was, as is often the case, the forerunner of a storm. The wind which had got up as the moon went down had freshened by degrees; it had become a strong wind and had finally taken on the violence of a gale. It was no longer in my power to work the sails or to take them in, and I was forced to scud before the hurricane.

In giving way before it, it was still all I could do to keep out of danger. The squalls were so strong that at times they lifted the ship above the waves like a flying-fish, whereas an instant later they plunged her under the foam as though they wished to bury her. This terrifying series of immersions had the one advantage that it caused all trace of our bloody struggle to disappear from the deck. At daybreak the storm died away, but the sky remained dark and threatening, and the horizon was shrouded in a thick mist.

I was terribly cold and tired to death; I felt myself giving way, and had neither the courage nor the strength which the situation demanded. I continued for a long while to carry on towards the North before I could summon the will power to trim sail in order to make the French coast, which I judged must be to starboard. I was about to start this manoeuvre when I noticed, in my wake, a war cutter which was following me and which, during my somnolence, had come within range.

I expected a shot on board, or at any rate through my

sails, to order me to heave to; but she did nothing, either by courtesy, which was scarcely customary, or else because her superior speed was bound to bring her up with me sooner or later. In effect she soon caught me and then, to my great astonishment, came abreast of the schooner without saying a word and followed the same course, sailing in company as she would do with a friend. I could not, however, congratulate myself on the meeting, for the two boats were so close together that I could hear my neighbours speaking English; and I could not doubt but that this time I was a prisoner of war—I who had escaped that fate so often and so luckily.

After a considerable time, which seemed to me an eternity, a distinguished looking young man appeared, leaning on the port rail, wearing the uniform of a midshipman in the British Royal Navy; he saluted me with the greatest politeness and said in French:

"You are making for the Nore, sir?"

Was this remark a question or a hint? I did not consider it necessary to ask for an explanation, and instead of answering made an ambiguous gesture, as much as to say, "You are better placed to judge of that than I am!"

It will be readily understood that I was far from happy about my situation. I was caught without colours, without papers, without a uniform, on a ship which there was every reason to suppose had been stolen, and whose captain and crew had completely disappeared.

It was quite useless to tell the truth, since all the witnesses had disappeared and the appearances were against me. I could see no better solution than to leave the explanations to the other side, and made up my mind to prevaricate. This system, entirely foreign to my character, succeeded beyond the wildest hopes.

"You have a charming schooner there," remarked my questioner. "A real Bermudan; she could sail under water."

"I know something about that," I replied.

"Ah," replied my midshipman laughing, "you were out last

night; she took you out to sea and you were badly prepared to face the dangers of the North Sea alone. If I recollect aright it is difficult to gauge the approach of a southerly gale from your town of Dunkirk. I was so happy when I was a prisoner in France that it would give me great pleasure to send you back there at once; but I am obliged to show considerable zeal so far as my Admiral is concerned, since he suspects me of being in sympathy with the men. Anyhow don't worry, I'll arrange your business; I will say I took you at anchor in order to find out whether it is true that delegates from the Republic are about to be despatched to put themselves at the head of our mutineers."

I had need of all my presence of mind to conceal the surprise which these revelations caused me. What! had the storm driven me so hard that I had covered almost the entire length of the Channel during the night and was now beyond the Straits of Calais, far from the French ports which I had imagined to be quite close? Still more! whilst the mutiny died out at Portsmouth it threatened to revive with no less violence and still more stubbornness in the English fleet at the Nore, at the mouth of the Thames, some twenty leagues from London, where sat the Government of Britain.

The urbanity of my courteous enemy surprised me almost as much as his confidence; but I searched vainly to find what interest he could find in dissimulation. Besides, his gaiety spoke in favour of his frankness; and I was obliged to admit that his stay in France, doubtless developing his natural qualities, had made of him a veritable Frenchman. With perfect courtesy he invited me to lunch with him, and I was received on board in so solemn a manner that I might have been excused had I thought myself a personage of some importance. The conversation was lively and unrestrained during our meal, which was lengthy, as becomes the most important event in a sailor's day. Recollecting that I had passed a terrible night, my young host advised me to take a nap on the divan, and went about his duties.

I went to sleep asking myself whether this scion of the British aristocracy was not more democratic than I and whether he would not have preferred to conduct a delegate of the Republic to the Nore rather than a prisoner of war. I was far from imagining that he had taken his desire for the reality and that a simple allusion to the password of the mutineers, which I had learnt from the papers in the commissary's portfolio, had sufficed to persuade him that I was entrusted with a mission concerning them.

The shuffling of sailors executing some manoeuvre woke me with a start and brought me on deck. I was dazzled by the brilliant spectacle I saw. The sun of the 1st Prairial (20th May 1797) had chased away the storm clouds and now shone upon one of the most beautiful marine scenes that one could possibly imagine.

We were moving under full sail into the immense circular basin which serves as Estuary to the Thames. Bearing towards the mouth of the river from all quarters came numberless barges laden with the merchandise which fed the rich commerce and colossal population of London. But the principal *trait* in this magnificent picture was the roadstead of the Nore, opening on the Southern coast of the bay opposite the picturesque town of Sheerness. It was covered with warships, and enclosed at the one anchorage twenty ships of the line and as many frigates. The entire fleet had just hoisted the red flag, the sign of mutiny.

As soon as he saw me the young commander ran up and took my hand with quite official gravity.

"*Monsieur le délégué,*" he said, "I hope you are satisfied with our sailors' punctuality. At the very moment of our arrival you behold them manifesting their resolve to rejuvenate old England. The flag of Admiral Buckner, who commanded the fleet, has just been hauled down; the crews have thus revoked his authority and have doubtless chosen leaders amongst themselves. You see," he added, "boats are leaving each ship and rowing to the *Sandwich,* which is packed with people. It is there that the representatives are meeting to consult, and we must go there at once."

The nearer we approached the anchorage the greater became the crowd of boats which were arriving from all directions. Everybody was extraordinarily animated; it was evident that the matter was of genuine popular interest and not a mere political fiction. A remarkable circumstance was that this revolution was carried out cheerfully and that the Admiralty had not a single supporter. Our boat was launched to take us on board the *Sandwich,* but the multitude of boats of all kinds made access to her difficult. Whilst we were waiting we saw a man come down the companion, who was being so roughly handled that I thought he would be killed; but I was reassured by his grotesque appearance. The sailors had tarred him from head to foot and rolled him in feathers, which covered him completely. The bird in question was a surgeon, found guilty of espionage, whom they were taking to Sheerness. The captain of one of the sloops did not get off so lightly; his men having damned Admiral Duncan for his severity, beat him cruelly, and on being taken aboard the *Sandwich* he was duly tried and condemned to be hanged. I saw him during his detention and contributed towards his escape. Although inexorable so far as his men were concerned, he was extremely alive to his own misfortunes and did nothing but lament them.

We finally reached the companion ladder and went on deck; we found it crowded with silent and attentive spectators. The twelve delegates chosen by the crews of the fleet were ranged at the foot of the poop and were receiving deputations from the ships which had mutinied, who brought them an energetic adhesion to all they might decide for the good of the common cause and who expressed, in a picturesque and powerful language similar to that of a character in Shakespeare, their firm determination to see their wrongs put right.

I was interested and touched by these speeches, filled with

the animated eloquence of a people wishing to deliver itself from oppression.

At the head of the delegates was their chief, Samuel Parker, a tall young man of a kind and melancholy expression, about thirty years old and, although a Scot, of dark complexion, with black hair. He was an ordinary seaman in the *Sandwich*; but like his countrymen, he had been well educated, and was esteemed for his knowledge, his conduct and his character. Although in fact he had become High-Admiral of England he had not altered his manners, and had kept his suit of coarse blue cloth.

My introducer took advantage of an interval between two deputations, and approaching, announced me with a few words which made an impression upon Parker; for he came towards me, took my hand and presented me to his colleagues. He told me in very good French that I was welcome and must consider myself a guest of the ship. Seeing that I was installed my young midshipman took leave of me, promising to come and see me the following day. That evening he sent me a trunk and some clothes which he had found in the schooner, and which he imagined belonged to me; he added a large stock of cognac from the same source, the excellence of which testified to the good taste of the Newhaven smugglers. This brandy argued strongly in favour of the Republic and its supposed delegate, for this title, with which I had been so curiously invested by the commander of the cutter, had now been given me officially by the admiral of the mutineers, and it would have been extremely difficult to deny and cowardly to avoid it.

I dined with headquarters and, although they were a sober and serious company, requested permission to take my meals in my cabin, which was accorded me. During the night I had a long conference with Parker. I told him that the real delegate had been killed and that I was merely his heir, but that the instructions from the government of the Republic, which were in my hands and which I should follow word for word, were such as the mutineers would wish them, and that their enterprise would be learnt of in France with the greatest interest and a real desire to help if it was necessary and possible. I found the head of the insurrection to be an excellent man, unreservedly devoted to his cause, but perhaps not so sure of its success as was essential to convince the rest. He had no illusions as to the power of those he had to fight nor as to the means they would employ to conquer him. He seemed to be persuaded that whatever might be the result of his undertaking he would not live to see it, since too many dangerous enemies were plotting his downfall.

Depressed by these ideas, I went for a walk on deck to get rid of the impression. The night was calm and beautiful, and through her veil I could make out a part of the fleet lying at anchor in profound silence, not as though it was in full mutiny. Order reigned in each ship, and routine was observed as though there was no question of a reversal of the ruling hierarchy. It is one of the wonders of civilisation that it is capable of giving an impulsion to the social machine which enables it to keep in motion when the spring of government is broken. The lights were out in each ship, as prescribed by the regulations. Watches were held with the same strictness as though the crew had been under officers' orders. The patrol boats made the rounds as necessitated for the public safety; and not a sound rose from this multitude of men, agitated by so many unchained passions; the only evidence of human life was the deep call of *"All's well,"* which corresponds to our *Bon quart* and to the night call of our sentries, *"Sentinelle! prenez garde à vous!"*[2]

In the morning a long line of barges left the bank and steered for the squadron; they flew the great square flag of the Admiralty, which announced the supreme power, and carried three members of that redoubtable authority who

2. Sentry beware!"

140

were coming aboard the *Sandwich* to negotiate. Admiral Buckner had transmitted a message which had only resulted in increasing the irritation felt by the crews; the tenor was an order to abandon their pretensions and solicit the King's pardon. The Lords of the Admiralty appreciated better the gravity of the circumstances when they were at the Nore, and to begin with adopted a more conciliatory or tactful attitude in their interview with Parker. One of them, Admiral Young, appeared to be well intentioned; but another, proud and haughty in appearance, Lord Arden, I think, humiliated at scoring no advantage over an ordinary seaman who opposed him by an invincible logic, wished to try intimidation. It was an unfortunate experiment; Parker, who had hitherto been extremely calm and deferent, changed completely when faced by this sudden attack; he interrupted the emissary from the Admiralty and in a strong and resonant voice, heard distinctly by three thousand sailors on deck or in the rigging, he told him:

"What! my lord, when we welcome you like the dove bearing the olive branch of peace and co-operation, you have threats in your mouth and vengeance in your heart! It is your duty to be a father to the men, but you threaten them with punishment and are prepared to send them to the scaffold; you need blood to wash away your sins. Well, you shall have it. But may the innocent blood you will have shed fall on your own head; may it be an indelible stain on the last of your descendants, and may everyone, on seeing you, cry: 'There goes the butcher of the fleet at the Nore, damn him!' Good-bye, my lord, you persist in injustice and oppression; we persist in trying every means to free ourselves from it. God will judge between us!"

The effect of these words is impossible to describe. A cry of approval arose from the crowd which sanctioned them and vowed themselves to support them. At the moment when the negotiations had been broken off in this manner a brig at the entrance to the roadstead began to signal, and its crew manned the yards with signs of joy; they had sighted four ships of the line making for the anchorage of the Nore; their red flags announced that they had come to join the rebel fleet. They were the *Agamemnon*, the *Leopard*, the *Ardent*, and the *Iris*, belonging to Admiral Duncan's squadron cruising off the coast of Holland, which had come to reinforce their comrades in the Thames.

This apparition filled the emissaries from the Admiralty with consternation, and they hastened to leave the *Sandwich*, where I counselled keeping them as hostages.

"They thoroughly deserve it," said Parker, "but I do not wish to give an example of violence."

Two hours later we learnt that on landing at Sheerness the Lords Commissioners had outlawed the leaders of the insurrection and offered a reward for their betrayal; they had called up the militia and invested General Sir Charles Grey with the command of fifteen to twenty thousand men, who were assembled to defend the coast. The buoys marking the Thames channel were removed by their orders. Chains were stretched across the fairway, and they commenced to construct batteries with furnaces for red-hot shot.

Before deciding on reprisals the mutineers' delegates determined to appeal from the Admiralty to the King. The captain of the *Montague*, Lord Northesk, had been kept a prisoner by her crew. He was offered his liberty on the condition that he gave his word of honour that he would give the King a faithful account of the men's grievances and expose all that they had suffered prior to revolting. Several days were lost waiting for the reply; finally, as I had predicted, we had to admit that a reply could no longer be expected. Thereupon the council ordered offensive measures which should have been employed from the very beginning. The blockade of London was declared and all communication of sea between the capital, its provinces, and foreign countries was interrupted by means of four ships moored athwart the Thames. Ships carrying provisions to the town were captured, and there was no doubt that the continuance of these measures, in bringing famine to the inhabitants of that populous city, would have led to a general uprising. To show the Lords Commissioners how little they were intimidated by their aggressive measures, the mutineers one morning manned a flotilla of barges and landed ten thousand men at Sheerness. The terrified inhabitants fled as far as Chatham. No disorder took place. The crews contented themselves with marching through the town with their delegates and the terrible red flag of insurrection at their head. I blamed this vain parade during one of my nocturnal conversations with Parker, who told me that he shared my opinion, but that it was very difficult to control the council and to avoid constantly giving way to popular passions. I had already realised how, at times, his position was critical and dangerous, and what obstacles he had to surmount in order to carry through the most urgent measures. Half the delegates on the council were as turbulent as Frenchmen. It was young England with Irish sailors. The other half, composed of old sailors, reminded me of Cromwell's puritans; they possessed their stubbornness, their phlegm, and their slyness. They were the men who, by their spirit of contradiction, caused the best plans to fail by delaying their execution; but they were the first to lend their ears to treachery and to the gilded hand of corruption. The crews became suspicious and changed certain of their delegates, without, however, changing their mentality.

To keep the insurrection alive it was necessary, in my opinion, that each day should show some progress, and I considered that waiting and inaction were fatal. Parker was of the same opinion, but when it came to acting he allowed himself to be hampered by adjournments, questions and refusals. It was of evident necessity that, as a first measure, the fleet at the Nore should be joined by all the naval forces of Great Britain. Parker therefore proposed setting sail for Portsmouth in order to join the St. Helena squadron, which was regretting having returned under the yoke of obedience, which it had done out of respect of their old Admiral, Lord Howe. Controlling forty sail of the line the insurrection would easily have attracted to itself the entire squadron blockading Holland, commanded by Admiral Duncan; it would then have disposed of the maritime strength of England, and the conditions it imposed would have been law. This step, which I dared to propose, was adopted; but instead of sailing for Portsmouth immediately, they sent off delegates who were never heard of afterwards. Whilst awaiting their return it was possible to swell the crews by calling on twenty to thirty thousand sailors belonging to the ships in the Thames; they could have been used to man the ships at Portsmouth and Plymouth which were capable of putting to sea. An attack on London would have complemented this. This project, which was welcomed with enthusiasm, boiled down eventually to a surprise reconnaissance carried out by armed boats with a password available to anyone who cared to pay the price for it. The merchant seamen made promises which they did not keep, and the authorities, enlightened by this abortive attempt, took steps to prevent another.

All these checks, and above all the lack of energy and union amongst the members of the council, led me to ask Parker whether, before coming to extremities, he would not consider taking refuge in a French port, and whether the squadron would not agree to enter Brest subject to whatever guarantees they might consider necessary. I reminded him that I had written in this sense to the Minister of the Marine in a letter which he had himself sent to Dunkirk by a fishing boat, and I added that it was very probable that orders had been given from Paris to warn the commander of the French squadron at Brest of this important event. He replied that when he had raised the standard of revolt he had sacrificed his life, for he knew that he had to fight a power which never pardoned. It was repugnant to him to fly from a danger which he had defied; also, he shrank from taking a step which might deprive his country of its principal defence and which would have the appearance or even the consequences of an act of treason; finally, he was resigned to await his destiny at his post, until such time as all hope had vanished.

Seeing his fatal resolution I turned to his colleague Davis, the other delegate from the *Sandwich,* who appreciated the pressing reasons for sending the fleet to sea to make Brest harbour if necessary. The proposition was put to the council and adopted by the majority; it was understood that it would be carried out the following day. But during the night the Admiralty, probably informed of the design, redoubled their efforts among the crews whose leaders had been bought, and at dawn we saw that four ships had cut their cables, had hurriedly and silently quitted the Nore fleet, and had entered the Thames. They had already passed Gravesend, and to escape the vengeance of those they had betrayed they mounted the stream as far as Woolwich, where numerous batteries were prepared to assure the success of their objective. From that moment treachery broke out everywhere. Parker was nearly poisoned, and pushed clemency so far as to pardon the assassin, whom he put ashore at Sheerness. Many fights took place on board the ships between the two parties into which the crews were divided, and although the mutineers remained the stronger, it was easy to foresee their approaching collapse. Parker himself was of this opinion; in the evening he sent for me and told me that being about to go under he did not wish to reproach himself with having involved me in his ruin by keeping me with him. He had made all arrangements for my departure which, despite my protests, he refused to postpone for a single day. We said goodbye to one another tenderly and sadly, and he guided me himself to a rope ladder which descended from the ship's gallery to the level of the sea. A skiff was waiting below, into which I threw myself, and was rowed silently to a point on the river bank above Sheerness. It was impossible to see anything in the obscurity, and it was just as well, as a body of fire-eating militia which occupied the place had certainly posted sentries. A slight noise was heard; the boatman gave a signal which was repeated; I jumped ashore and was met by a tall girl who took me by the arm, laughing as though we were bound for a wedding. On our way I learnt that my cheerful companion was Miss Kitty, a poor child taken in by Mrs Parker, educated by her, and in possession of her entire confidence. She was an excellent girl, hard-working, good, devoted to her masters, and employing in their service a rare intelligence, an unalterable good humour, and the courage of a man of war. She had made drunk the post of militia which should have arrested me on my landing, and she traced a clever course which, through a succession of lanes, court-yards and gardens, brought me safe to Mrs Parker's house after having ten times traversed the line of enemy posts. She had quickly grasped that if a sentry stopped us we must strangle him on the instant without pity and without noise; never had I such a companion in adventure who, by strength and resolution, was better able to face danger and to share it.

Mrs Parker received me with the greatest kindness; her husband had told her of our close relationship and had recommended me as a proved friend. She told me that hitherto her house had been protected because of the affection in which the inhabitants of the town held her, but since the militia had occupied Sheerness she could not count upon the same security, and fearing the rounds, she would be obliged to lodge me elsewhere pending the moment when I could cross to France. "Besides," she added, "it will be less unpleasant for you to be alone than to stay with an unhappy woman who does nothing else but weep." In effect she scarcely stopped crying and praying, and was already in mourning. The respect in which she was held by the entire town was a testimony to the goodness of her life and a return for the charity which she had always extended to the unfortunate.

The excellent Kitty installed me in the top room of an

isolated and broken-down house in the midst of a number of small gardens, whose owners had decamped in fear of a collision between the sailors and the militia.

On waking I ran to the window, whence was visible the entire roadstead of the Nore, and I noticed, with a terrible tightening of the heart, that the majority of the ships had hauled down their red flag. I could only count five which still flew it: the *Montague,* the *Dictateur,* the *Belliqueux,* the *Inflexible* and one other. I saw with dismay that even the *Sandwich* had capitulated. The previous evening Sir Charles Grey had received a communication from the reactionaries among the crew, offering not only their submission but proposing to arrest and hand over Parker and Davis, the vessel's two delegates to the mutineer's council. This abominable act was carried out the following day and earned the reward of twelve thousand five hundred francs which had been officially promised. A few hours later I should have faced the same fate.

The 22nd June (1st Messidor), the unfortunate Parker was brought before a court martial held in the *Neptune* at Greenwich and composed of eleven officers. Vice-Admiral Paisley presided. The victory of the Admiralty, bought with the help of the Exchequer, was as yet so uncertain that instead of holding the court at the Nore, on the scene of the insurrection, they held it, for more security, twenty leagues away behind the batteries at Woolwich, which defended the entrance to the Thames. The sitting lasted from ten in the morning until four in the afternoon, and consisted of the hearing of the witnesses for the prosecution, the cross-examination of the accused, and his replies to the charges brought against him. The following day five persons he had named were heard. The death sentence was pronounced the third day and its execution ordered at once, despite the appeal for mercy addressed by Mrs Parker to the King, who had left immediately for Windsor. Throughout this terrible ordeal, and up to the very moment of his death, the condemned man preserved his unshaken calm and his heroic resolution. He replied to the judges with the greatest presence of mind, and upheld the justice of the cause he had defended.

During these deplorable events, I was threatened every minute with being hunted down by my enemies and dragged to the scaffold, although I counted for nothing in the part which I had taken in the uprising and in the role which had been given me. I passed there fifteen of the most discouraging days in all my life; in absolute isolation. I tried to distract myself by reading, but could not. My eyes were constantly fixed on the panorama of the roadstead. I followed all the movements on board the ships, and I saw the last of them surrender to the Admiralty to receive one after another a garrison of marines. Then followed each day the spectacle of those barbarous floggings which recalled that of the Christ and disgraced a civilised and Christian people.

Realising that the warship's telescopes might well discover me I had altered the position of a mirror so that it reflected the roadstead and I could see without being seen. Kitty saw to all my wants in sisterly fashion. That intrepid girl was an angel of kindness and of patience. When she came to see me she had frequently to wait for an hour or two in some hiding place until the way was clear. She believed, with the inhabitants of the town, that they could not send to his death a man like her master, who had always shown himself the enemy of violence and had constantly refused to shed blood. "You know well," she told me, "that on a sign from him the Lords of the Admiralty would have been thrown into the sea, and that had he made the signal the English fleet would be in one of your French ports today. It depended on him to send twenty thousand sailors who would have sacked everything up the Thames as far as London Bridge, and everybody says that he would not have fallen into the hands of his enemies had he used his power to render evil for evil." The people, who are not acquainted with the lessons taught by history, readily believe in the justice, the moderation, and the clemency of the stronger party. It was rumoured therefore that a reprieve had been granted the condemned man, and that his wife's prayers had obtained a commutation of his sentence. I could not believe it, and seeing in my imagination a very different ending to this drama, I was so distressed that repeated bouts of fever nearly made an end of me and presented Kitty with an unexpected problem; that of burying me with her own hands in some deserted corner of the garden. I had the greatest difficulty in preventing her from bringing a clergyman and a doctor, whose intervention might have brought about that of the Admiralty and prevented me from dying a natural death.

Finally, after having been disappointed several times in projects for escape, which redoubled my impatience and increased the badness of my health, I was warned by Kitty to hold myself in readiness for the following night. Disguised as a fisherman, with my face darkened, a net on my shoulder and arms concealed in my clothing, I left the town in the footsteps of my guide, who succeeded in avoiding a thousand dangers with admirable presence of mind. After a long walk we arrived at a distant cove, where a large boat stolen somewhere along the coast had just been brought by four vigorous and determined looking sailors. All had taken part in the rising, and they had agreed to take me at the request of Mrs Parker, whom they worshipped as a saint. Kitty recommended me to them as a brother, and the devotion she had shown for the mutineers on many a dangerous occasion had earned her the esteem and affection of all the seamen at the Nore. Forgetting her puritan reserve for once, she put her arms round my neck and kissed me tenderly, with tears. We pushed off at once and did our utmost to reach the mouth of the Thames by daylight. But time and tide were wanting, and we were no nearer than half way when we saw a brig-of-war observing us, which immediately gave chase. Our position was desperate, for we had not a chance of escape from a ship so much faster than we; well aware of the fate reserved for us if we were captured, we had all agreed to escape it by death. Each of us had taken measures in consequence and according to his predilections. One unsheathed a knife and thrust it up his sleeve ready to plunge it in his heart. Another, wishing to die a sailor's death, had attached himself to a lump of lead which would prevent his coming to the surface when he jumped overboard. The two others had prepared the means to poison themselves. As for me, I had a pistol for this purpose hidden between the various vests which all sailors in the Channel then wore, to the number of three or four. Man's courage is a curious thing. Each of us had certainly faced death in a dozen bloody engagements and would not have winked an eyelid at seeing the ports of an enemy ship go up preparatory to loosing a broadside at us; but we were terrified at the prospect of the gibbet, and our faces plainly showed it. This influence was so strong that we had the greatest difficulty in dissuading our two companions from poisoning themselves by precaution when the brig was still a good league off.

We put about in order to escape this redoubtable vessel, and hoped that upon seeing us approach the anchorage of the Nore she would cease her pursuit. Sailing in this direction we soon fell in with a crowd of boats of all sorts making for Blackstake, as though a fair or a regatta was about to be held there. We threw ourselves into the midst of the flotilla, which increased at every moment, and flattered ourselves that we should be lost among all these boats, many of which exactly resembled our own. In effect the brig gave up the chase, either because she had lost sight of us or because she was persuaded that we were there for our pleasure. Our satisfaction was damped by the fact that when we made the anchorage we should be faced by sixty enemy ships instead of one. But we were powerless to leave the flotilla which sheltered us, for we should draw undeniable attention to ourselves in quitting them. We were soon obliged to follow the stream, for the boats were crowded side by side, and it would have been impossible to make a passage to get away from them. Besides, the people in them were kindly souls, who would probably be more inclined to help us than to hurt us, but the risk of trusting ourselves to others was too dangerous to be attempted. The situation brought us one considerable embarrassment, that of replying to the questions put to us and of carrying on the conversation which commenced from boat to boat concerning the tide and the weather which, between sailors, furnish an inexhaustible mine of controversy. My companions knew the subject by heart and replied in most praiseworthy fashion. A woman remarked my silence and my drawn features, and asked if I was ill. One of my friends replied that I was suffering from Lincoln fever (an English county where the marshes poison the air like the Pontine marshes of old). As a matter of fact it was not far from the truth. A fresh bout of fever had hold of me, and violent shivers made my teeth chatter and ran through my body. I threw myself on a net at the bottom of the boat and remained there half conscious. A long time afterwards, doubtless, I was brought to by the voice of one of my comrades whispering in my ear and exhorting me to make an effort to get up in order to scotch a rumour that I must be dead. On coming to my eyes opened on one of the saddest spectacles imaginable. Ahead of the countless boats of which we were one was a flotilla of boats and barges containing the majority of the crews of the Nore squadron. They were ranged in a semi-circle before a ship flying the yellow flag. It was the *Sandwich*. A platform, level with the deck, had been erected outboard, supported by two stays. Above hung a long cord attached to a yard. A man was led on to this platform; I recognised the unfortunate Parker who, even at this terrible moment, preserved his courage and his calm; he communicated his last wishes to the clergyman who accompanied him and, walking firmly to the edge of the scaffold, he spoke from this terrible rostrum to the sailors massed in their boats beneath, who heard him bareheaded and in a religious silence.

At the signal of a cannon shot the platform gave way beneath his feet. I shut my eyes at this scene of horror and saw no more. Only when Parker, at the very doors of Eternity, uttered his wishes for his ungrateful country and expressed his hope that his death might be the last, I heard a great cry, that of *"Amen"* the biblical formula used by Protestant peoples when they implore God against the evils of the great ones of the earth.

Late that evening the authorities transported Parker's body to Sheerness cemetery and buried it in secret; but the townspeople discovered the spot where the coffin lay, and an immense crowd having assembled, despite the presence of the Lords of the Admiralty, they exhumed the body and carried it to the Horseshoe Tavern. There his funeral rites had been prepared, and he was carried solemnly, followed by the entire population, to the White Chapel. Fervent prayers were raised by twenty thousand people who only dispersed when they had seen the body lowered into the crypt of the church.

A strange race, who let their tribunes perish miserably, as the Romans let the Gracchi; and who, like them, honour their memory and sanctify their sepulchre!

When this barbarous execution was finished and the thousands of boats dispersed, my companions hastened to make the open sea, at first with their oars and afterwards under full sail. They joined a group of boats bound for Margate, a little port situated at the furthest limit of the Thames estuary on the North Sea. This companionship served them as escort and enabled them to pass the coastguards without trouble. Night had fallen and favoured their daring; under its cover they weathered the dunes and finally, leaving the shores of England, they crossed in two hours the Straits of Dover which separated them from France. At daylight an English cutter gave chase to the barque, but could not catch it, and only served to witness its entry into Calais harbour.

I remained in ignorance of all these circumstances, in which my companions showed so much skill and courage. I had lost consciousness, and only came to my senses when those fine fellows carried me ashore to a hostelry kept by an old woman known to sailors as "Mother." The following day an American captain signed on my comrades in misfortune, and they left at once. I am convinced that, brave and intelligent as they were, they did honour to the navy of the United States; and I have often thought that one of them may be found among those intrepid commanders whose name one likes to hear of amongst the hardy navigators of North America.

Before their departure they had found time to sell the boat which had saved us; and, with a spirit of justice and liberality which proved the greatness of their character, they had divided the proceeds into five parts. They handed my share to my old landlady, to serve either to care for my illness or to pay for my funeral if I died. At the moment of sailing they came to see me, shook me by the hand and wished me *Farewell;*[4] which is at once an affectionate parting and an expression of good wishes.

I recovered slowly but surely, either owing to the strength of youth or thanks to the old wives' remedies applied, which are often more efficacious than all the learning of the doctors. When I could walk, a ship's captain, who had taken a liking for me, assured me that what I needed for convalescence was the sea, and offered me a passage to Morlaix. The voyage passed off without incident despite the English cruisers, and I was practically in normal health when I left Morlaix to return to Brest and rejoin my half brigade.

I had remained forty days in England, from the 22nd May, when the sailors of the Nore squadron took possession of their twenty ships of the line, until the 30th June, the date of the unfortunate Parker's execution. During all my unsettled existence I have never been so unhappy, nor have I run into such terrible dangers as those I encountered on this fatal expedition.

The Irish Rebellion

Ireland, that uneasy country, wished to break the English yoke. Secret societies prepared a general uprising; but frequently, betrayed by false brethren at the very moment of success, their leaders were arrested and brought before tribunals on which the judge and jury were picked with a view to condemning the accused, were they innocent and pure as Socrates.

Besides, acquittal counted for nothing with those in power. No proof existing against the celebrated Arthur O'Connor, he was solemnly declared "not guilty"; but a warrant from the Lord Lieutenant, the Earl of Portland, sent him to the cells on leaving the court-room. Reasons of state did not boggle at injustice; they went much further. Lord Fitz-Gerald,[1] brother to the Duke of Leinster, the daring leader of the Munster rebels in 1796, was so foolhardy as to come to Dublin. His hiding-place was discovered, and to earn the sum of 2500 francs promised to the man who captured him, a captain and an alderman put themselves at the head of a band of cut-throats with a view to taking him by force, but he resisted furiously and wounded the two of them. Overcome by numbers, he was taken prisoner to the Castle and separated from his wife Pamela, who was ordered to leave Ireland immediately. He was guarded so strictly that even his brother was not allowed to see him. One morning he was found dead in his cell; he had been strangled.

1. See Chapter 6.

An Irish Chief, O'Coigley by name, having been arrested, a letter addressed to the French Directory was found in the lining of his waistcoat and traced to the Secret Committee of the rebels in England. He was condemned to death for high treason. After hanging for twelve minutes his head was cut off by the executioner, who lifted it by the hair and showed it to the crowd at the foot of the scaffold, saying: "This is the head of a traitor."

The Irish were more infuriated than frightened by this system of terrorism. In the County of Wexford, where the rebels were in force, they stood up to the troops of the line although they were only armed with pikes. At Carlow they defended the town by shooting from the windows of the houses, which at that time was considered extraordinary. At Ross they attacked Colonel Walpole in a defile, killed him, and routed the six hundred men he commanded. At New Rock they chased a herd of oxen into the town, throwing the royal troops into complete disorder. The place was taken and retaken three times and half burnt.

The audacity of these attacks gave rise to the fear that something might be undertaken against Dublin. The posts were strengthened, and three ships were moored in the bay to protect the town and its approaches. Nevertheless, the rebels were forced to admit that hatred, anger, and a thirst for vengeance were not adequate allies to free them from their oppressors; they turned to France and called for succour. Their delegate, Theobald Wolfe Tone, was untiring in his efforts to obtain it. He was a young man some thirty years old, of medium height and feeble health, but full of spirit and the highest qualities. When I saw him at Brest he had just been appointed Brigadier-General by the Directory. His manners and his conversation pleased me immensely.

After long delays, most prejudicial to the Irish cause, the French Government decided to make an effort to help. In the middle of June an expedition was prepared at Brest under the command of Captain Second, who was much in favour at the time. It consisted only of the frigates *la Fraternité* and *la Béllone,* with the cutter *l'Aiguille.* Four hundred men of the marine artillery were embarked, picked troops who were especially suitable for this kind of warfare. I was detailed for this expedition, which fell through for some reason of which I was ignorant; but I received an order to proceed to Rochefort and to embark as second master-gunner in the frigate *la Concorde.* When I arrived she was about to go down the Charente in company with the *Médée,* the *Françiade* and the corvette *Méduse.* The landing force awaited us at Ile d'Aix and was of necessity in proportion to this limited squadron. At the outside there were one thousand two hundred men detached from various different corps, which, as usual, had not picked their best men for this service. General Humbert, commander-in-chief, had under his orders two adjutants, Generals Sarrazin and Fontaine. We sailed on the 6th August, before our troops were properly stowed, which resulted in indescribable confusion and muddle. We had the greatest difficulty in clearing the deck sufficiently to permit us to manoeuvre, and had we been attacked it would have been impossible to send the battery among the crowd which pressed around our gunners. There was not a square inch to spare either in the hold, which was filled with the rations needed for so large a ship's company, or on the orlop deck, where we had to stow the cases of muskets and ammunition. A crossing like that must be experienced to understand what tortures can be endured by four or five hundred men shut up night and day between a ship's decks, without air, light, or the means to move, walk, work or even distract themselves. Under those circumstances all habits must be forgotten and all desires suppressed; the food is repulsive, the air vitiated, and one is thrown about by the pitching and the rolling until one feels within an ace of dying. This wretched state of affairs was aggravated by an unhappy idea of the commander of the expedition, Captain Savary, who, to put the enemy off his track, went beyond the latitude of Ireland and led us through the rough seas of the northern Atlantic almost as far as Iceland, which prolonged our voyage and rendered it more troublesome. I had but little sympathy for our passengers who, from the officers downwards, seemed to me to have been badly chosen in every respect if we wished to give the Irish a good idea of the discipline, the bearing and the instruction of our troops. I had therefore resolved to have nothing to do with any of them, but by the force of somewhat peculiar circumstances I was led to abandon this line of conduct.

Every day at dawn when going on deck I found seated on a gun an artillery officer, middle-aged but tall and strongly made, and carrying rather more stomach than is common among men of war. I noticed his distinguished air and calm and dignified bearing, also the patience he showed when during some manoeuvre the sailors hustled him about. He was constantly engrossed in a small book, the corners of which gave evidence of long and frequent service. I was extremely surprised to discover that it was a Horace. The fact was so extraordinary that I could hardly believe my eyes. I took the earliest opportunity of making this learned officer's acquaintance, and I was charmed by the kind confidence he extended to me, despite the difference in our ages and position. He was at this time a captain in the artillery, but when the Revolution had broken out he had been one of the Fathers of the Oratory, a religious order whose scientific renown equalled that of the Benedictines of Saint-Maur. His life had been passed in the deepest study, and he possessed a profound knowledge of archaeology and mathematics. He had welcomed the Revolution as a blessing for humanity and had served it with zeal; but on being denounced for having saved a family of *émigrés* he had been gravely compromised, and only owed his safety to his worthy *confrère* Daunou, who had found the means to save him from arrest by obtaining him a commission as an officer of artillery in the army. He had arrived at Rochefort, thinking to find there the company he was called upon to command. A counter order had sent this company to Brest, whence the second division of the expedition was destined to set sail. In the offices in Paris it was imagined that he would find his company in Ireland, a hypothesis which took no account whatever of eventualities and which traced the lines of operations across the seas like marching orders. Captain d'Herblay had the most lovable character; but whether as a result of his first vocation or because it was a natural trait, he was endowed with an extraordinary abnegation in all that concerned him personally, and, for example, he had allowed the sleeping place assigned to him to be usurped in spite of his rights, and had ended by having no refuge but the deck. Notwithstanding loud complaints I succeeded in finding him a corner in the powder magazine, where he could at least be undisturbed. This trifling service made him happy. We became attached to one another and he made our unpleasant voyage extremely agreeable to me. It was, however, a satisfaction dearly bought, for my desire to be of use to this excellent man led me into the most dangerous adventures.

Finally, after having drifted about the sea for fifteen days, we made the north-west coast of Ireland on the 20th August and entered the vast gulf of Donegal, at the bottom of which is the town of Sligo. The frigates anchored in the bay of Killala, on the southern side of the gulf. An hour later the adjutant-general Sarrazin, at the head of the grenadiers only, landed before the town, which was defended by three or four hundred men.

He took their trenches at the point of the bayonet and made them prisoners; his success was so rapid that the bishop had not the time to leave Killala and was captured in his carriage. Nevertheless, the fight was fairly murderous, since there were more than one hundred men killed. We remained as spectators of this vigorous *début,* which earned Sarrazin the grade of Brigadier-General. That evening, when the landings of the troops had been carried out, Humbert promoted him in the name of the Directory, and such was the enthusiasm that nobody doubted but that we should march from victory to victory to Dublin.

A glance from my learned friend confirmed me in the thought that this opinion had best be accepted with reserve, and in effect, when our troops were on the beach, although they had been joined by every man the crew could spare, it was found that our army scarcely amounted to the strength of a battalion. It was even worse when it came to organise the material necessary to enable us to advance. Naturally, in the campaigns of the Republic, no provision was made for camp equipment, hospitals or clothing, and one had no provision either for the subsistence of the soldier or his pay; the enemy was supposed to provide for all that. But here negligence went even further: we had omitted to provide our four field-guns with the means either to manoeuvre, be transported, or even to fire. When we had landed we realised that these articles must have been sent elsewhere. At the time of this discovery I was about to say farewell to Captain d'Herblay and return to my post in the frigate. "My boy," he said, "don't leave me in this difficult situation; if you do not help me with your youthful energy and ability I am a dishonoured man." I assured him of my willingness to help him, but called attention to the objections which the captain of the frigate was bound to raise. The obstacle was flattened in a moment by General Humbert, who swore with an energy of expression which cannot be committed to paper that if the Navy refused him what was necessary he would render the commanders of the ships responsible for the expedition and would accuse them before the Directory in the event of failure. The general's anger gained d'Herblay a dozen gunners and my assistance; a quantity of promises were added, whose execution we awaited in vain; for the frigates provided very badly for our needs and, pretexting bad weather, soon got under sail. Their return was effected without incident, and when they entered the harbour they had more than two hundred men on board who had been of no service to them and who would have been a considerable reinforcement to the expedition had they left them to us. Thus it was that I found myself, much against my will, second in command of the artillery of what was pompously called the Army of Ireland. In reality we were the foremost of a forlorn hope which could never rejoin the main division.

The general, whose axiom it was that French troops could do anything, had ordered the artillery to leave with the column in the morning; and his fiery temper forbade the observation that nothing was ready and that everything we needed was missing. He was capable of shooting on the spot anybody even vaguely connected with such a state of affairs. I was of the opinion that instead of complaining we would be better advised to make the best of things; my captain strongly approved my idea, and justified it by a quotation from some antique philosopher entirely unknown to me. I also took advantage of the dictatorship which victory confers to bring our gun teams up to strength. I seized the bishop's excellent horses; I used the postal wagons as limbers; I commandeered the bell ropes of the cathedral; finally, by many other similar expedients I succeeded in lining up at daylight four field pieces, tolerably well-equipped, which earned a satisfied smile from the General when he inspected us before our departure. My most difficult problem was to find a horse for the captain, who was quite incapable of marching. All the rich inhabitants had left at full gallop when we landed, and it was not easy to persuade any of them to return us his palfrey for our own purposes. One, nevertheless, in whose house we had billeted ourselves, possessed cellars as large as an Egyptian labyrinth, which furnished us with a quantity of exquisite wines. The captain and I, who drank nothing but water, refused the kindly offers made by the majordomo, but in return I asked him to arrange for his master to lend us a saddle horse, which we should certainly be unable to transport to France and which he would therefore not lose sight of. As a recompense I promised to keep secret the existence of those excellent cellars and prevent our men from visiting them, provided that when we left the captain was no longer afoot. One good turn deserves another, even in Ireland; and in due course a veritable charger was brought to M. d'Herblay, to the accompaniment of courtly phrases.

In our happy days of lawful peace my methods will undoubtedly be considered as terribly revolutionary; but it must be remembered that my duty obliged me to take military action in favour of a popular uprising, and in the name of the Republic. Let us hope that the troops of the Holy Alliance, who invaded us in 1815 under the auspices of the Holy Trinity, committed no graver depredations.

On leaving Killala we marched towards the town of Castlebar, where the enemy was in force. Our advance guard, commanded by General Sarrazin, found at Balayna, our first halt, a body of cavalry which made as though to dispute the passage, but thinking better of it they made off helter-skelter. The rebels, instead of meeting us, were late, but they eventually arrived, and if they could with reason have criticised the smallness of our numbers we had every reason to be alarmed at seeing our allies in such a pitiable condition. They all wore the uniform of the greatest misery; not a beggar in France could boast of rags to compare with theirs. They were scarcely armed, and the rest was in keeping. The Munster rebels, whom I had seen at Cork, were their superiors in every respect. General Humbert received them very kindly, but could not hide from us his surprise and dissatisfaction; it was evident to those who were with him that he had ceased to count on the co-operation of his allies.

The morning of our departure from Balayna we found

ourselves faced with an English force commanded by General Lake, one of the heroes of the war in Hindustan. Our columns charged his positions at the double and carried them. General Lake endeavoured to rally his troops in the town and posted his guns in the main street of Castlebar, but they were captured with the bayonet, and the rout was complete. We pursued the fugitives for more than two leagues, and our soldiers took several colours and some thousand men, whom we allowed to escape the following night, having no means either to feed or to guard them.

It was a fine day's work; the success was due entirely to the dash of the officers and men, which was irresistible. The enemy could nowhere stand his ground; he was dislodged from his positions so rapidly that the battle was lost before he knew where he was. The rebels were chiefly of use in the pursuit; they tracked the fugitives with an ardour and a courage which was not without reward, for that evening the majority had boots and some even shirts.

The General-in-Chief in the guise of conqueror organised the province of Connaught as a Department of the Irish Republic. As President of this Republic he recognised John Moore who, after twenty days in power, was taken by the English when they re-entered Castlebar, condemned to death and hanged on the spot.

The army marched south for four or five days without meeting any resistance from the enemy, but we learnt that a considerable number of troops were assembling under the command of Lord Cornwallis between the towns of Limerick and Galway. The farther we penetrated into the interior of the country the greater the obstacles became. Ireland has not the resources of the continent; provision of corn, hay or wine for the subsistence of the troops is not to be found there; it was necessary to glean, so to speak, amongst the potato fields.

The country consisted of pasture, from which the herds had been driven away, or else vast downs, or even vaster bogs.

Our allies brought us no provisions, and even often lived at our expense. Our ammunition was running low and was a cause of great anxiety. On the other hand the mass levy of the rebels had been deferred because of our small numbers and also, doubtless, because of an amnesty which pardoned all rebels who repented of their sins, with the exception of Napper Tandy and thirty other chiefs. Our greatest worry was an entire lack of news from the other expeditions which had left France to act in concert with us; there was even reason to believe that they had been intercepted by the English squadrons, and in that case our fate was sealed; we were abandoned in an island without issue and exposed to the attacks of a hostile force whose strength was at least double our own. The rumour started to spread among our troops who, as it always happens, passed from an unbounded confidence to an excessive diffidence. It was remarked that the rebels from Roscommon, commanded by an intelligent man named Plunket had withdrawn two days after their junction with us, and it was alleged that they had done so without orders. We concluded, with reason, that they were playing for safety, and it was in fact probable that they knew that an army twenty thousand strong was about to fall upon us. The captain had no need to consult others in order to appreciate the bad state of our affairs; we were fully enlightened by the sullen mien of our General-in-Chief and by his tendency to burst into a fury at the slightest contradiction. After a troublesome march we reached the Shannon, the largest river in Ireland, which flows into the North Atlantic. We crossed it at Ballintra by a bridge which was to be destroyed by the General's order. But this operation was not carried out with the care it merited. During its execution the company detailed to cover the workers, being attacked by superior forces, retired and allowed Lord Cornwallis to cross the stream with his entire army. In war an initial fault inevitably leads to others even graver. Furious at having been over-reached in the matter of the river crossing, the General wished at first to shoot the Captain who had been kept to guard the bridge; then he ordered the troops to turn about and attack the enemy. After several marches with the object of occupying positions which General Lake had succeeded in seizing before us, Humbert, giving full rein to his impatience, attacked with twelve hundred men an enemy line which was defended by at least twelve thousand. This action, which was furiously disputed, despite the enormous disparity in numbers, took place near the village at Ballina-muck. It was very deadly; our artillery fired at point-blank range on the enemy ranks for an hour, and we saw whole files fall at each discharge ; but it must be admitted that there are no soldiers in the world who stand up to fire with more courage and resignation than the British. We retired in fairly good order after losing three hundred men, or the quarter of our attacking strength.

During our retreat we were harassed by a corps of Rang-ers. The General sent an *aide-de-camp* with orders to the infan-try to beat them off. The captain detailed for this service was a man of middle age whose arm was in a sling; he came up to me and asked me whether I would render him a very essential service. On my agreeing without hesitation, he begged me to keep his young son with the artillery; the latter was weak and ill, and he thought he would be better with me if his father was killed in the impending attack. I accepted, and he brought the young man to me at once, kissing him most tenderly, and recommended him to me with tears in his eyes, by the love my mother bore me. A few minutes later they brought him back dead; he had been killed by a bullet through the head. This occurrence greatly touched me; getting leave from d'Herblay I advanced two guns at the gallop and took those skirmishers in flank; they were hidden behind a stone wall marking the boundary of a field. A cannon ball *à ricochet* put them up like a flight of crows and a charge of grape laid half of them flat. This tardy vengeance repaired nothing, but the

General loudly remarked that that cannon shot had afforded him the one moment of pleasure he had experienced during the last eight days.

When I returned to camp I found the unhappy orphan clinging to his father's corpse, from which he refused to be separated. We had to use force. The marching orders having arrived, I was obliged to place the boy in a fainting condition in one of the wagons; his father was buried in a ditch, and our men did their utmost to insure that his sepulchre should rest inviolate. The unfortunate Captain's wallet was saved and handed to d'Herblay, who told me that evening that he had been an *émigré* who had been authorised to re-enter France, and that his name was Henri de la Tour. They had restored him to the rank which he had held in a regiment before the Revolution, and his record proved that he had been a brave and worthy man.

Fortune, which had always been against him, had led him to Rochefort to embark in one of the frigates of the expedition, and his wife had caught a fever there from which she died. Not knowing, in his distress, to whom he could entrust his young son, he had been obliged to take him with him into uniform in order that the authorities should allow him to share his father's fate. This was the child he had entrusted to me before going to his death.

The desperate situation in which the loss of the battle had placed us left me no means to carry out this pious duty, and every hour added to our difficulties. Whilst I was discussing our prospects with Captain d'Herblay a gunner informed me that a rebel chief, who doubtless had capitulated, had arrived at head-quarters accompanied by a soldier, who was said to be an English General come to arrange the terms of our surrender. I immediately declared that I would do anything rather than become a prisoner of war, and that to avoid the fate of the army, I should leave it immediately and trust in God for a successful issue to my enterprise. I urged the Captain to make the same decision, and he was much inclined to do so. After reflection, however, he changed his mind; but he fully understood my reasons and made no attempt to combat them. I made my preparations at once, and asked my gunners whether any among them would care to follow me. All welcomed my resolve with joy; they appreciated my motives better than most, since several had learnt to their cost what imprisonment on the English hulks could mean.

I summoned young de la Tour and acquainted him with my plan, telling him also that M. d'Herblay was prepared to take charge of him, and had assured me that he would consider it a matter of honour to fulfil the promises I had made to his father. At this unexpected news the poor boy burst into tears; but making up his mind with a firmness which his age did not lead one to expect, he told me that since I was going he would follow me whatever might happen; that it was to me that his father had entrusted him, and that he would do nothing to counter his wishes, which undoubtedly had their reasons and which in any case was sacred to him. He urged me so strongly to approve his decision that I agreed, not, however, without warning him of the perils to which it would expose him.

We were interrupted by heavy firing. Our rearguard had taken position on a mound which was difficult of access. The enemy officers got into touch with ours, we could not tell how, and persuaded them that we were completely surrounded; they pretended that our advance guard had already laid down their arms. Our officers, whose spirits had suffered from under-feeding, replied that they would willingly do the same were they certain of the fact, and they sent messengers to find out. Whilst waiting they continued their confidence without remarking the increasing numbers of enemies around their bivouac. Suddenly the English soldiers threw themselves upon the piled arms and seized the muskets. Taken by surprise our grenadiers drew their sabres and charged these robbers so vigorously that they recaptured their arms and opened a murderous fire at point-blank range on the authors of this treachery. Colonel Craddock was among the first to fall.

If General Humbert had attacked the enemy at that moment I do not know what the troops in their indignation would not have been capable of doing; but he had allowed himself to be tied up in negotiations, and on the 28th Fructidor (14th September) he signed the capitulation. There remained eight hundred and fifty men and ninety-six officers, with two pieces of artillery; I had spiked the two others, which the rebels threw into a bog to be recovered when the opportunity offered. The troops were taken to Dublin under escort, then sent by sea as prisoners to England, where the majority found their end aboard the hulks. The landing at Killala had taken place on the 5th, and the expedition had therefore lasted twenty-five days. There had been three actions and a battle; it had captured two towns; taken a dozen guns and as many colours, and it had needed an army of twenty-five thousand men commanded by the leading English General to arrest its march and put a turn to its successes. Its success would have been even greater had the rebels been more unified and had they supported it better, and above all if its General, instead of being merely an extremely courageous soldier, had been a clever and resourceful man, as becomes a partisan leader.

I did not wait for the capitulation to quit the army. At daylight I passed our furthest sentries, giving them the password, and made for the open country with my little troop, separating henceforward my fate from that of our unfortunate expedition. It was undoubtedly risky to start in daylight in the presence of the enemy, but we had to see ahead of us if we were to guard against danger, which would have been impossible at night-time; and so far as meeting English troops was concerned I worried little, being persuaded, and rightly, that their General had concentrated them in view of the capitulation, an event which took up their entire attention. In effect we made rapid progress across the fields and reached a distant chain of hills, whence we were able to reconnoitre the country and discover that we were beyond the chain of posts which encircled the French army.

Our party should have consisted of a dozen gunners, but half were missing at the rendezvous, as is always the case when a risky undertaking is toward. Two others disappeared on the way and probably returned to camp; only five remained, but they were the *élite* for courage, intelligence, and devotion. Young Henri de la Tour held his position among this number, if not by his strength which on occasions was below the level of his courage, at least by his vigilance, his activity, and his piercing eyesight, which, coupled with great perspicacity, caused him always to be the first to discover anything of interest to us. Every one acknowledged his superiority; we called on him to confirm our opinions, and the satisfaction of being useful to us softened the deep sorrow caused by his misfortunes.

My intention was to reach the Shannon and follow its course until it became navigable for large ships. I hoped that by surprise we might get possession of a boat, which would furnish us with the means to capture some vessel large enough to keep the sea. In that case we were saved; but the plan could not be carried out.

On reaching the river we saw a boat which was used to cross it and which could have served us for this purpose only; it was too small for any other. A gunner suggested taking possession and throwing the owner overboard. This simple expedient was undoubtedly the best; it was not adopted because Henri undertook to enter into negotiations with the ferryman; he knew enough English to get us taken across with no other payment than some bread, a sacrifice which already seemed sufficiently large. At this price we were taken over in two trips, and the old boatman threw in his prayers as well;

but the traitor sent a shepherd to follow us with instructions to find out where we hid ourselves and sell us to the Yeomanry who were roaming about the country.

We followed our route until nightfall; it was then necessary to find a shelter, for the day had been a long one and we were dead beat. I advised hiding ourselves among the thickets and blocking the entrances with bush-wood, but a gunner had discovered a barn on some rising ground which offered an excellent lodging. It had been built when this part of the country was inhabited and cultivated ; it was now in the midst of a desert, shepherds, outlaws, and rebels used it as a halting place, and beds of briar were already prepared for us. It seemed to me that this sumptuous dwelling had one great drawback; it was "in the air"; in other words, it offered no means of covering a retreat. A sentry was placed before the vast opening which served as a door, and his orders were to watch all possible approaches up the slopes. After a frugal repast, and after making a round which showed nothing suspicious, we threw ourselves on our leafy beds. Three gunners lay opposite and across the doorway. I took place at the further end of the barn with Henri, who always stayed by me. Before going to sleep I assured myself that in case of need it was possible to find a way out between the wall and the thatch. I noticed that the thatch was of great thickness, having been renewed several times without removing the straw beneath.

I went to sleep with the recklessness which constant and apparently inevitable danger brings. I was suddenly awakened by Henri, who told me that he had heard a suspicious noise. I seized my musket and was about to rise, but happily had not the time, or I should have gone to meet my death. At that very moment a discharge of musketry was fired into the barn at point-blank range by a troop who had surprised our sentinel asleep and who, after killing him, had advanced as far as the door. The three gunners sleeping in front of it were riddled with bullets and died without making a sound. We should have shared their fate if the fire, instead of being direct, had been slightly oblique. We profited by the moment when the enemy were reloading to reach the top of the wall and shelter between it and the thatch. I thought that from there we could jump down on the outside and escape whilst the attackers continued to fire into the barn; but we were bitterly disappointed to find that we were surrounded by cavalry, of whom only a party had dismounted to shoot us.

We were forced to remain hidden under the thatch, exposed to the enemy, without the possibility of defending ourselves or selling our lives by fighting. Finally, the yeomanry ceased their fire, satisfied that they had exterminated their victims. Nevertheless one of them, to make sure, lit a torch of straw and waved it over the bodies of our unfortunate comrades, then going out announced that all were dead. We were the invisible witnesses of this sad scene, and were threatened with being added to the massacre at any moment. Our muskets, which we had left hidden in the briar where we were sleeping, should have given us away, and we thought ourselves lost when we saw a light brought to illuminate that bloody scene; but whether he was dazzled by the torch he carried or else was moved by the sight of the men he had just slaughtered, the trooper who had entered the barn pushed his search no further and did not notice our arms.

As he remounted the commander of the troop shouted imperatively to someone who had hitherto kept out of sight. He told him that as a reward for his zeal he could keep anything he found in the pockets of the dead, enjoining him, nevertheless, under the threat of condign punishment, to carry the arms and clothing to his excellent uncle the boatman, where the company would collect them on their return.

Hope returned to us when we heard the Yeomanry depart and the sound of their horses' hoofs gradually dying away in the distance. Henri was commencing to thank God for our deliverance when a light showed in front of the barn and announced the presence of another enemy. It was the shepherd who had sold us, come to take his pay. He stuck a piece of resinous wood upright in the earth to serve him as a torch, and knelt down to despoil our poor comrades' bodies at his leisure; but he had no sooner commenced this odious sacrilege than he was laid low by a sabre stroke which stretched him at the feet of those his infamous treachery had assassinated. We took up our packs and our muskets, and left the scene rapidly and silently. When from a distant hill we looked back towards the barn, we saw it in flames; the shepherd's torch had fired the briars which were strewn upon the ground and furnished a funeral pyre for our unfortunate comrades.

By that time we had reached the country of Munster, the inhabitants of which were rebels in heart if not in deed. Our risks, in consequence, were diminished; we could even dare to communicate with the peasants, who, poor as they were, shared their potatoes with us. It was all they had to eat. They directed us towards the coast and warned us of the points where we might meet danger. One night we had a peculiar experience which reconciled us to our lot by showing us that the fate of many others was no better than our own. Looking down into an open valley we discovered a traveller having the appearance and uniform of a French sailor. We called him and he turned out to be a signalman from the *Hoche,* which had left Brest with the troops destined to support us. This expedition had met with contrary winds for eighteen days; it had made the Bay of Killala one month and a half after us and twenty-eight days after the capitulation of General Humbert.

The *Hoche* was attacked by three English ships and a frigate; she defended herself intrepidly for four hours, and only surrendered on seeing three other enemy ships preparing to join the others. Captain Bompart, who commanded her, was incapacitated by wounds. Of the four frigates accompanying her, one, the *Embuscade,* was sunk; another, the *Résolue,* which had been dismantled by the storm, was forced to surrender, and two escaped, the *Romaine* and the *Loire,* which succeeded in getting back to Brest.

Wolfe Tone, one of the chiefs of the Irish Union, who was said to be its father, was taken with the ship; he would have been confused with the French officers, but one of his old school friends recognised him. He was taken to Dublin and brought before a court martial, which condemned him to be hanged. He produced his commission as Brigadier-General in the French Service, and asked as an only favour to be shot as a soldier. His request being refused, he anticipated his fate: on being taken back to prison he cut his throat from ear to ear with a small knife he had hidden. He was a brave and clever man.

Luckier than the rebel leader, our signalman, despite numberless dangers, had escaped the terrible fate of an English prison and was going gaily off to find the shores of St. George's Channel, where he hoped to meet with Some American vessel which would enable him to get back to France by going round the world! His cheerfulness reconciled Henri to our position and gave us the hope of better times to come, precisely at the moment when an unlucky and unforeseen accident was about to place us in an appallingly awkward situation.

During the evening we had had a glimpse of the sea between two hills. For us it was the Promised Land. Not hoping to be able to reach the shore that day we decided to start before daybreak. After passing the night in bivouac in a thin coppice, we continued our route, which seemed easy and without other obstacle than the uncertainty which darkness brings to all travellers over unknown country. Suddenly the ground gave way beneath my feet, and I fell from a height of several feet into a quagmire formed of thick and bottomless mud. All my efforts were useless; I was sucked down by degrees into this ghastly mud-hole, and I was already in up to the shoulders, shortly to disappear altogether and perish by slow asphyxiation. Nor was this all; I had the remorse of having led Henri to his death; he had followed me with confidence and had shared my fate; he was behind me, struggling with death in the filthy and tenacious slime of this appalling bog.

Never, thank God, when I have been called upon to save another's life have I lacked for inspiration, but when on this occasion I had to save my own my imagination failed me. It was true that I was chilled through and through by the icy coldness of the mud, and that our misfortune was so unexpected and so bitter that it might have paralysed faculties more vigorous than our own.

The day which dawned just then brought with it less hope than horror, for it showed us that we had fallen into one of those vast Irish bogs which extend for many square leagues and are of a depth so great that it has never yet been calculated. They are, so to speak, real seas of mud which like the ocean have a progressive movement, by which the river borders are invaded and submerged under a semi-liquid peat, whose powerful flow cannot be arrested.

A glance at Henri left me in no doubt but that he was about to go under; I called to him to look after himself without worrying about me, but he refused, and protested that he would die with me. This devotion put me on my mettle. I had dropped my musket when I fell, and my arms were as free as the clinging mud allowed; I succeeded in taking off my pack and pushing it straight down to the bottom of the marsh; it served to raise me several inches further above the surface, and was a great relief to me. I could then help Henri to do the same thing, which rendered his position less intolerable, but did not raise our hopes of escaping our unhappy fate. The embankment bordering the lake formed an escarpment five or six feet high above the surface of the mud, and from the surface to the bottom was about the same, so that we had a wall nearly twelve feet high to climb. In the open country such an obstacle would have been difficult to pass; what then must it be to us, weighed down by our arms, our mud-soaked clothes, and the quantity of peat adhering to our bodies? In addition all our movements were hampered by the fear of losing footing on the slippery bottom, whose rapid slope led to nothingness two paces further on.

At the moment of our fall Henri had his musket slung, which had prevented his losing it. I told him to unsling it and fix the bayonet. It took him an interminable time to do this. When he had this weapon in hand we stretched it out at arm's length, and pointing it towards the embankment thrust it into a horizontal fissure in the stone. We thus obtained a fulcrum which I utilised to cover the distance which separated me from Henri and join him at the foot of the embankment.

This progress encouraged us. My young companion, who was light and slim, clambered with my aid up the side of the embankment and set foot on the bayonet which had been solidly thrust therein. Standing up he could not yet reach the top and had to make another fulcrum with his sword, whose blade he thrust between the stones. He was then able to climb to the top and reach port. Instead of rejoicing in his safety this excellent lad reproached himself because I was still in deadly danger, and when in my turn I endeavoured to get out of the loathsome quagmire he ran the risk of falling in once more in his efforts to help me. I had more difficulty in getting out than he. My greater height gave me a certain advantage, but I was heavier and less nimble, and I trembled, when taking Henri's hand, at the thought that by an involuntary movement I might pull him back with me into the ever open tomb below us.

As soon as I had reached firm ground we fell into each other's arms like men escaped from shipwreck. Henri's emotion was so great that he burst into tears and fell on his knees to thank God for having saved us.

We had great need of the intervention of Providence if we were to profit by the favour it had shown us. Never in all my life had I been reduced to such a state of misery. We had lost everything, arms, provisions, ammunition, service papers; even my watch was stopped and my compass put out of order by the peaty ooze with which our clothes were soaked. We were covered from head to foot in a layer of stinking slime which, hardening in the air, covered us with a sort of mineral product and turned us into fossils. In this desperate situation there was nothing further we could attempt for safety; all my plans had fallen through completely, and there remained no alternative but to give ourselves up to the first constable we came across. It would have been better had we gone to Dublin straight away. I think now that the icy bath we had just taken was acting on my brain, and that its influence deprived me of all firmness and resolution.

A high road, which seemed to be frequented, and which we had followed for some time, being likely to lead into the hands of those yeomanry whom we so well remembered, we turned into a wood of young trees, carefully planted and pruned. We had seen nothing like it in the country we had passed through. At our approach a large number of rooks flew away, cawing as if they had seen some extraordinary animals. I argued from their presence that we were near some aristocratic manor, since they are always to be found near country houses in the British Isles. This conjecture was soon realised. On the reverse slope of the hill which the slope covered we saw a lawn, and beyond it a Gothic castle framed in a wonderful view of the sea. Its towers and belfrys stood out against the blue and brilliant background of the western ocean, and at the sides we discovered terraced gardens, sheltered by great plantations from the wind.

We stopped, Henri and I, to enjoy this beautiful view, as though our troubles were not sufficient to absorb us. We had, however, to look after ourselves, and we sat down on the lawn to talk matters over. My young companion thought that if we presented ourselves at the castle we should find succour, and that it was impossible that civilised and Christian men should not take pity on fellow creatures whom misfortune had so hardly treated. I was considerably less credulous; I predicted that the owner of this magnificent house was some Anglican bishop who would curse us in the name of the established church, or else some old and crusted Tory whom the very sight of a Frenchman of the Revolution would be like to strike with apoplexy. Henri interrupted the course of my sinister presentiments; with his lynx-like eyes he had seen some ladies on a balcony who were observing us through opera-glasses. We were so appallingly clad that an inspection of this nature was quite sufficient to damn us. Nevertheless, I noticed that my young comrade had succeeded in wiping his face clean from the layer of mud which still covered mine, and I augured a favourable result; for the human virtues are such that pity is much more easily excited by a pleasant face than an ugly one.

Soon, in fact, we saw a footman coming towards us who told us that Lady French desired to know who the travellers might be, and whether it would suit them to stop at the castle. Henri replied that we were Frenchmen who had greatly suffered, and that in our present state we could not possibly present ourselves before ladies. This reserve—somewhat elaborate, be it said, and very rash coming from two poor devils who had eaten nothing—succeeded perfectly. We easily divined, from their vivacious gestures, that the company on the balcony was doubtless protesting that Irish hospitality would not permit of such a thing. The footman returned with a formal and pressing invitation from the Chatelaine, whatever our costume might be.

An arched and scalloped gateway led us to a vast court surrounded by hot houses, which were open and showed a profusion of exotic flowers. At the end of a gallery which led to the castle was an elegant doorway, where the guests of this fine house were gathered. They were evidently very great ladies and distinguished gentlemen. We approached respectfully, but without embarrassment, and I explained in general terms that after a series of misfortunes we had met with one which had nearly cost us our lives and was the cause of our present miserable condition; we had fallen into a bog during the night.

At this redoubtable word a cry arose and we were asked how we had managed to escape, since that kind of accident invariably resulted in the death of those who experienced it. With a happy choice of expressions, and under the inspiration of his gratitude to Divine Providence, Henri told how our efforts had been crowned with success. His story was most sympathetically received; Lady French reproached me kindly for my hesitation to confide myself to her hospitality. I justified myself by the feeling of disgust which our appearance must inspire, and by the painful apprehension of being taken for adventurers, since our papers, which could have proved our identity, had remained at the bottom of the marsh. This reminded Henri that the little pocket book in which he kept his was on him when we fell. He looked for it and presented it open to the oldest and most distinguished of the gentlemen present. At this moment a young man who had an arm in a sling, and whose soldierly look had struck me, told me that we were not strangers to one another.

"We saw each other," he said, in a dry voice, "at Ballina-muck, on the battlefield."

Lady French showed signs of nervousness on hearing her nephew take this tone; but the hardy young man continued imperturbably:

"You remember, sir, that leaving your guns you accosted the body of rebels on your right and asked an officer what was the nature of the land in front of the enemy's line. I was that officer. I replied that it was stony. Thanking me, you returned to your battery, and a few moments afterwards your cannon balls by a series of ricochets were ravaging the ranks of the Leicestershire regiment. Our astonishment and admiration found vent in loud applause. I congratulate myself, and consider it an honour to be your comrade-in-arms," he said, taking my hand.

When I turned my eyes to Lady French, who I feared would be annoyed by this rash and compromising confession, I found her very agitated, it is true, but with joy and pride to know that her nephew had followed in the steps of her ancestors in fighting for Ireland side by side with the French. Neither the circumspection which habitually reigns in high society nor the danger of calling down the conqueror's vengeance could repress the instinctive enthusiasm which these words called forth.

At this moment the gentleman who had been glancing interestedly at Henri's papers handed them back to him saying, "It would be impossible to find a finer or nobler line than that of *monsieur.* There is there the proof that one of his ancestors fought at Saint Jean d'Acre with Phillippe Auguste and our Richard the Lionheart."

This declaration, which transformed into a descendant of the Crusaders a poor lad who had shortly before been taken for a beggar, was welcomed by a most flattering murmur. The gentleman added: "I suppose, Monsieur, that Mademoiselle Henriette de la Tour is your sister?"

"I am she, Monsieur," replied Henri. This unexpected reply caused the greatest surprise. I was absolutely dumbfounded.

"Forgive me, my worthy friend," said Henriette to me, "if I have kept this secret from you; I had not the right to entrust it to anyone, even to you, who saved my life. My father made me solemnly promise to keep it, even in the last extremity. Besides," she continued, "had you known what I was you would have tried to spare me some of the fatigue and danger of your perilous journey; I should have been a burden and embarrassment to you; to spare my weakness you would have exposed yourself the more, and I might perhaps have been the cause of your loss, which would have brought about my own."

This strange metamorphosis had so astounded me that I must have replied very badly, if I replied at all. As to our audience, so romantic an incident aroused the greatest interest. Everyone embroidered the theme that it was a descendant of the doughty knights of the twelfth century who was fighting for the French Republic and the liberty of Ireland. Besides, it must in all humility be admitted that, even were we descended directly from Vercingetorix and Civilis, as we were inclined to boast, we should have been but *petits bourgeois,* men of little standing, compared to our noble hosts, who, as the chaplain told me, could for the most part trace their descent to the Kings of Munster before the preaching of Christianity in Ireland. Their genealogical tree stretched even further, with certain lacunae, it is true. Its roots sprang from Carthage, and in antiquity greatly exceeded the oldest patrician families of Rome. I cannot vouch for the absolute truth of this, but it is certain that the origin of the Irish is surrounded by so much obscurity that it must be older than any other race in Europe.

We were taken great care of, and, what was beyond price, were allowed to rest after our terrible journey. Either from agitation, or because I had lost the habit of sleeping in a bed, I could not go to sleep. Towards dinner time Captain Patrick, the young rebel leader, came to take me to the drawing-room, where a large company was assembled. Thanks to my borrowed clothes I bore little resemblance to the half drowned victim of the bog, and an old lady who had lived in Italy, and had there acquired the habit of saying what she wished, remarked slyly that in the morning I had kept my mask on, as is the custom in Venice, in order to create the greater sensation when one takes it off.

Henriette entered with a young woman who had kindly seen to her toilette; I could not realise that it was she, she was so pretty. Her black robe emphasised the whiteness of her skin, and every one admired her tall, slim figure, which her father had so carefully hidden under a delusive uniform. This disguise was all the easier in those days, when soldiers were not tailored like wasps, and when their measure was taken by the size of a sentry box, as the saying went; an assertion which, if not true, was at any rate plausible.

Our hostess overwhelmed us with kindness and attention; she kept a place for Henriette by her side, and when the circle was complete she took her arm and presented her to the ladies, all of whom welcomed her charmingly. She took possession of me when passing by a group where I was talking to the chaplain, and leading us into another room she told me that realising the impossibility of my ward and myself seeing anything of one another during the evening, she was arranging for us to be together for a few moments under the guard of the holy gentleman by whom I was accompanied. An instant after we were alone. My emotions prevented my speaking, and it was Henriette, blushing, who began the burning conversation. Giving me her hands she begged me not to think that the change which had taken place had altered the tender affection which she bore me, and which I had merited by so much service and devotion; she justified this affection by the choice her father had made of me, by the confidence I had inspired in him, and by the last words he had uttered when kissing her before going to his death. With a sweet kindness she recalled to me the engagement I had taken in that sad moment, to protect her and let her share my fate.

"Nothing," she added in a touching voice, "will cause you to change that resolution, I hope; and whatever happens you will keep your friendship for me, which today is dearer to me than ever. I earnestly desired this interview," she continued, "because since I disclosed my sex I have noticed an unaccustomed coldness in you, and you have not once tried to talk to me. You will know that I was forced to make the avowal to avoid a lie, and also to avoid the suppositions which might have arisen were my secret eventually discovered. But despite these motives I must mortally regret it if it has wounded you or has changed the affection which you had for me. Perhaps you have thought that I was unbalanced by the luxury which surrounds us, that it pleases me to wear these clothes? Make no mistake! I am ready to quit them if you tell me so, and to put on those I wore when you loved me; I have kept them with that intention."

This last thrust, which fell in with my unworthy thoughts, touched me to the heart; and I do not know how this interview might have ended if the chaplain, who had left us quite alone with perfect discretion, had not returned to say that the guests were going into the dining-room. He led out Henriette, who on seeing me going away from her nearly burst into tears.

This passion of a young girl, ingenuous, devoted and resolved, this affection born in the breast of misfortune, this reward which my friendship had unexpectedly found in a sentiment full of charm and which promised happiness—could I refuse these gifts, this greatest treasure in the world, the love of a sweet companion? I was so fascinated by these powerful attractions that, under their irresistible influence, could I have spoken to Henriette, I would have proposed to her to put on our old clothes once more and fly the castle to brave fortune in a life of adventure which, in restoring us to each other, would have fulfilled all our desires.

There is doubtless some mysterious communication between hearts moved by a common affection. This fine project, mad enough to be original, had been conceived by Henriette also. That same evening, at the piano, she sang with delightful expression, and side glances full of tenderness, the Italian verses whose refrain is: *A Cottage and his Heart.*

When, during our perilous flight, Henri and I had crossed Ireland, we thought only of danger, and the arts were too far from our thoughts even to be alluded to. I would, however, never have imagined that a young man who seemed to be three or four years younger than Henriette had had time to learn anything but the elements of a good education. I was therefore singularly surprised when, after the ceremony of tea, my pretty ward become without warning the leader of a concert which had been prepared and in which nobody supposed she could take a part.

Despite the fury of war, the Italian music had continued its triumphal march across Europe to soften the savage customs of its inhabitants. It had even come to Ireland. Good company in the island was delighted with it, the national airs being remembered only by patriotism and the English airs by policy. All these, being familiar to the noble persons performing, were played with remarkable skill. But the second part of the programme, consisting of Italian music, found itself somehow held up by want of an accompanist. Our hostess was much distressed. Henriette seeing her anxiety, asked if she could not do something. She was asked whether she knew the piece, and replied that she did not, but hoped that that would not cause any difficulty.

On the invitation of Lady French she was led to the piano. A lively anxiety and perhaps even an accusation of presumption must have been visible on my countenance, for on taking off her gloves, Henriette gave me a smile which I took to be a mockery of my uneasiness. I nevertheless persisted in my fears, which were justified by the consequences which a check might have for us. Happily I was soon put out of my agony. As soon as the lady who was to sing was ready, Henriette commenced the prelude: she played it in profound silence, and with the greatest charm. It seemed as though beneath her fingers the instrument had another tone and a harmony hitherto unheard.

The effect was magical; every one was carried away ; and around me I heard her playing compared with the best to be heard in Naples or Milan for skill, grace and feeling. Henriette obtained the greatest success in all her life for the lady she accompanied; and as soon as it was over this lady kissed Henriette and asked her friendship. Each vied with the other to congratulate the young French *émigré,* for it was under this quite unmerited title that our hostess had hidden another which it was dangerous to make known. I was the last to offer my respects.

"If I played well," she said, in an undertone, "it was to please you. I am satisfied if I have succeeded."

At the end of the concert she was pressed to sing, but excused herself, and it was only when politeness forced her that she sang in a low voice, with a purpose which she explained to me by a glance, a verse of the Italian song of which I have spoken, and which the present generation has seen translated into French. As an excuse she said she would try and do better another time: and immediately a big concert in which she could figure as Prima Donna was suggested for the day after tomorrow. All the aristocracy in Munster was invited. The concert was magnificent; there were more Dukes present than in our entire House of Lords, and they were Dukes with duchies as large as German principalities. Henriette was at the piano during a part of this splendid *soirée*. She was constantly asked to give the song she had promised; she always put it off in deference to other ladies, who wished to sing themselves. Finally, when the impatience of the audience admitted of no further delay, she sang in a melodious soprano, Cimarosa's great air from the *Secret Marriage: Pria che spunto in ciel l'aurora*. It was another eloquent challenge to leave the castle and take our love for guide. I have heard Madame Catalani in the hey-day of her fame lend her extraordinary talent to this air, and I can say that if Henriette was not her equal in musical technique, she carried the day by the equality of her voice, which was of a softness and a purity unequalled.

The Irish race is as sensitive to music as the people of the south, and it is one of their passions. It can be imagined what effect was produced by the *chef d'oeuvre* of the greatest of Italian masters; a *chef d'oeuvre* which hitherto had only been known by hearsay, and which a beautiful young creature executed with the greatest skill. The enthusiasm was so extraordinary that, throwing etiquette to the winds, the ladies rose *en masse* and, followed by the men, rushed to congratulate Henriette on her brilliant triumph.

I am forced to admit, however, that there was one there who was saddened by these plaudits and alarmed by this success. It was I. I reflected that the intoxication of such a success would shake the balance of a man, and that it was bound to have a harmful effect on that of a woman, too young as yet to appreciate the value of the opinions of the world. Although entirely immune from caste prejudice, it did not please me to see a daughter of the Crusaders reap an applause which would have better suited a daughter of the Opera. I was frightened by this talent, so great that home-life could never hold it, so attractive that crowds were drawn into its wake, so greedy of admiration that even when it was but pleasure it perforce became a spectacle. In my stormy state of mind I was irritated by this imprudent revelation which had thrown the girl I loved haphazard into unknown company. I trembled at this publicity which had taken hold of her, of the praise which was lavished on her and which tacitly implied the right of criticism. Above all was I revolted by the examination of her person, carried out microscopically with the impertinent curiosity peculiar to good company at the end of the eighteenth century. It reminded me of a slave in the Antilles being inspected on the auctioneer's table by prospective buyers. Instead of offering my meed of praise to the beauteous singer I left the concert-room, where I felt like suffocating.

In the evening I had seen the flowers; the morrow brought forth the fruits. The chaplain told me in confidence that many rich and advantageous offers had been made to Lady French for the hand of Mademoiselle de la Tour. He showed me the armorial bearings of the various candidates, which was extremely charming for me. This information gave me deeply and sadly to think. If Henriette really loved me she would refuse the advantages offered with these gilded chains, and from then on her destiny, not to mention my own, would be delivered to all the chances of adversity.

If, on the contrary, she accepted, even after a respectable resistance, I was cast for the unpleasant role of the gulled tutor in the Italian comedy, and my passion, daily increased by deceitful hopes and perfidious allurements, would be repaid by the bitterest disillusion and the most cruel sorrow. I think, nevertheless, that in spite of the counsels of common sense I was about to ask an explanation of Henriette and take her wishes as a guide, when Captain Patrick arrived and proposed that we should ride round the new plantations which his aunt had just had made. I accepted, and for more than two hours we followed the coast, which offered the most picturesque of views.

In a deep bay, hidden by islets of basalt, tall and lace-like as the cathedrals of the Middle Ages, I made out a brig which I recognised at once as a French privateer. Patrick told me that she had probably come to land arms during the night, and I suspected that this was probably the object of our excursion. I urged him to go about his business whilst I visited the privateer to get some news from France. He raised no objection, and a fisherman's ferry took me on board. The captain, to whom I made myself known, welcomed me like a friend; he suggested that I should join his company and take my revenge for the unhappy Irish expedition. I was in just the mood to exercise any kind of reprisal. I agreed without even weighing the advantages.

The sacrifice to which my heart had resigned itself could find no other compensation. I wrote a letter on the spot to Lady French, full of gratitude; and another to Mademoiselle de la Tour, full of love and sorrow. I gave them to the fisherman whose boat had brought me on board, with orders to hand them to the domestic holding my horse, with instructions to return with them to the castle at once in order that Patrick, seeing that I was not at the rendezvous, should think I had returned there. An hour later, as the tide went out and the night began to fall, the privateer made sail and was quickly out of sight of land.

I have often remarked the powerful effect of sea air on the passions. It seems that man, faced with the immensity of the ocean, is forced to gauge his interests and finds it more easy to appreciate them. Thus it is that the following couplet comes from a sea song:

Chagrin d'amour ne va pas en voyage
Chagrin d'amour ne va pas en vaisseau.[2]

Calm slowly entered into me, although my heart still suffered.

Twelve days later we entered Morlaix river with two prizes, in which I had my part, following the stipulations made by my honest privateer himself. A local Jew gave me a thousand francs for my share, worth four times as much, and after taking leave of my worthy friends I returned to Brest. I enquired vainly after my old friends; the officers and men of my old company had given place to new-comers. They looked for my name on the roll without success, and it was necessary to refer to the books of the half-brigade, where it was found crossed off with the mention: "Dead in the Irish Expedition under the orders of General Humbert." I was reinstated without much difficulty, but when it came to paying me my past pay, I was told it was impossible, since my death was an accomplished fact so far as the pay rolls were concerned! Happily the privateer had treated me in kinder fashion.

Thoroughly convinced henceforth albeit somewhat late in the day, of the truth of the proverb that no one is a prophet in his own country, I was leaving the marine head-quarters,

2. "Love sickness never takes to travel.
Love sickness never takes to sail."

asking myself whether any trace remained of my existence, when an apple-woman established at the barrier threw herself in my way with exclamations of joy. She reminded me of Ulysses' hound, who alone recognised him on his return. How came it about that she remembered me; why was she so glad to see me? And what ties were there between us? This is what I am about to recall, while saying at once that this poor woman opened up a new career to me and that I owe to her intervention the employment which eventually succeeded in mitigating the sorrow caused by being separated forever from the Daughter of the Crusaders!

A Chouan Adventure

There are some happy people, favoured by fortune or a period of peace, who can choose their own profession. There are others who instinctively follow the profession of their fathers and learn it by the power of imitation. Neither know the tortures which a young man must endure when he is saddled with the duties of a profession of which he is entirely ignorant, but which he is bound to carry out for his own honour, that of his country, and for the sake of humanity. A hundred times in my agitated existence have I been told: "Carry on!" and I knew not what to carry on; nobody had taught it me, nor had I ever imagined that I should be called upon to learn it.

During a military reconnaissance a general once picked me, out of ten perfectly capable officers, to make a map of the ground we had covered. This mission was doubtless very honourable, but was a desperate one for a poor student who had never sketched anything but an eye or a nose in profile and whom an unanswerable order suddenly transformed into an engineer.

"Sir!" cried an accused man, "if you do not undertake my defence before the court martial I am lost." In vain I pointed out my inexperience, the impossibility for me to undertake so difficult and so serious a task; he would not listen, but embraced my knees as though his life depended on me. He said he had dreamed a dream, had had his fortune told, and that I alone had his entire confidence. Could I refuse to become his advocate?

"Captain!" cried a chorus of men in hospital, "the last of our surgeons has just died; save us; you are learned, you must know everything; do the rounds, look after us; for God's sake don't leave us without help! If you can't stop us dying at least you will console us." Who could refuse the last wish of these unfortunates?

It was thus that by an invincible fatality I became, turn by turn, engineer, poor man's lawyer and doctor to the sick abandoned by men and Heaven—without ceasing my trade as gunner.

I will give an example of one of these arrows of fate.

One morning when crossing in the boat from Brest to the Recouvrance I remarked among the passengers a woman who was weeping bitterly. I asked her the cause of her sorrow, and this is what I learnt. Her husband, who was steward's mate in a ship, in other words, charged with the handling of the crew's rations, had just returned from a long cruise. The vessel had come into port to pay off when the authorities had unexpectedly come aboard, and had verified the quantity of wine delivered at departure, the amount remaining and the daily accounts of distribution during the cruise. It had been shown that according to the accounts, kept by the steward's mate himself, ten barrels of wine were missing.

Now, the day before, a similar number had been seized which had been secretly landed on Brest quay, and which undoubtedly originated in a theft from some vessel in port. It had not been possible to arrest the persons who intended to carry this wine into the town, but on discovering the deficit in the steward's mate's accounts it had been taken for granted that he was the guilty party; he had been sent to prison and brought before a court martial on the charge of the theft, committed in port, of articles entrusted to him and belonging to the outfit of a ship of war. Public opinion was strongly against the stewards, who were suspected of double dealing; in consequence no interest in favour of the accused could be expected, and if he could count upon impartiality he would be lucky.

The woman's protests were coldly received by the passengers and I was the only one who was touched by her sobs. Nevertheless an old sailor who, like myself, had doubtless remarked this prejudice, spoke up, and said that while he held no brief for steward's mates, a rotten lot who, during his lengthy cruises, had invariably encroached upon his wine ration, this woman had been his neighbour for ten years, and that he could vouch for her reputation and affirm that she was a mother who brought up her children in respect of God and other people's property. This sufficed to dissipate suspicion and open the floodgates of benevolence. Everybody searched for some means to alleviate the woman's lot.

"I can see no other," remarked the sailor, "than to examine the case, which is perhaps not so clear as it may seem. Go ahead, young fellow," he added, speaking to me, "I see by your clothes that you know how to read and write, you can do something for this poor woman; perhaps you will save the family from ruin."

All the passengers backed up the old sailor and persuaded me to go to Pontaniou prison to visit the accused, and endeavour to elucidate some fact which might be useful to his cause.

Although in those times there were many less rogues than there are today, I had already met a few, and I knew their habits and how to recognise them. The prisoner in no sense resembled them. He told me ingenuously that he knew nothing whatever about the business which was likely to prove his ruin. The deficit could not be contested, but he nevertheless assured me, on his hope of Paradise, that he had never misappropriated a pint of wine. As to the barrels seized on the quay, the first that he had heard of them was when he was questioned about them. On the other hand, he had heard from the other prisoners that his case was one for the galleys, and in order that his children should never be reproached with having a convict for a father, he had decided to drown himself when they took him across the port to go before the tribunal. The unhappy man having told me nothing of any use, I decided, after reflection, to ask the clerk to the court martial to show me the documents bearing on the case. I had hoped to discover that the wine seized differed from that on board, of which it was said to be a part; but it turned out that the thieves had effaced all identification marks; and to complete my disappointment the quality of the wine in one barrel differed so greatly from that in another that no deduction could be made from a disparity.

The only recourse remaining to me was to examine the accounts of the steward's mate. It was a collection of notebooks, inscribed in the obscurity of the orlop deck, by a heavy and unaccustomed hand, and the figures being written in wavy columns were difficult to add up. The original documents which justified them were even more undecipherable. I asked what verification had been made of these numerous notebooks and was told that the totals only had been checked, in order to avoid what, they gave me to understand, would have been an immense amount of work. The totals showed that in this accountancy there was missing precisely the ten barrels of wine fraudulently landed on the quay. But were the additions which formed these totals right? There was a grave question, the solution of which seemed to me to have been taken for granted by the prosecution.

I came across certain errors of which I kept the secret. I confined myself to proposing to make a general verification by means of a sufficient number of service marine artillerymen. My request was submitted to the judge-advocate, who agreed to it; and at once half a dozen young men, with no incentive but that of a good action, set to work to go through this farrago of figures. After eight days of calculation I was able to establish, with evidence, that the wine carried to deficit had been distributed to the crew, and that the journal and supporting documents proved it. The error consisted in the additions of the pages. I placed the papers before the judge-advocate, and showed him that incorrect additions had been carried forward. This discovery caused a sensation, and was a fresh instance of the errors to which justice is exposed by misleading appearances, which seem to show the proof of crime in what may be a simple turn of chance.

Thus the whole of this grave accusation reposed upon two figures: that of the barrels missing and that of the barrels stolen. In this affair, M. Bergeven, the judge-advocate, proved himself worthy of the name he bore, and which was honoured both in the navy and in the administration of the marine. He decided that in order to rehabilitate the unfortunate steward's mate the case should be brought before the court. There he abandoned the case, and was kind enough to say that it was entirely due to me that the necessary evidence was forthcoming to clear the accused.

The latter, as frequently happens, had understood not a word of the legal jargon constituting his charge-sheet, and when he was told he was free he was so overcome with joy that he fainted. An apoplectic fit followed which carried him off in forty-eight hours. In consequence the sole result of my efforts was to save the family honour, and in acknowledging its error, justice was as fatal to its victim as if it had declared him guilty. Happily some kind-hearted woman, who had followed this case with interest, took charge of the orphans, and obtained a permit for the widow to sell fruit at the entrance to the marine artillery quarters.

On my return from the expedition to Killala I was leaving those quarters when this same woman recognised me, and came to greet me. She had looked for me everywhere. Her husband's case, about which she had but the haziest ideas, had made her believe that I possessed a sort of miraculous power of liberation, like the Lord of Kellern who burst a prisoner's chains asunder merely by looking at them.

Following this line of thought, when a young soldier was condemned to death for insubordination, she had not hesitated to say that I would save his life were I at Brest; and this opinion had been borne out by the crew of the flagship when the verdict had been rendered. The woman's prayers won me over, and I drew up a demand for revision of the sentence on the nearest grocer's counter. There was not a moment to be lost, for the delay allowed was nearly spent and the pontoon, destined to serve as a scaffold, was already being prepared. As soon as Admiral Latouche left his room, the woman handed him the document, which he took, assuring her that the execution would be countermanded and the Counsel of Revision convoked. An hour before it was held I went on board and examined the procedure: as I had imagined it was most irregular and, despite my inexperience, I was able to attack it before the Counsel with a dozen reasons for cancellation. I fully succeeded and a new enquiry was ordered, which would be submitted to another court martial. It was certainly a respite: but in fifteen days the accused would inevitably find himself in the same situation, with the only difference that the president, profiting by my intervention, would see that the procedure was irreproachable.

This idea upset me and I worried myself to death trying to find some means to save the poor devil. The following day a *fête* was to be held in harbour to celebrate the victory of Marengo. I decided to take advantage of it. When the French and Spanish generals were assembled on board the *Ocean,* around a table laid for a sumptuous banquet, Admiral Latouche, commanding in chief, found under his plate an epistle in verse wherein the condemned man asked for mercy, and the right to shed his blood on the battle-fields of the Republic instead of the scaffold, which would kill his brothers for very shame, and cause his mother to die of sorrow.

The Admiral, who was cultured and kind-hearted, immediately took a kindly resolution; he read the verses aloud, and after speaking to his ally Admiral Gravina, he descended with him to the battery where the condemned man lay in irons; he had him set free before his eyes and announced his unconditional pardon, in order that on a day of thanksgiving nobody under his orders should be unhappy.

That evening on returning home I found a young soldier seated on the stairs who threw himself at my feet and kissed my knees. He had received his marching orders for the army of Italy, and the permission to see his mother and family. His happiness and gratitude filled me with joy; and I do not think that any other profession can give the satisfaction felt by a lawyer, who has succeeded in saving from the scaffold a man more unhappy than guilty, and who is spared to serve his country for twenty-five years or more.

From that day on I set myself seriously to study law, and I became the lone hope of the many awaiting judgement in the prisons of Finisterre. I had clients who called for me from all the prisons, military or civil. I had to plead as many as three cases a day before three different tribunals.

Among the cases with which I had to deal there were very few crimes against property or persons. Theft was rare in Lower Brittany and, on the other hand, drunken brawls were so common that they never came to law. Broken heads arranged themselves without recourse to justice: but many a time I was called to Quimper to plead in cases of the highest importance before the Assize Court. Its President, M. R. Keréon, who had taken a liking to me, pressed me to accept these missions, very honourable doubtless, but which on occasions led me into dangerous traps, as we shall shortly see.

One day, at the request of a soldier brought before the divisional court martial, I went to Brest castle. This poor fellow, who was said to be most dangerous and unscrupulous, had been imprisoned in the dungeon of Caesar's Tower, forty or fifty feet below the ground. When the turnkey opened the door of this dreadful place the stench which came from it was so terrible that I recoiled in horror.

I succeeded in arranging with the gaoler to bring the prisoner up to the court-room, surrounding him by warders. He was a tall man, whose face had been rendered sinister and unpleasant by many scars which marked it in all directions. He was covered with the rotting dung on which he slept in his dungeon. He told me that in his quality of Master-at-Arms he was not particularly sweet-tempered, and that an officer having deliberately taken him to task he had, unhappily, been unable to resist the temptation to give him a hiding. He was well acquainted with the Penal Code, and had no illusion as to the fate reserved for him; but, resigned as he might be, he wished, for his personal satisfaction, to consult me in order to be *quite* certain that his case was hopeless.

The man was a real scamp, but on going through his papers I found records of so many meritorious actions that I could not make up my mind to leave him without a glimmer of hope.

"You are ill," I told him, "be still more ill and you will be sent to hospital, to the prisoners' ward; in your turn you will be taken to the yard for exercise; its walls are thirty feet high, and you will be guarded by a sentry. A young tree might facilitate your climb, and enable you to reach the top of the wall in a bound. The sentry will fire at you; if he misses you can let yourself fall into the neighbouring street and you are saved."

The prisoner thanked me effusively and was led back to his horrible dungeon. I heard no more of him. Several months later I met the captain who had been detailed to preside at the court martial destined to shuffle this poor devil off.

"I strongly suspect," he said to me, "that it was you who played me the dirty trick of arranging that rascal's escape."

I asked him how he arrived at that conclusion, and he gave me a detailed account which showed me that the prisoner had carried out what I had suggested to him with the exactitude of a military order. I was astounded at the man's smartness, courage, and good fortune.

Some time after that I went to Quimper to plead before the Assize Court: the case finished, I discovered, when I wanted to return to Brest, that the communications were disturbed by a band of Chouans. Their methods were well known. As soon as the coach arrived at the foot of a steep hill the brigands, who were waiting in the gorse, attacked the escort, killed a few men before showing themselves, and forced it to abandon the coach. They turned the passengers out at once, and instead of robbing them, passed the hat round for the benefit of Notre Dame de Recouvrance. In the meantime, the more nimble-fingered among them rummaged in the hiding places where the money destined for the tax-collector was placed, and took out the sacks, which they counted carefully to see that nothing was missing. They then put the passengers back in the coach and wished them a good journey. This story sounded too good to me, and I learnt in effect that at times these honest brigands did not bother to ask for what they could take.

It all fell out exactly as I had been told, when the coach, in which I had taken my place, was held up on the way by a large troop of Chouans. Only, what I did not expect, was that their leader, on seeing me, should give a shout of joy and make me most affectionately welcome. It was the Master-at-Arms, the prisoner of Caesar's Tower, the escaped hospital patient, who had taken refuge with these highwaymen, and who by his intelligence and courage had forced them to accept him as one of their leaders. He kept repeating that he would never forget that I was his liberator, and instead of taking my purse he offered me his own. I urged him to quit so base a calling as soon as possible, and he promised me to follow this second piece of advice as faithfully as he had the first. He had sufficient resources, he said, to live honestly in the United States. In consideration for me the other passengers were not held to ransom, and the tax-money in the coach paid for everybody.

The Chouans and their leader overwhelmed us with attention, and made a point of acting towards us in a most courteous manner. When they let us go, very content to have got off so cheaply, I was obliged to explain how I became the object of so much tender affection.

"Which proves," remarked one of my travelling companions, "that it is as well to have friends everywhere, even amongst highwaymen."

I had considerable success in other people's business, but remarkably little in my own. It has always been so all my lifetime.

One night after pleading successfully in a long case at Quimper I was supping with M. R. Keréon. After a long and agreeable evening I was returning to my hostelry, when I stopped to admire the spectacle of the cathedral lit up by the moon. A lady, who seemed young and pretty and appeared to be elegantly dressed, was crossing the square; an exclamation which escaped her when she saw me led me to ask her politely whether I had the honour of her acquaintance.

"I owe you, sir," she said, "a day brimful of emotion. I was at the hearing today when you obtained such a fine success."

She continued to tell me many pleasant things, the hearing of which was rendered all the more agreeable by the sound of her voice. The conversation became courteous and gallant on my side; lively and witty on hers. I was intensely curious to know whom I was speaking with. It was evident that the beauteous unknown knew all the great families of the district by heart and shared their royalist opinions; but her animation, her frankness, and the broadness of her views left me in doubt as to whether she was a great lady or merely her frisky maid. After all, in those fabulous times of social equality it very little mattered, since she was a charming person anyway, and in spite of all the experience which she boasted, she could not have been more than twenty at the most.

When I asked her if this walk, on which I should look back with tender memory, would leave me with the regretful knowledge that it would never be repeated, she replied that the regret was shared but unavoidable, and that she was leaving at dawn for a destination where tender or affectionate feelings were unknown. I thought she was going to some strictly-guarded convent; it was worse than that, she assured me; her home was an old feudal castle in the middle of the woods and downs, and she frequently remained for eight days without speaking a word other than Gaelic, and seeing no other faces but those of the peasants. I protested against such a horrible fate, and asked her to take me with her to keep her company.

"*Mon Dieu,*" she replied, "I had thought of it and could well do so, since I am told I shall be absolutely alone in the castle; but," she hastened to add, laughing, "the thick walls of my tower and my groves of honeysuckle would furnish too favourable an opportunity for the birth of a *grande passion,* and we should be unable to guard ourselves against it. Without having too profound an intuition, I think that you would learn to love me; and when yesterday I saw you in the court-room, I could not disguise the fact that you seemed the man that I had always dreamed about."

This flattering avowal only served to prolong our interview and increase the pain of parting.

Finally we said goodbye without hope of seeing one another again, when she suddenly came back and asked me how I intended to leave. I replied by the morning coach, unless there was trouble on the road; and I added that even in that case the passengers had little to fear.

"Splendid," she said, "but if by chance things look bad, remember without fail to call out: '*Ohé! Jacquot, que le diable t'emporte,*' nothing else; but if you find yourself still in a tight corner, do not forget to say: '*Je suis des amis du Marquis, ventre-de-biche.*'"

I had not the time to thank her for this sign of confidence. She had already disappeared in the shadow of the cathedral. Back in my room I asked myself whether I had not mistaken some old Chouan leader for a beautiful young girl, and if the insurgent password, which a charming mouth had seemed to give, was not a trap set for my credulity. I was, nevertheless, forced to admit that this vision was not entirely false, for I was haunted by the glance of the charming unknown and the silhouette of her figure, a seductive promise which is nearer the reality in Finisterre than in any other country in the world.

The following day at noon the coach which should have left at dawn was not even loaded. It eventually started on its cumbersome way accompanied by an infantry escort which made it even slower. I slept for sheer boredom, and only opened my eyes to find the coach stopped in the midst of a band of Chouans. Our escort, intimidated by their superior numbers, had retired without firing a shot. It looked as though everything had been prepared beforehand, which reminded me that at the posting-house the delay in starting had been attributed to the supposition that the brigands were not yet ready to attack the coach. All these crimes had become a matter of business in which everybody had a share.

All passed off with a regularity worthy of a siege; the passengers were ordered to get out and we were lined up like prisoners of war against the wall of an inn near the high road; two sentinels guarded us while the rest turned the coach inside out in a search for a large sum of money belonging to the Treasury. I was studying these peasants, turned robbers by profession, and was thinking that their rags proclaimed their profession as a pretty bad one, when suddenly our escort, which had rallied, charged the Chouans with the bayonet. The coach was recaptured, turned round, and dispatched at a gallop to return to Quimper. Furious at seeing their prey carried off under their very eyes the brigands ran after it, harassing our soldiers with their fire without daring to come to close quarters. I foresaw that they would soon return to the passengers in an endeavour to recoup themselves. Profiting by the fact that our sentries had gone to join their comrades, I made off at the double in the opposite direction, without worrying about the coach which, far from promising safety, was more likely to attract the enemy and lead one into his hands.

I was beginning to find the day somewhat fatiguing and was proposing to stop at a village, which I could see in the distance, on a height; when, unexpectedly, two armed peasants came out of a sunken road and aimed their muskets at me, accompanying the action by menaces of which I understood the meaning. Their appearance was so sudden that it was a moment before I remembered the password. As soon as I recollected it I looked my two rascals in the eye, and called out:

"*Ohé! Jacquot, que le diable t'emporte.*"

I was not particularly confident in the power of this talisman, and was much relieved to note the result. At the words the two rogues lowered their muskets and regarded me with a most promising air of surprise and stupidity.

"I know," I said to the elder of the two, "that you speak French as well as I do; come now give me some news of the marquis; am I far from the castle?" He started to answer in a quick and unintelligible manner, but when I said: "*Ventre de biche,* I'm a friend of the marquis," he talked sense, and showed me, above the oaks of a neighbouring wood, some high walls as dark as the dwelling-house of Cyclops. It was the old house which contained my beautiful unknown. I ordered the two brigands to lead me there, and they obeyed without hesitation; but it was not easy to enter this sombre abode; the bridges were broken and the posterns walled up, so that we had to climb over ivy-covered breaches in the wall in order to reach the courtyard. Finally, under a vaulted porch, we found a door which gave on a large dark hall resembling the refectory in a monastery. Before a chimney-piece as large as a room, where a great fire was burning, a woman sat in an immense armchair, which only showed her hair.

"Here," said my conductor on entering, "is one of the friends of the marquis."

Annoyed, doubtless, at having her thoughts disturbed, the

lady replied in an imperious voice, and without bothering to turn round: "Take him for a walk, Jacquot, what do you expect me to do with him?"

"This," I cried, "is a charming welcome!"

Hearing my voice the lady, who was none other than my beautiful unknown, jumped up, and giving way to surprise and unexpected pleasure ran up and threw herself into my arms.

"I was thinking of you," she said, "and bitterly reproaching myself for refusing to allow you to accompany me here; it seemed that in leaving you I had forfeited the one happy day in my existence." She perceived, somewhat tardily, that our transports had been witnessed by my old guide. She thanked him for the prisoner he had brought and told him to go to the kitchen and order an excellent supper in which he could share; she added kindly, "I was short with you, my poor fellow, but you know how many causes I have for ill-humour and for sadness."

Hearing his mistress speak to him so, the rough peasant was so touched that he burst into tears. This was the same man who, fifteen minutes earlier, would willingly have shot me like a rabbit and buried me in a ditch.

My charming friend led me by endless corridors and stairways to the part of the castle where she lived. It was a round tower flanked by four smaller ones, wherein she had installed her *cabinet de toilette,* her library and her aviary. Whilst I was looking at the books she changed her riding-habit for a light robe, which made her more ravishing than ever. Looking at her I was intoxicated by her beauty, and surely all the philtres of the East have never exercised a power to touch it. She was a young girl, strong, graceful, and supple. In her one recognised the Cymric type which, in its liaison with the Celts, sometimes keeps its distinctive features. She had long black hair, with large eyes of the deepest blue. One could see the life flowing under her white and satin skin, and the slightest emotion tinted her cheeks with rose. Her splendid health had endowed her with charms in advance of her age. Nothing could be more perfect than her shoulders, her neck and her arms. Like all her race, her hands were remarkably small, and she had the foot of a child.

Upon my word ! I forgot I was a soldier of the Republic. I went over to the enemy and gave myself up without reserve to lively admiration.

"My God," I cried ecstatically, "how beautiful you are!"

"I am so glad," she replied, with her Breton ingenuity; "I was just thinking when you arrived that the moonlight had probably flattered me and that if you saw me in daylight you might not love me nor even recognise me."

Happily this too tender conversation was interrupted by a third party. It was Ursula, a peasant girl who strongly resembled the strapping highwaymen I had encountered on several unfortunate occasions. She was the cook, the maid, and, if need be, the page of the Chatelaine, who, whilst she was laying the table, told me that on several occasions she had behaved like a veritable Caesar. Looking once more upon that cheery countenance I seemed to recognise it.

"But, Ursula," I said to her, "were you not at Kerzu this morning?"

"It wasn't I," replied the girl, "it was my brother."

"That's good," replied her mistress, "you are going to make our guest think he has fallen into a robbers' cave."

Ursula's laughter being capable of giving credence to this remark, my friend explained that her friends, having no tax collectors, like the Republic, had adopted the expedient of seizing the money as soon as it had been collected.

To attain this object it sufficed to keep oneself carefully informed of the movements of the public funds, as they were transported from one spot to another, by coaches or otherwise. A troop of men then intercepted them, and for a commission paid them into the Treasury of the Western Royalists. The money thus levied was legitimately recovered, since a usurping government had extorted it from the people in order to use it against the good cause. The various occurrences which had taken place since yesterday had left me little time for reflection; but I had nevertheless understood that, from a political standpoint, my adventure was not brilliant. I resolved therefore to keep off the subject; I asked for no information whatsoever for fear of unpleasant revelations; besides I was certain that anything I might learn would never equal what I could see. I did not even know my beautiful friend's name, and it was only by chance that I learnt from Ursula that she was called Mademoiselle Nanine. As deductions were not denied me I deduced from this: firstly, that she was free to dispose of her heart; and, secondly, that despite her education and distinguished manners, she was not of the aristocracy. This latter guess, however, seemed risky, when I recollected that I had once seen a charming young person at the Palais Royal[1] who was not a stranger to one of the noblest families in Europe, and who called herself Pamela. A somewhat curious scene dissipated my doubts.

Whilst Ursula hustled about, her mistress asked her what she thought of me.

"But," replied the girl maliciously, "I am like Mademoiselle, I find the gentleman good-looking."

"Well, my child," replied Nanine, "you will like him more when you know that he had my two cousins set free yesterday, when they were about to be shot."

"My God! my God! How grateful I am to you!" cried the young peasant-girl; and going down on her knees she crossed her arms over her large bosom, and started to pray with a fervour which deeply moved me. Then, dragging herself to me she took my hands and wanted to kiss them. I hastened to lift her up, and kissing her, told her she was a good and worthy girl who well merited the affection which her mistress had

1. The Palais Royal was at that time the rendezvous of the gay set and its appendages.

for her. Nanine, who without thinking had given away her identity, was touched to tears on seeing how I appreciated in her the qualities which inspired her servants to so much tender devotion.

Ursula had got it into her Breton head that a banquet was necessary to celebrate so great a day, with the consequence that she served supper at the hour when one usually holds *Réveillon*.[2]

It is true that she had employed the time marvellously well, she had raided the marquis' aviary and had transformed his tame quails into roast ones large as chickens. The grey parrot himself would not have escaped had he been less thin, and above all, had he not cried out:

"Good morning, my dear!" on seeing her, quite like a Christian.

To excite my appetite the cook explained to me the origin of the dishes, or rather the traditions attaching to them. I only remember that she served a lamb which had been nourished in a field watered by the well of Saint Yvonne, which guaranteed its absolute perfection. As to the precious wines which she had brought up from some secret cellar, she had recourse to my science in order to decipher the labels which were their title deeds. Nanine and I little deserved all this abundance; we only drank water, but we had to break the habit this time to satisfy Ursula, and touched glasses in the old fashioned manner whilst wishing luck to our love affairs.

Never was a meal gayer, more animated or the scene of tenderer outbursts. The dangers which menace lovers of our age, left alone in the middle of the night to a prolonged *tête-à-tête,* were becoming more and more imminent when suddenly Jacquot ran in, in fright, crying, "Madame, the Blues![3] The Blues are here!"

---

2. Supper on Christmas Eve after the Midnight Mass.
3. Synonym for the soldiers of the Republic. The Royalist partisans being known as *The Whites*.

He opened a window, and we saw in the moonlight a crowd of soldiers who were throwing bundles of bushwood into the ditches in order to cross them, and who were already climbing the outer walls of the castle.

"Come on, then," said Nanine, without showing the slightest emotion, "we must yield to bad luck, until the time comes to get our own back."

She asked Jacquot whether he had bolted the doors on the staircase, and on his replying in the affirmative assured me that we had time to get ready. She gave her orders to the old peasant, who left at once; she put on her riding-habit, threw some compromising papers on the fire, took some family jewels, and told Ursula to open when the soldiers came, to tell their leader that she was at Quimper and that the Marquis had left the day before. She promised her that, within two hours, help of some kind would arrive; and we left, carrying a candle each to light us. I have seen generals of armies give orders with the enemy before them, and I can guarantee that not one showed more *sang-froid* or intelligence than that young girl. The peril threatening her was nevertheless imminent; for the vaults of the castle still contained arms and powder; and the Military Commission would have shown no mercy to the guardian of these munitions of war if, as was quite possible, they were discovered.

A hidden door led us to a spiral staircase, which led to the very foundations of the old manor. There we entered a narrow gallery like those one finds in mines. We followed it for so long a time that I was convinced it must come out in the open country. In effect, we emerged in a thick wood outside the park. Two fine horses had been brought there by the faithful Jacquot; we mounted them in silence and left at a gallop.

A few moments later we were speeding across the downs, the sound of our hoof-beats deadened by the turf. The moonlight, so propitious the night before by the cathedral, protected our flight by directing our course towards the middle of this desert; but when it paled before the light of dawn it took away again the happiness which it had brought. As the moon disappeared we arrived, by a sunken road, at the high road. Nanine stopped and said: "Dear friend, you are now safe! God is my witness that my only fear was that you should be gravely compromised by the love you have for me. I must now think of poor Ursula. I have some relatives near by, who have made their peace with the Republic; I shall send them to her aid. I do not know what will become of me; perhaps I had better go to Paris like my cousins. Whatever happens I shall never forget you. Take this paper, it indicates a hiding place I have made in the park. If you have no news of me within a year, open it, it is my *dot* and will be my heritage." We kissed like friends destined never to meet again, and she left me for ever.

Half an hour later I was at Châteaulin. I handed my horse to an inn-keeper who knew it, and went to Port-Launay, where I boarded a boat about to go down the river and cross the Brest roadstead. I eventually reached the town, sad and heart-broken, and recommending to the devil the politics which separated me from my dear friend, because she was *white* and I was, and intended to remain, *blue*.

(From 1801-1802 M. de Tonnes was detached for Serv-ice in the West Indies.)

Caribbean Pirates

Yellow fever had carried off three-quarters of the troops in Martinique. When war with England recommenced, with the rupture of the treaty of Amiens, there remained eight hundred men including those in hospital.

As chief of staff I had the sad duty of handing the commander every morning a list of the losses during the last twenty-four hours, and of telling him which young and promising officer had unexpectedly died during the night, leaving his service in disorder and us without means to carry it on. Overcome by the responsibility the admiral could not sleep, and his worry was so great that his health was gravely compromised. One morning when I came to make my report he asked me whether I still knew many people in Paris.

"Nobody," I replied, "those I knew are dead."

"So," he answered, "you could stay there forty-eight hours, and leave again without being delayed by your acquaintances, your interests, or your pleasure? Very good," he said, when I gave him the assurance, "I will entrust you with a secret mission which concerns my honour and my life, you will leave tomorrow at dawn."

He told me that he had written countless times to ask for aid, and that having received no reply he could only suppose that he was being deliberately abandoned. He attributed this resolve to the minister, who saw in him a probable successor; and in effect, every time there was question of a change, the sailors named the admiral as being the best minister the First Consul could choose. In the last ditch, he was forced to apply elsewhere, and it was for this reason that he had decided on my departure.

An hour later I handed in my papers to the admiral; he granted me leave, ostensibly to continue my map-making in the hills of the Cavastirra; he handed me his signed letter and his instructions; I took a passport as a doctor, and exchanged my uniform for a black suit and my plumed hat for a grey felt. I added a pair of large gold spectacles which I still use when I wish to see long distances; at nightfall a post boat took me to the roadstead of St. Pierre, where I found an American vessel, a neutral, whose captain was awaiting me as a desirable passenger.

The thirtieth day out, as I was just finishing my last volume of Shakespeare, the ship entered the Gironde after an excellent crossing. I landed at Bordeaux and soon arrived in Paris. The following day I was introduced to a charming lady, living in the Rue du Bac, and who was a friend of the admiral, proved by the vicissitudes of the Revolution. She was the Ariel destined to guide me, and she turned to the task with untiring kindness; she overcame all obstacles, and leading me by the hand, she presented me to two great ladies and three other personages, to whom I handed the pressing letters of which I was the bearer.

I received a kindly welcome everywhere, and found much affection and esteem for the admiral, whose situation aroused the greatest interest. Nobody hesitated an instant to act in his favour, and the third day I received the positive assurance that two frigates, then being fitted for sea, would embark troops and war material for Martinique without delay. Two others would follow at a short interval, and this would continue until the isle was in a position to resist the enemy. I wrote the admiral a three-page letter to inform him of the complete success of my mission; my enigmatic recital was taken to him by a young woman, who had no idea what she was doing.

During forty days fortune never ceased to smile upon me, and I succeeded in carrying through my duty beyond my wildest hopes; but it was scarcely accomplished than fortune abandoned me, and I met with the greatest misadventures.

On my return to Bordeaux I learnt that the ship on which I had counted could not leave before a month, and that there was no other. It was a most unfortunate mishap, for the admiral's impatience was so great that it might endanger his life, and in that case all was lost. I was in the greatest anxiety, when I was told that an American vessel calling at La Rochelle was leaving for St. Thomas, one of the Northern Antilles; I leaped into a tumbledown trap, determined to profit by this unique opportunity. The journey was long, boring, and tiring, but I arrived at length. I found the captain in a *café* smoking a cigar and drinking grog, like a real American, but his appearance did not confirm these national characteristics. Instead of a large bony man with yellow hair and a white skin, I saw a regular nigger, whose tanned skin was half yellow and black, and his locks a mixture of wool and horsehair. Otherwise he was tall and strong, and carried a most pronounced air of effrontery and arrogance; his English costume was irreproachable.

"*Monsieur,*" he said, "my ship is not equipped to carry passengers, and I have already refused several, but your quality as doctor assures you my goodwill. I should even be greatly obliged to you if, during the voyage, you can rid me of a tertiary fever which torments me, and which no West Indian sorcerer has been able to cure."

I did not promise to succeed where they had failed; I merely undertook to do my best. This hope and doubtless also the tone of superiority which the habit of command had given me, gained me a better welcome from the captain than I had at first expected. However, his cast of countenance did not speak in his favour, and, to decide me to make up my mind, it needed no less than his promise to be at St. Thomas the twenty-eighth day of our crossing, otherwise he renounced all claim to my passage money. The hope of so short a voyage took my fancy, and two hours later a boat took me aboard the American ship, which had already hauled out of port and only awaited the tide to set sail. Her appearance was even less edifying than that of her captain. Instead of carrying a band of red or yellow paint and being straight masted like an honest merchantman, she was painted black all over and had her masts stepped back with a blustering air resembling that of the pirates of Landerneau river. It was even worse when, arriving on deck, I could appreciate the hangdog look of a dozen large rascals composing the crew, and who appeared to represent every variety of the human race which most nearly approached the animal. The good idea occurred to me that I had better get out of this wasps' nest, but a false pride held me, and I went on board.

The captain welcomed me most warmly, and gave me a cabin resembling his own, the only other on the level of the quarter-deck. When I arrived he was much preoccupied by a task with which he did not seem familiar, and which in no way diminished my mistrust. He was mounting two bronze carronades which he had bought, he said, at La Rochelle, having learnt that American ships, in spite of their neutrality, were visited by the English cruisers, and that he wished to circumvent this oppressive measure by his superior sailing qualities, and if necessary by his artillery. As a French officer I could not blame this decision. Only, when he showed me a twelve-pounder mounted forward, I remarked it was better placed to fire on a ship in flight than to defend his own vessel. He agreed, and excused himself on the ground that there was no better place to put it. This man, who was as ignorant as a plantation negro, was nevertheless gifted with any amount of common sense and perspicacity, and he had even greater cunning. He saw clearly that his clumsy method of mounting his carronades (purposely perhaps), irritated me to the last degree.

"Doctor," he said, "you have perhaps seen them mounted in a battery, try to remember and give me your advice."

I let myself be taken in by this flattery, and thoroughly persuaded that these guns, like those I had served throughout my life, would be used against the English only, I saw to it that they were mounted in perfect style. Captain Lazare could not contain himself for joy, and his crew considered themselves invincible with such a magnificent armament.

The following day before noon the sextants were brought up to take the sun, and the same scene was repeated. I was obliged willy-nilly to do the necessary myself, to control the calculations of the second officer, and to verify the course in reference to the speed of the ship. The second officer, who was blind in one eye, scarred, lame, and whom I had taken for an idiot, because he never opened his mouth, turned out to be an experienced sailor. I gave him this credit, and the captain was as proud as punch. If it be thought that I was too familiar with people whose character I strongly suspected, I would remark that we were then in the neighbourhood of the Sorlingues and that it was a question of avoiding their reefs, so sadly famous for shipwreck, without worrying so much about the company I was in, as the danger of getting off our course and going to pieces on the granite rocks of this terrible archipelago.

I must, however, admit that my good offices, coupled with my bad habit of living amongst honest people, threw me momentarily into great perplexity. I had bought a gold watch with a second hand from Lépine in Paris, and had had it modestly silverplated. I used it to determine the longitude of the ship by the difference with the meridian. Catching sight of it the captain's eye lit up with envy; had it not been hanging from my neck, I doubt if I should ever had seen it back again. He offered me any price I cared to name for it. I refused to sell, but prudently gave him to understand that on our arrival I might let him have it, and that in the meantime I would willingly use it to help his navigation.

"Excuse me," he said, coming back an instant later, "I am like a child which wants everything it sees. Look," he added, opening a large box, "here are many more watches than I shall ever need; there are eleven, all fine ones, but they do not possess the qualities of yours."

"What use then is all this jewellery to you?" I asked him.

He remained uncertain for a moment as to whether he could speak frankly, then making up his mind he told me:

"On the bluffs of Port-au-Prince there is an old hut where lives an old negress—free by birth," he added; "she is my mother; she nourished me for fifteen years with what she could spare from her poverty. When it was fine, she could tell by the sun the time for work, the only thing which interested us! But when it rained (and it rains half the year on the bluffs) she used to say: 'Ah, if only I had a watch!' On leaving her I swore to bring her one—no, a dozen—and I am not far off the total."

I reflected that mine would gratify this *idée fixe,* and decided that it should excite his cupidity as little as possible. The human heart is a curious thing! This man, who was genuinely affected at the thought of his mother, had undoubtedly stolen, probably by force, the eleven watches he had, and had seriously considered rounding off the dozen by adding mine to the collection. Remarking that I had no pride—I, a doctor, who could mount carronades like an officer of artillery, and take the high hand like a ship's captain—he had abandoned his role of American gentleman and had confessed that he was a mulatto from Saint Domingo plying the seas, probably as a pirate. The final proof was not long in coming.

The brig was sailing on a calm sea before a light and steady breeze which made her slip over the water.

"Well, doctor," said the captain, "I hope you like my ship, she's a real Bermudan, built of cedar, you'll not see her like in Europe."

"That's true," I replied, "but where did you take her?"

"Did I say that I had taken her?" he replied quickly. "Bah!"

he added, "since you've guessed it, I may as well admit it: here's the story." He took a stool and told me the following story, which I will abridge.

THE ACCOUNT

"We were a collection of rogues at Port-au-Prince, living willingly at the expense of others. What else is there to do when one is a free mulatto? One cannot work like a negro without degrading oneself; one cannot live like a white man because one hasn't a sou to one's name; one can only become a thief. But when three years ago the French came they spoilt our business and we decided to quit. A Spanish ship, laden, was in the roadstead ready to leave the following morning; we boarded her that night, ten of us; the crew thought it wiser not to defend themselves; we told them to take our boats back, and being masters of the brig and a rich cargo, we set sail for St. Thomas where we sold our prize, making certain sacrifices in order to soothe the scrupulous consciences of the local authorities. The business was so successful that I was encouraged to undertake others similar for my own account, which I did, without experiencing any difficulty. But the small ships, with which I was obliged to content myself, were so unsuited to the needs of piracy, that we had to perform extraordinary deeds of courage and cunning to make ends meet. I dreamt unceasingly of a ship like this, but despaired of the possibility of acquiring one. My good angel, however, decided not to let me die without giving me this satisfaction.

"In Hamburg I met some Irish refugees, who were returning in all haste to Dublin to take part in a revolution, which was about to break out. This seemed to me a good opportunity to fish in troubled waters. I took a cargo at a low price, for a respectable firm whose name would serve me as passport and recommendation, and I left with a rotten brig which I hoped to sell at a profit.

"On reaching Saint George's Channel, which as you know separates Ireland from England, not a single coastguard did we come across. The armed ships were in port, stationed along the quays to defend the marine establishments against an incursion by the rebels, who were rising everywhere. In the evening, to my great astonishment, the country was lit by thousands of beacons, and the echoes resounded to shouts of joy. I thought, in my innocence, that the local calendar had advanced the *fête* of St. John, which is our great day in Saint-Domingo. In fact it was quite another matter—the commemoration by the Irish of the 14th of July 1789, the anniversary of the French Revolution, and the deliverance of enslaved peoples. We were so enthusiastic, that for a little more we would have sacrificed ourselves for the liberty of Ireland! However, on the way I did some good business. A ship from Ostend had been charged to deliver a consignment of pike-heads to the rebels; arms which would suffice, so it was said, to reconquer liberty; but the captain was much worried about his cargo, which rendered him liable to be hanged by the speedy justice of England. I proposed to take it off his hands, undertaking to deliver it to the parties interested; he agreed, and it is one of the best bargains I have ever made. I resold it in detail at unheard of prices.

"I found Dublin in confusion. There was no guard-ship, and one entered the port as easily as a church; the navy, and the garrison, had other things to do but look for contraband: eighty thousand peasants were converging on the town from all directions, and the Lord-Lieutenant did not know where to turn. I handed my cargo to my consignees, who gave me discharge but put off its delivery until the morrow. Whilst I was looking around to find a ship which might suit me, one came to anchor alongside, so close that a plank sufficed to pass from one ship to the other. Imagine my joy when I saw she was a beautiful Bermudan brig, the very object of my dreams, the one you see here; she had evidently been sent me by Providence. We welcomed the crew like brothers, and two hours later we went ashore together arm-in-arm, to assist in the overthrow of English Government in Ireland.

"You doubtless imagine, doctor, and with good reason, that a filibuster like myself only thinks about the profits of his honest profession. Well! I swear that I forgot not only my own interests but even my coveted brig, when I found myself in St. James's Street, in the middle of that passionate crowd ; shouting, bawling, gesticulating, and calling down Divine justice on their oppressors. Yes, for two hours I was dominated by the same sentiment as all those people, I felt their exaltation, and even their fury. If I returned to my senses it was the sad sight of the people's excesses which did it.

"The leader of the insurrection was named Robert Emmett. He was a young lawyer, good looking, full of talent, which he employed to defend the poor and the Catholics, who were the victims of religious or political hatred. His enemies themselves esteemed him, for they had more than once experienced his generosity. He had but one fault, his chivalrous character; which rendered him incapable of directing a popular uprising, filled with hatred and the lust of vengeance like revolted slaves.

"At the signal of a shot, which he fired from a window, three rockets replied, and were welcomed by hurrahs loud enough to kill the birds in the sky. Immediately this immense multitude of men formed themselves in a dense column and marched against the enemy. It was a fine sight, this great population rising in mass to affirm its rights and to reconquer them; I thought to witness something like the great scenes of your own revolution which, after all, has made you a free people and a great nation. I was out of my reckoning and my hopes were short-lived.

"There were three things to do: blockade the barracks, where eighteen hundred English soldiers were shut up, and who would willingly have sold or handed over their muskets in exchange for their lives; capture the Lord-Lieutenant, who represented the English Government, and hold him as a hostage; attack and capture the castle, derisively known as the Pigeon House; it is a poor fortress capable of holding four men and a corporal, but which attracted the uprising like the Bastille: for the best of the Irish leaders had been tortured there.

"The distances being considerable, at least two hours were needed to finish with England. But the column had scarcely made a hundred paces when it was held up by a tumult, which was at first taken for the appearance of English troops on its flank. It was simply a dragoon orderly who had been seen in a side street; they tried to arrest him but he only galloped the faster, and they fired at him without hitting. Thereupon two or three thousand men started in pursuit, leaving their ranks and throwing everything into disorder, since not one knew the reason of the hubbub. When it was explained, half an hour had been lost by this ridiculous event.

"A manufacturer named Clark had learnt the secret of the undertaking from his workmen: to claim the merit of having discovered it, he mounted and went to the castle. On his return he fell into the midst of those he had betrayed; he tried to escape; he was pursued, and before he had been arrested and condemned to death another half hour had been lost.

"Finally the column formed again and continued its route, but its confidence was no longer so firm as at the start. It seemed to me that although quite white, all the lot had vanished into thin air like niggers. When I asked them if they had no soldiers among them they replied that they had all been hanged; when I remarked that they should not have allowed them to be hanged, I was assured that there was no means of doing so because the English were always the cleverer, and the more persistent, and ended by being the stronger. 'In consequence,' they added, 'every revolution in Ireland is nothing but a stroke of desperation.' That looked bad, and I determined to keep my crew in hand in order to be able to go about my own business and to renounce my role of amateur revolutionary. The necessity of this was proved a few paces further on. A guard-house occupied by some twenty soldiers was on our line of march. Instead of asking them to drink the people's health, they demanded their arms; they said, rightly, that they could not give them up; we insisted, they refused; we menaced, they ran indoors, and while we beat down the door, they disappeared by another issue giving on a neighbouring street. The march had been delayed another half hour. I was boiling with impatience.

"Suddenly a state coach appeared at the tail of the column, driven by an English coachman in his official peruke, and accompanied by a lackey in full dress livery. By an incredible lunacy, instead of getting away from this crowd of armed men at top speed, they drove into it as though to brave it and make their way by force. Furious cries came from every quarter:— 'He's the Lord-Lieutenant! No, it's the Lord Chief Justice! Yes, it's the Lord Chief Justice. Yes, it's him! Death to him! Kill! Kill!' Immediately twenty pikes were plunged into the carriage and pulled out stained with blood. Lord Kilvarden and his nephew were assassinated in this manner! Lord Kilvarden's daughter, a poor child of scarcely fifteen years, distracted, mad with horror and terror, threw herself into the midst of the murderers, who opened their ranks to let her pass. The sight of her excited the deepest pity, and changed what seemed implacable anger into compassion. Emmett, on learning of this massacre, cursed the cause to which he had consecrated his life and, in his indignation, thinking it dishonoured, he abandoned it and left the town immediately to show that he separated himself from the assassins.

"I followed this example and escorted by my men I reached the harbour which was still deserted. The watchman of my ship had made such a night of it with the watchman of the Bermudan that the latter was dead drunk. I distributed my crew between the two ships and we made the open without the slightest challenge. A few minutes later we were under sail descending St. George's Channel towards the open sea. All along the Irish coast we could make out troops of armed men going to Dublin to join the revolution, of whose unfortunate outcome we had just been witnesses. Our voyage was lucky and we reached the Spanish coast without incident. A friend of mine helped me to sell the two cargoes and my old ship. I kept the Bermuda brig, which suited my purposes, and to find guns I was forced to go to La Rochelle. It is to that trip that I owe the pleasure of your acquaintance, doctor."

* * * * * * * *

Parbleu! I said to myself, I could have done without it; but confined myself to asking the captain what his plans were.

"They are very simple," he answered, "I shall take three prizes, it is enough for my modest needs; afterwards we shall sail direct to Saint Thomas; I shall sell my ship and her cargo of cognac, which is very valuable in any country of the world; I shall give my good men their shares; I shall also give you yours, doctor, for your service at sea and for having cured me of the fever. I shall then go to the United States, where I shall set up as a ships' chandler and become an honest merchant. There now!" he added on finishing, "I trust you approve my plan of campaign?"

"I do," I replied, "if you carry it through the other way about." He took this for a joke: it was sound advice as events turned out.

"A sail!" called the lookout.

In a minute the captain was in the cross-trees with his telescope. The ship sighted was very far away, and was only visible because she lay in the path of the setting sun. The brig took her in chase; and as I could not prevent it, I went to bed. At daylight a cannon shot informed me that we had come up with the unhappy ship. I turned over and went to sleep again to avoid unpleasant reflections. On awaking I found the deck littered with cases, trunks, and barrels, brought from the prize, and which were to be shared up with the most scrupulous equity, as though they constituted a perfectly legitimate profit. The pillaged owners had been shut in their own hold and four men from our crew had been charged to take the captured ship to Spain, and hand her over to the faithful friend aforementioned. Captain Lazare recounted me this wonderful feat with great excitement, albeit it had nearly cost him his life. When they were manning the prize, a young passenger, furious at the treatment he had received, had revolted, and seizing a cutlass had loosed a blow at the captain which would have cut his head off had the cutlass not turned in his hand, which transformed the blow into an excellent bludgeon stroke. The culprit had been trussed up, taken aboard our ship, and thrown into the *lions' den*, a filthy sump, so-called because it was inhabited by enormous rats, so ferocious that they were reputed to have gnawed away the hook of a ship's anchor.

"Doctor," said the second officer to me in a whisper, "get the prisoner out of there or he'll be dead to-morrow morning."

I said immediately to the captain, that since he had offered me my share in the prize I had the right to ask him for it, and that I asked him to give me the prisoner on parole as an officer prisoner of war. He swore by all his gods that he ought to execute a rogue who had committed an act of hostility contrary to international law when his flag was hauled down.

On hearing a pirate calling this great principle to witness I could not help laughing. The captain, satisfied with his success, calmed down, and finally gave me the key to the padlock of the *lions' den*. The second officer helped me release the unhappy prisoner from that appalling place. He was a fine young man, having a most distinguished bearing, speaking perfect French, and whose clothes, despite their tears, announced the English gentleman. I cut the ropes which bound him with the aid of a dagger twenty inches long which I always carried on me, and which the crew regarded with surprise and admiration, only half persuaded that it was a surgical instrument, as I took pains to inform them it was.

The captive I had delivered, on hearing of my ambiguous position and the danger of his own, decided to give his solemn promise to undertake nothing against the ship or her captain. His name was Robert Alan, and he had been born in Cork, like the unlucky Emmett, whose cousin and friend he was. He had shared his projects and was in despair at their failure. He told me that the chief of the conspiracy had rashly returned to Dublin. He had been arrested and brought before a Royal Commission which had condemned him to death for high treason. In an eloquent speech, made to his judges after his sentence, he was silent as to his own case and only defended Ireland against her oppressors. He was executed amidst the lamentations of the crowd, praying fervently for the peace of his soul.

Condemned to death as an accomplice, Alan succeeded, after running the greatest risks, in reaching an American vessel which was under sail, and had thought himself at last in safety when the pirate boarded them. His attempts at resistance not having been supported by his companions, had nearly been fatal to him.

At daybreak a large ship was sighted and we gave chase. A cannon shot gave her the impression that she was pursued by an enemy warship and she stopped, hauling down a French flag which she had just hoisted.

"She's French," I said to the captain, "take care."

"Bah!" he replied, "I have seen many others at Saint Domingo! If I fall, doctor," he added, "take command of my brig and get away as best you can."

He leaped into his boat with seven men, leaving only one on board; he went alongside the vessel, on which appeared but three or four men, and since there was no sign of defence

I thought this unhappy success was assured. But suddenly the flag reappeared at the mizzen, and a hot fire sent bullets whistling even as far as us. A dozen fighters, sailors and passengers, charged the pirates, killed half of them on the quarter-deck and went after the others. The captain and the second officer took refuge in the shrouds. The first, wounded by a musket ball, fell into the sea and disappeared; the other threw himself into the sea and swam towards us.

The French ship, although free, still feared the pirate's guns and set sail without attempting reprisals, which would have given her a fine prize without firing a shot. The falling night shut her from our sight. The poor devil who was wrestling with the waves, and whom I expected to see disappear at any moment, caught hold of a chicken coop I had thrown overboard; he hung on until I could get the ship near him by means of the current; he was half drowned when we succeeded in fishing him out, and it needed several hours of hard work to bring him back to life.

I had not lost a moment in setting the brig's course for the Antilles. As soon as the half drowned man, who was called Jean-Pierre, had come to, he took service under me as though I was Captain Lazare, his defunct master. I told him that I considered the spoken will which had left me the brig as null and void, and that if we arrived at Martinique I would see that his rights as successor were regularised, since we knew nothing of his previous master. So fine a reward would have made an honest man of the devil himself; at the same time I am sure that he would have been just as devoted to me, merely in gratitude for having saved him from the sea. Accustomed as he was to the ship, he could get a pace out of her which I never could. He succeeded so well that on the twenty-fifth day we made our landfall at Martinique, and two hours later we sighted Vauclin head.

An English brig-of-war was cruising in Saint Lucie's channel, but she was to leeward and could not bar our access to the island. It was an important advantage by which I hastened to profit, for at any cost we had to avoid falling into the hands of the English, in order to preserve the lives of my companions, one of whom was already condemned as a traitor, in his quality as an Irish rebel, whereas the two others would undoubtedly be considered as pirates.

As for me, although I was innocent, it would have been extremely difficult for me to prove it, had I been taken in command of a ship stolen in the port of Dublin, and carrying on the profession of sea-rover. Happily I had fallen on a coast I knew, and which I had even charted. I rounded the long peninsula of the Tartane, and made the port of La Trinité, the only one in Cavesterre which possesses a town, a fort, a garrison, and batteries affording a crossfire. I hoisted the tricolour, and a gunshot brought a pilot aboard, who took us in and anchored us almost ashore at the further end of the basin.

A mounted officer examined us from the bank. It was Colonel Miany, who commanded on this coast and who was greatly astonished to see me land when he supposed me to be at Fort-de-France, where he sent me his reports. I confined myself to remarking that I had just finished a very tiring trip about which I was not free to speak. I introduced Robert Alan, and asked him to look after my ship and her captain.

After a copious lunch which he gave us and which was most welcome, we mounted, and amidst the finest of tropical scenery we arrived, Alan and I, at the town of Lamantin, receiving everywhere the greatest attention. A boat took us to Fort-de-France, where we disembarked at midnight.

The commander-in-chief was not yet in bed. I gave him the report of my mission, the success of which caused him the greatest satisfaction, and he thanked me heartily. The following night two frigates carrying troops, guns, and munitions of war entered the harbour, escaping the English cruisers which, misled by false information, had gone to intercept them off Guadaloupe. The frigates re-sailed within twenty-four hours, taking with them Robert Alan, who could not have found a better opportunity to get to France. At my request, the Admiral gave him a commission as a French officer, to cover him in the event of trouble. Sailors and a pilot were sent to our ship to take her to St. Pierre, where the new captain sold his precious cargo of cognac, not without making certain presents, which were appreciated as such nectar merits. I succeeded in regularising the position and the ownership of the captain, who left for the United States full of gratitude for the services I had rendered him, and resolved, so he told me, to efface the sins of his past life by the excellence of his future conduct.

The title of statistician which I have earned by sixty years of work, official or otherwise, impels me to put the result of my mission into figures. By its means France continued in possession of her fine colony of Martinique for five years longer: 1803-1809. I hasten to add that, in all this, my role was that of the fly on the coach horse, and that its success was due to the kindness, the easy access and the superior judgement of the men whom I succeeded in interesting in Paris. Besides I should have been greatly mistaken had I supposed, like the fly in the fable, "that *Messieurs les chevaux* would pay me for my trouble," for when the Admiral put in a demand in my favour to the Ministry for the Legion of Honour he received no reply. The object of my mission was certainly no recommendation so far as the Minister was concerned.

War in the West Indies

A people who once governed and civilised the then known world were firmly convinced that if one started off with the left foot foremost one had a bad journey. This must undoubtedly have happened to me when I left school for the army in 1792. Had I stepped out with my right foot, I should have gone with drums beating from victory to victory, conquering the finest countries in Europe: fruitful Belgium and fertile Germany, finding everywhere good wine, good lodging, kindly hosts and above all hostesses; and what hostesses! Mignon, Charlotte, Marguerite! Charming creatures with long plaits of golden hair and tender devoted hearts always compassionate for the soldier whether wounded, ill, or prisoner of war.

But that happiness was not reserved for me, for I had stepped out with my left foot. During twenty campaigns did I expiate this original fault, and submit to the double misfortunes of living in the most savage places under the most murderous climates, and having to fight the most vindictive and pitiless of enemies: the Chouans of the Morbihan, the Sectionairies of Toulon, the *Émigrés,* the Orange-men of Ireland, the negroes of Saint Domingo, and the English, such as the wicked passions of their statesmen had then made them.

The Kafir and Ashanti wars afford examples of the kind of war we had to wage. It was a war of ambushes, of surprise attacks by night, of spying, of treachery and barbarism. The wounded were finished off on the battlefield, the prisoners were massacred or, if they fell into the hands of the best of our enemies, they were sent to perish on the hulks at Portsmouth. The torch and the gibbet were added to the arms of war. Twenty-two towns in Saint Domingo were burnt, and I know not how many Irish leaders, or allies, or even officers in the French Service, perished miserably at the stake or in their cells from sudden death.

Terrible reprisals and the prodigious successes of our arms had somewhat abated the frantic cruelty of our enemies; and since Campo-Formio and the Peace of Amiens they had lost the hope of treating us like Poles in the suburbs of Praga, or the protestants on the day of Saint Bartholomew. Nevertheless the war retained its savage characteristics in the West Indies, as if it was not sufficient to kill one another, without adding thereto the sin of impoliteness. During two years on the southern coast of Martinique, of which I had the military command, I had English warships in sight, and often near enough to smell their powder, without ever having any other relations with them save those of musketry and cannon shot. The Spanish garrison of Melilla, who for five hundred years have lived at daggers drawn with the Moroccans who surround them, have to deal with enemies less harsh than the Christians who blockaded us. However, it must be admitted that they regarded us as revolutionaries, that is, people of the same kidney as the famous men of the English Republic, who were dug up and re-interred at the foot of the gibbet on the restoration of the Stuarts.

A war of cunning and disorder not succeeding as Sir Samuel Hood, who commanded the enemy squadron, desired, he conceived a plan during the endless boredom of the blockade, which in default of utility was effective by its originality and hardihood: it was to occupy and fortify the Diamond; but before speaking of this undertaking it is necessary to know the rock which was its objective. Martinique ends to the south-west in a long peninsula which lies between the bay of Fort-de-France and the Channel of Sainte Lucie. It is a solid mass, formed by eight volcanoes joined one to the other, the united area of which is about eighty thousand metres in circumference. The highest of these hills, known as the Great Morne, advances southward into the rough seas of the Channel, and forms an enormous pyramidal promontory, steepened by the waters, covered with woods on its landward side and thrusting its bald head upwards to a height of more than fifteen hundred feet, shaded only by two cabbage palms inviting the lightning.

At eight hundred metres from the Great Morne, in the middle of the tossing waters of the Channel, rises a vast and picturesque rock, steep on every side, and all the more unapproachable in that it is surrounded by violent and perpetual surf. It is called the Diamond, a name doubtless derived from its prismatic shape which gives to the summit the appearance of a pyramid with four walls. Its height is almost equal to its diameter and is at least three hundred metres. It is surrounded by a cliff, vertical or inclined towards the sea which has eaten away the base, and the slopes on the summit do not extend for more than one quarter of its height; the ridges which separate them, and join at the topmost point, give this rock the appearance of a colossal crystallisation. On each face there are a dozen fissures or crevices which serve as a refuge for thousands of sea birds, and when a ship passes near a cloud of seagulls arises from the summit, filling the air with the strident clamour of their voices.

Sir Samuel Hood who, in order to intercept our arrivals from Europe, kept his vessels ceaselessly in the Channel of Sainte Lucie, passed and repassed daily before the Diamond rock. He resolved to take possession of it, and use it to forward his blockade by installing a lookout who would signal the ships making land to windward of Martinique. To assure a better welcome for his plan in London he exaggerated the results and described as a new Gibraltar the fortress he was about to build on this sterile rock, which was almost unapproachable and hitherto unknown. Whilst setting down his undertaking as nothing more than a piece of bluster, it would be unjust not to recognise that the works he erected were done with a master's hand, and that he overcame the difficulties with a high intelligence and a rare activity.

In the month of January 1804, when the season of regular winds renders the sea calm and gives all security for navigation, detachments of English sailors were landed on the Diamond. This extremely dangerous landing, on a cornice at the foot of the eastern face, was facilitated by a mobile landing stage made of timber. A vast anfractuosity opened above, and was enlarged by a mine; he built at the further end a sort of small fort which was only accessible by a very steep slope, and designed to offer a last refuge to the garrison.

Forward and below this, they built two circular batteries armed with twenty-four-pounders. Entrenchments defended the entrance to several lateral caves, which could only be entered by narrow paths running along the flank of the rock. The barracks and storehouses were established there. The only path to the top of the rock led to the main cave; at half distance it was cut by a platform, on which they had mounted a heavy gun, whose fire took the approaches in enfilade. From there, rope ladders allowed the sailors to reach the summit of the Diamond. But it was such a terrible undertaking that a French officer, who, in the heat of combat, had first climbed this cliff when the Diamond was taken in 1805, dared not trust himself to repeat the feat a few months later. The greatest merit of these daring and complicated works was the lookout established on top of the rock.

There was there a signal mast and, which is very remarkable, two eighteen-pounders to back it up. To haul them to such a height the cleverest and most difficult manoeuvres had been needed. The Commodore had succeeded in getting so close to the rock as to be able almost to touch it when he was to leeward; he had then thrown grapnels and anchors into the caves, which opened at different heights, and by means of these fulcrums, blocks and tackle had enabled the two guns to be hauled to the top of the Diamond. Lookout men were posted there to warn the cruisers of the approach of any ship to windward of the Channel; and a garrison of gunners and marines manned the lower batteries, living in the caves which communicated with them.

By means of my telescope I followed the progress of these works, and gave an account thereof to the commander-in-chief. I appreciated them at their useful value, and I offered the opinion that a brig-of-war sailing in the Channel would render better service. I described the undertaking as a vast bluff, and the Admiral used the expression in his official despatches. The proof that it was no more lay in the fact that our ships continued to arrive at Fort-de-France with no more difficulty than heretofore. But in London the Diamond became a triumphal monument. The hundred mouths of the press proclaimed it as a miracle, and published a series of coloured views of the rock from all its aspects, and all more or less false.

Many fabulous tales had been told about this savage spot. I am afraid I cannot add to them, but I do owe to the Diamond the most annoying and idiotic military venture of my lifetime. I will relate it in all humility, as a sad example of human vicissitude.

The commodore, having victualled and garrisoned his rock, went to Antigua to repair some of the ravages caused by so long a blockade, and the other ships of his squadron profited by his absence to sample the pleasures of a call at Sainte Lucie. There being no enemy left I returned to Fort-de-France and to my duties as Chief of Staff. My studies were not of long duration and the calm was soon troubled by a violent squall.

On the 3rd May 1804, a day of ill-omen, Colonel Miany called on me in great agitation, and taking me in his arms asked me whether I would forgive him for being the involuntary cause of my death. As he was extremely hotheaded I thought a duel must be in the wind, and told him that I would bear him no malice if the reason justified it. It was much worse than I imagined. The commander-in-chief had just sent for him and had told him peremptorily that he was to command an expedition destined to capture the Diamond rock by a night attack. This order presupposed that four heavy old port barges could row across the rapid current of Sainte Lucie's Channel and, despite a surf six feet high and the fire of ten twenty-four pounders, disembark forty soldiers, who would leap from their barges in the darkness on to a ledge eighteen inches broad, bordered by a rough sea twelve hundred feet deep at least.

Now, the admiral was aware of all these facts, for the sketches which I had sent him showed up the localities in great detail, as well as the works erected by the enemy. He had never uttered a doubt as to their accuracy, and besides, he could have checked them by means of a reconnaissance carried out by engineer officers. But he did not think it necessary to do so. He made so great a secret of his intention that that very morning, when I spoke to him as usual, he never said a word about it, and seemed much put out when Miany pointed out that my help was absolute necessary, nobody having studied this part of the island as I had, who had commanded it for three years.

All this seemed so peculiar to me, that I thought the admiral's sound judgement must have suffered the influence of some evil counsel. I asked Miany whether, when he received his orders, there was anybody present whom I could accuse of such a thing. He recollected having seen, standing aside and pretending not to listen, a small, ruddy, weasel-faced man, wearing his epaulettes on his chest, as the dandies of the old *régime* were wont to do. I recognised him at once; he was an *émigré,* an officer who had taken service in England in 1794 and who, when Admiral Jervis' squadron and the army commanded by Sir Charles Grey attacked Martinique, contributed most efficaciously towards the capitulation of General Rochambeau, by instigating the escalade of Fort Royal, a success which changed the nature of the attack of which Fort Bourbon had been the object, and which forced the latter to surrender forty-eight hours later.

The whole merit of this treachery reposed upon the knowledge of the place which he had acquired when under M. de Bonillé during the American War. He had been generously rewarded by the English, who gave him the lucrative post of Superintendent of Military works in Martinique. He exercised it until the day the colony was handed back to France, and he then obtained a better and certainly more honourable situation by presenting himself to the commander-in-chief in the guise of a repentant *émigré*.

In his favour was put forward his knowledge of matters and men; but he was above all welcomed for his interesting conversation, his easy-going character, his gift for raising a word of praise under all circumstances and his skill in all games of chance. It was said that he always won or lost to suit the circumstances. Like the old noblemen of his time, he possessed both wit and courage, only his wit was false, and his courage was at the disposal of the highest bidder. He was profoundly antipathetic to me, all the more because I suspected him of being in the English pay, whilst wearing a French uniform. The three generals to whom I had been *aide-de-camp* must have shared this opinion, for during seven years they had never invited him to their table, which was open daily to the officers of the army.

When Miany, who lived some distance away from us at the Trinity, heard this charming biography he at once thought that our plan had been sold to the enemy; and he believed it all the more when he learnt that since my return, the turncoat had made a trip to the Diamond on his own account. The Colonel swore that if ever he came across him he would cut him in two, and he was a man of his word.

We had scarcely an hour to make our preparations and our visits. Miany passed the time half with a solicitor and half with a confessor. I got rid of mine more promptly; I went to say goodbye to the charming women who had helped me when in trouble, and in the black silk apron of a pretty child of thirteen years I placed some hundred moidores, my entire fortune; I asked her to keep them for me and if I did not return to add them to her *dot*. I left the whole family in tears and praying for my safety.

It was much worse when I arrived at the embarkation point. This secret expedition was, I know not how, known to everybody, and half the town was there. The whites protested that we were being sent to be slaughtered and that the author of the plan was either a traitor or a madman. The coloured women sobbed, and after we had left the bank we could hear them for a long while. Captain Halgan, a distinguished naval officer, to whom the naval side of the expedition had been confided, told me that its promoter had come down to the port, but that having been advised of an unpleasant reception he had disappeared.

The conception of this expedition was so utterly mad that it was believed that by leaving at nightfall we could attack the enemy at daybreak. It turned out that, at three in the morning, we were scarcely half way, and that having merely passed the inland water of the bay of Fort Royal, we were in reality much less advanced than we seemed.

We called in at Mathurin's cove which, at Ramiers, is only separated from the islet by a narrow channel. Our crews, who were already fatigued, landed, and I raised some provisions for them from the commander of the fort. We were supposed to have with us a barge loaded with bread and wine, but she had gone astray and only joined us on the morrow. So that to my task of arranging the slaughter of some hundred picked men, officers, grenadiers, and sailors included, was added that of nourishing them, somehow or other, until their decease.

In the midst of these preoccupations I had the presence of mind to hail my old friend Parmentier, the fort's ordnance officer, who was perched in his stronghold some hundred and twenty feet above our heads. He clambered down three ladders, and gathering that I was in trouble, appeared before me equipped with his excellent short sabre and a pair of boarding pistols. I had him taken aboard the commander's boat with us, and it was to him that we owed the one solitary satisfaction our unhappy undertaking brought forth. Long before daylight we set out again. The course had become more difficult, but our halt had rested the men and everybody felt the better for it. We rowed for some ten to twelve leagues, and towards three o'clock we landed in Diamond Cove between the slopes of the Cross Hill on one side, and those of the Great Morne on the other. Behind the vast mass of the latter, at eighteen hundred metres from its base, rose the Diamond Rock.

The halt I had chosen had several advantages. It left us but two leagues to do to reach our objective, so that we might hope to get there without being overwhelmed by fatigue. We doubtless found fewer resources in this little cove than in the larger one, in which the town of Arlet is situated; but it would have been most unwise to put the men in touch with the inhabitants, who would have told them they were going to their death. Moreover I had a secret plan: to send Parmentier to the Great Morne in order to make certain that no traitorous warning of our approach be given to the enemy. I sent my friend off at once by a track, which turned the mountain, and led up its reverse slope to a spot facing the Diamond. Although he was only accompanied by a sergeant I had no further fear, such was my confidence in his courage and intelligence.

I had another inspiration which I will mention, in order to show that it is possible to do some little good, even in life's most precarious situations. Among the coves of Arlet we were in the midst of the country growing the finest coffee in the world, not excepting the Moka. I succeeded in making some, and distributed it to the entire troop, who had their fill of it. Halgan, become Vice-Admiral, State Councillor and Peer of France, still recollected this forty-four years after, and went into raptures over my excellent idea.

Darkness being a condition of our rash undertaking, we waited two hours after midnight before leaving the shore. As soon as we were outside the cove, and following the cliffs of the Great Morne to enter the channel of Sainte Lucie, our boats were lifted, rolled, and shaken roughly by the swell. Each stroke lost half its strength and efficacity. Nevertheless our progress was merely slackened, as long as we were under cover of the convex base of the Morne; but when we reached the furthest end of the long promontory, the current of the channel, that of the tropical Atlantic precipitated between the Antilles into the Gulf of Mexico (the Gulf Stream) arrayed itself against us like the giant Adamastor of the Cape of Storms. The sea's appearance suddenly altered; it seemed to boil, and to be animated by a disordered spirit.

Despite the complete absence of wind, it was as violently choppy as though we were over a reef. We were then in the deep and narrow channel between the Diamond Rock and the Great Morne; it had to be crossed, and its width did not exceed one third of a league. Desperate efforts to conquer the current enabled us to cover half this distance, and already we thought we had reached the rock when the sea which was breaking against it, enveloped us in surf, twisted the barges about, and thrust them into the middle of the current, which carried them away so quickly that in the twinkling of an eye we had lost sight of them.

"Oh, well," said Miany, "we'll attack alone! Carry on!"

But he had scarcely uttered the words than our boat, manned by ten strong oarsmen, was carried away like a skiff on the flood waters of the Seine or Loire. We were struck with consternation. None thought about the danger of our situation; all were dumbfounded by this sudden misfortune, at the moment we were about to reach the enemy. We had been near enough to distinguish the red glow of the lanterns lighting the batteries. The sound of our oars would have reached them had we not taken the precaution of muffling them. Besides the surf was deafening; its violence was such that no boat or barge could have come alongside the ledge where we were supposed to disembark, and which was only a few inches long; our boats would have been broken to pieces at the bottom of the cliff, and so one piece of bad luck preserved us from a greater, and one which would have been the last of our existence.

The waves which had come aboard in the confusion had wetted us to the skin, without, however, putting us in any great danger, and we soon regained our presence of mind; but the current had already carried us far into the gulf of Mexico; and when day dawned the sight of the mountains of Martinique, showing above the horizon, enabled me to estimate that we had drifted at least six leagues. I assured my companions that we had only to strike across the current for a few minutes to get out of it, and enter the backwater which lies parallel to it; my words were borne out, and we emerged into slack water. This was a great relief to us and a first gleam of hope.

Finally the sun scattered the mists which obstinately covered the sea, for in this latitude it is either day or night, there is neither dawn nor dusk. We searched anxiously for our lost barges. Our telescopes eventually picked them up far away, like black spots on the horizon, in the Gulf of Mexico. They were at least six leagues out to sea, un-decked, without sails, and manned by crews half dead with fatigue. I was desperate. My deadly fear was the arrival of an English cruiser, armed only with a few cannon, who would summon them with a megaphone, without approaching:

"Surrender or I sink you."

We fired primings, we sent up rockets, and burnt flares. Reluctantly the barges replied. But how many were they? We counted and recounted, but one was always missing. Had she sunk or was she lost in the Gulf? What would happen to the twenty-five men on board? If they succeeded in putting in at the Iles d'Aves, some ninety leagues away, the only nourishment they would find would be crabs and stinking seabirds' eggs; if they missed those islands, the pitiless current of the Gulf Stream would carry them to Florida, but the length of the route would oblige them to eat each other to live. We were terribly anxious, and the thought took away the joy of finding the others, whom we had thought were lost as well. The crews of the three barges plucked up courage on seeing our signals, and favoured by the mass of Martinique, which suspends the action of the current to leeward of the island, they rejoined us more rapidly than I expected.

Their cries of joy, when the junction was made, showed the affection the good fellows had for us, whom they had given up as lost.

It was high tide when we arrived at Arlet cove; we were all at the end of our strength, and despite the happiness of having escaped and reached the hoped-for land, we were unable to leave our thwarts and go ashore, we were too broken with fatigue. The rowers had their arms paralysed, or dislocated; and in the pinnace, where we had spent two days seated and half covered in sea-water, we were seized with such violent cramps that they wrung cries of agony from us. Halgan kept them all his life. To lessen the evil I turned doctor once more. I had the men rubbed with burning hot *tafia*[1] before large fires, which we found lighted on our return. This is how and why:

On leaving the coast for our unpleasant nocturnal expedition, our only expectation, if we returned, was a meal of bread and cheese. This had seemed to me a harsh ingratitude, and I had sent off the negroes of the neighbouring village to find, and purchase from the inhabitants of the *mornes,* some

---

1. An inferior rum.

Siamese pigs in order to give the sailors and grenadiers a treat. The inconvenience lay in the fact that a large number would be needed, as they are not much larger than cats, but they are perfectly good to eat. They succeeded in getting together three of four dozen, and when they saw us approaching the coast they had lit the fires to cook them. Their excellent smell and the sight of all this splendid fare contributed not a little, I think, towards reviving the courage of our companions in misfortune. At the same time I had another satisfaction of a higher order: this was the return of Parmentier, whom I had despatched the day before to investigate during the night any possible criminal relations with the enemy.

Following my instructions my old friend took, at dusk, a wooded path, narrow, winding, and often steep and difficult, which ran round the base of the Great Morne towards the sea and led to a platform facing the Diamond Rock. Parmentier and the sergeant accompanying him lay in ambush near this spot on a thick bed of dead leaves, without worrying whether they were sharing it with serpents or not. At eleven o'clock they heard voices, and the footsteps of two men who were making their way through the wood, and who passed close by them; one was a negro and the other an English sailor. As soon as these people had reached the platform they used their flints to light a candle, with which to light a signal lantern they had brought with them, and which was to show a red light. But they had not the time to carry out their plan. Attacked by the two gunners they were killed on the spot, before being able to use their arms. Parmentier had brought back their effects. It was evident that if these men had been able to make their signal to the garrison of the Diamond, our boats would have been blown out of the water when they were at four hundred yards range, and not one of us would have escaped to tell of the ambush whereby we perished.

We were all furious at the announcement of this discovery when the Colonel was informed that the post-boat was bringing a stranger alongside. Our troop being duly posted the boat was arrested and confiscated and the officer therein obliged to make himself known. It was the promoter of our expedition.

Recognising him Miany roared with fury, and without listening to the information that it was an officer sent by the admiral to get news of us, he called him two names, which have the same effect on a man as a piece of cold steel in his entrails. Then snatching the sabre which I had in my hand, he threw his own at his opponent, shouting to him to put himself on guard. Without crossing swords he instantly disarmed him with a wrist-stroke, and cut at his head with such violence that he would certainly have split it in two, had not the other stepped back so quickly that he fell full length on the sand ten paces away. The Colonel insisted, violently, on the combat being restarted. Whilst Halgan held him back, I led the unlucky paladin to his boat, advising him to tell the admiral that he had not seen us, and adding the warning to keep out of the Colonel's way if he valued his life.

The impression made by this unpleasant occurrence was quickly dissipated by an unexpected event, which overjoyed us. A sail, which we had made out approaching the coast for some time, was recognised as an American whaler, who had on board the twenty-five men of our lost boat. She had picked them up when they were sinking and had brought them back to us. It was a great satisfaction for us, as we believed them lost for ever. A fine reward was due to those who had saved them, and we promised to see they had it when next they touched at Saint Pierre or Fort-de-France. The commander-in-chief agreed to this, but they never came back to claim it.

We lodged our poor comrades as best we could, and I arranged for their return across the mountains to the islet at Ramiers, where a schooner would come to take them into port. As for us, our boats took us there without trouble by a calm sea. There are many sailors who make a pilgrimage to Notre-Dame de Recouvrance,[2] without having as much reason as we to praise her divine kindness.

An unpleasant duty remained—to give the commander-in-chief an account of our unfortunate expedition. Miany having been the leader I decided to abstain; but he was so unhappy at the idea that I had to support him. The admiral had been worried to death when he learnt that we had disappeared; nevertheless he feared we might burst into recriminations against a project which had nearly cost us our lives, and he received us entrenched behind his dignity; but Miany contented himself with a short, dry report and added that his state of mind and body did not permit of his saying more. As we were about to retire I called Parmentier, who placed a *caraïbe* basket at the admiral's feet.

"What is that?" he asked.

"The effects," I answered, "of the men posted on the coast to reveal our approach to the enemy."

"And the men?" he replied.

"They are dead," I said. And I made a gesture showing that justice had been done by my brave comrade. The admiral's expression relaxed, and going to his desk he took a handful of gold pieces which he held out to him; but the old soldier remained at the "Present," and only accepted when I told him that he could not refuse.

When we were in the street Miany wanted to take us, Halgan and I, to his adversary's house to oblige him to fight.

"Can't you see," he said, "that it is a conspiracy against the flag? What those fellows failed to do at Coblentz they will succeed in doing here; they need only take a contrite air and disguise themselves as valets to open the door of the antechamber, which leads them to the hall of the war council, and from there they can deliver us to the enemy."

---

2. The patron saint of sailors.

238

Although I was struck by the justice of his anger, I made the greatest efforts to stop him realising his bloodthirsty resolve. I thought I was doing a good action by saving the life of a man, whoever he might be, but I made a grave and fatal error. Four years later the same turncoat, whose life my pity had prolonged, renewed the treason which had led General Rochambeau to surrender to the English; and this time he caused the death, at two paces from me, of brave officers and men: Captains Trobillant and Allègre and Squadron-Leader Morancy. I escaped their fate but was seriously wounded. This disaster was only the commencement of a long run of misfortunes.

The fact is not generally known, and the Emperor should have been informed of it, but in the West Indies, the turncoats, who carried our cockade the better to deceive us, were in the English service and betrayed us at every turn, long before the explosion in the Rue Saint Nicaise, the battle of Leipsic, and the eve of Waterloo.

The loyal and trusting character of Admiral Villaret was known to our enemies, and they profited so well by it that they were perpetually deceiving and betraying us— and experience never served us for anything.

The arrival at Martinique of the fleet of twenty-five ships of the line, commanded by Admirals Villeneuve and Gravina,[3] gave the commander-in-chief the means to attack the Diamond. On the 2nd of June 1805, two seventy-fours and several frigates and corvettes left the harbour of Fort-de-France, ascended the channel of Sainte-Lucie by tacking, and descended to within half cannon shot of the eastern face of the rock. Their guns completely destroyed, with two broadsides, the enemy works and batteries. The boats, towed by the ships and loaded with colonial troops, set off, protected against the current by the bulk of the ships. They landed two hundred picked men on the Diamond, who obliged the garrison to

---

3. The fleet which was to perish at Trafalgar.

lay down their arms. It remained to take the summit of the rock, where the English commander had installed himself. An *aide-de-camp* of General d'Houdetot, Cortes by name, climbed a slope of sixty degrees, above a sheer cliff dropping five hundred feet into a rough sea. The enemy officer politely handed him his sword, and a few hardy sailors who had followed Cortès, substituted the French flag for the English; the two eighteen-pounders, which Samuel Hood had mounted on the summit with so much trouble, were thrown into the sea; half an hour after the attack nothing of his work remained: the Diamond was once more in possession of its customary inhabitants, the sea-birds.

But to attain this result it had needed two ships carrying one hundred and fifty guns and two thousand four hundred men, plus two hundred troops from Martinique, and the protection given them by the big ships against the current, which rendered their landing possible. It should be added that these operations were carried out in broad daylight.

I did not take part in this expedition, being in the *Formidable* at the time, in the quality of Chief-of-Staff to Admiral Villaret and General Lauriston, who was *aide-de-camp* to the Emperor and commanded the troops in the fleet. I was to go towards new adventures in war, and in effect I met with many, most unexpected and less agreeable than those I had hoped for.

(End of M. de Jonnès' Memoirs.)

LEONAUR

ALSO FROM LEONAUR
AVAILABLE IN SOFTCOVER OR HARDCOVER WITH DUST JACKET

THE JENA CAMPAIGN: 1806 *by F. N. Maude*—The Twin Battles of Jena & Auerstadt Between Napoleon's French and the Prussian Army.

PRIVATE O'NEIL *by Charles O'Neil*—The recollections of an Irish Rogue of H. M. 28th Regt.—The Slashers— during the Peninsula & Waterloo campaigns of the Napoleonic wars.

ROYAL HIGHLANDER *by James Anton*—A soldier of H.M 42nd (Royal) Highlanders during the Peninsular, South of France & Waterloo Campaigns of the Napoleonic Wars.

CAPTAIN BLAZE *by Elzéar Blaze*—Elzéar Blaze recounts his life and experiences in Napoleon's army in a well written, articulate and companionable style.

LEJEUNE VOLUME 1 *by Louis-François Lejeune*—The Napoleonic Wars through the Experiences of an Officer on Berthier's Staff.

LEJEUNE VOLUME 2 *by Louis-François Lejeune*—The Napoleonic Wars through the Experiences of an Officer on Berthier's Staff.

FUSILIER COOPER *by John S. Cooper*—Experiences in the 7th (Royal) Fusiliers During the Peninsular Campaign of the Napoleonic Wars and the American Campaign to New Orleans.

CAPTAIN COIGNET *by Jean-Roch Coignet*—A Soldier of Napoleon's Imperial Guard from the Italian Campaign to Russia and Waterloo.

FIGHTING NAPOLEON'S EMPIRE *by Joseph Anderson*—The Campaigns of a British Infantryman in Italy, Egypt, the Peninsular & the West Indies During the Napoleonic Wars.

CHASSEUR BARRES *by Jean-Baptiste Barres*—The experiences of a French Infantryman of the Imperial Guard at Austerlitz, Jena, Eylau, Friedland, in the Peninsular, Lutzen, Bautzen, Zinnwald and Hanau during the Napoleonic Wars.

MARINES TO 95TH (RIFLES) *by Thomas Fernyhough*—The military experiences of Robert Fernyhough during the Napoleonic Wars.

HUSSAR ROCCA *by Albert Jean Michel de Rocca*—A French cavalry officer's experiences of the Napoleonic Wars and his views on the Peninsular Campaigns against the Spanish, British And Guerilla Armies.

SERGEANT BOURGOGNE *by Adrien Bourgogne*—With Napoleon's Imperial Guard in the Russian Campaign and on the Retreat from Moscow 1812 - 13.